CHURCH:
COMMUNITY FOR THE KINGDOM

CHURCH: COMMUNITY FOR THE KINGDOM

by

John Fuellenbach, SVD

Manila
2000

The Society of the Divine Word (SVD) is an international missionary congregation of priests and brothers serving in more than fifty countries all over the world. Through the Logos Publications, the SVD in the Philippines aims to foster the apostolate of the printed word in the biblical, theological, catechetical and pastoral fields in order to promote justice, peace and human development. The opinions expressed by the author do not necessarily reflect those of the SVD community.

ISBN: 971-510-140-2

Contents

Preface 11

Acknowledgment 14

Introduction 15
    Presuppositions 15
        The Distinction between individual salvation and the
        necessity of a Church 15
        Salvation as bound to community - in contrast to a purely
        subjective and individualistic understanding of the
        Christian faith 17
        Being a Christian as a call to mission 18
        The meaning of "the keys of the Kingdom" given to Peter 19
    Essential Relationships: Jesus - Kingdom - Church - Israel 19
    Jesus and the Kingdom 19
        God's intention - his plan for the world 20
        Kingdom as belonging to this world 21
        The Dream of God for creation 22
    Jesus and the Church 23
    Jesus and Israel 25
    Procedure 25

Part 1: THE CHURCH IN SCRIPTURE AND IN VATICAN II 27

Chapter One: Jesus and the Church 29

    I. Return to the Jesus who walked over this earth 29
    II. Biblical findings concerning Israel, Kingdom, Church 30
        The Exodus story: God's election of a "counter society" 30
        Kingdom and Church in the Gospels 35
        The Kingdom vision mediated through the Church 37
        Conclusion 40
    III. Jesus and the foundation of the Church 41
        1. The most common positions today 42
        2. Four representatives of the common positions 44
            Richard McBrien: Catholicism 44
            Gerhard Lohfink: Did Jesus found a Church? 44

Walter Kirchschläger: his common points can be
summarized as follows: 45
Leonardo Boff: Church, Charisma and Power 46
Conclusion 47

Chapter Two: The Church in Vatican II 51

I. The Council's vision of the Church 51
II. Images of the Church in Vatican II 53
 1. THE NEW PEOPLE OF GOD 54
 A gratuitous election by God. 55
 The communitarian aspect 57
 A people of equals 57
 A pilgrim people 58
 Conclusion 59
 2. THE CHURCH AS BODY OF CHRIST 59
 The image as used in the Council 59
 The origin of the "Body of Christ" symbol in St. Paul 60
 The Body of the Risen Christ and not the physical body
 of Jesus 63
 The "broken mirror" Model 68
 3. THE CHURCH AS TEMPLE OF THE HOLY SPIRIT 70
 Conclusion 73

Chapter Three: The Church in the Context of the Kingdom 77

I. Church in relation to the world 77
II. The Church as not identical with Kingdom of God now 78
 Arguments for an identity 80
 Arguments against an Identity 81
 Biblical foundation for a non-identity 81
 The theological fruits of such non-identity 84
 Voiced 'reservations' to a 'Kingdom-centered Church' 85
 Conclusion 88
III. The Kingdom of God as present in the Church 89
 The Kingdom in 'spatial' and 'dynamic' terms 89
 Difficulties voiced with this view 91
 Conclusion 93

Part 2: MODELS OF THE CHURCH 95

Chapter Four: Emergence of a World-Church 97

I. A Theological Interpretation of Vatican II 97
   Introduction 97
   The emergence of a World Church in Vatican II 98
   What are these three epochs? 99
      First the period of Jewish Christianity 99
      The second period of the Church: the Gentile Christian
        community freed from Judaic Law 101
      The third epoch: the transition of the Western Church
        to a World Church 103
   Conclusion 105
II. Megatrends affecting the Church Today 106
   Resurgence of Cultural Traditions 107
   Globalization: the trend towards socio-economic and
      political globalization 107
   Revival of Religious Experiences 108
   Basic Ecclesial Communities: the need for personal
      encounter of God within small faith communities 108
   Problems in Ministerial structures: 109
   The Western Church in Crisis 109
   The Poor as the New Evangelizers: the centrality of the
      poor and oppressed in the plan of God for humanity 109
   New Presence and Significance of Women 110
   New frontiers for Mission 110
   Conclusion 110

**Chapter Five: The use of models in Theology to describe the
Church today** 111

I. What is a model? 111
II. Different Models of Church 116
   Introduction 116
     1. The Church as "community of disciples" 117
       The group around Jesus: Community of Disciples 117
       The Church based on the Community of Disciples 117

Discipleship a constant becoming 118
Disciples in community 119
Disciple and ministry 120
2. The Church as Institution 120
The strength of this model 122
The weaknesses of this model 123
The Council and the hierarchical model 125
The Ministry of Prophets: succession of prophets in the Church 130
What are the proper functions of the prophets? 132
Further development 133
Prophets in the Church today 134
Religious Orders as "Institutional Prophetic Ministry" 136
The origin of religious orders: "a prophetic protest" 139
The three basic functions of religious life in and for the Church .. 140
(1.) The "innovative function" of religious life 140
(2.) The "corrective role" or the "shock therapy" of
religious life 141
(3.) The Witness of "community living" 142
Conclusion: Prophetic criticism applied 143
(1). The crisis in the Church herself 145
(2.) The rift between Church and society 145
(3.) Consumerism and materialism 146
Who are the Successors of the Teachers? 146
Conclusion: 147
3. The Church as Communion 149
Strength of this model 152
It has a very good biblical basis. 152
This image of Church is based on good tradition. 153
This view corresponds to the present experience 154
Weakness of this model 154
Conclusion 156
4. The Church as Sacrament 158
What does it mean to say the Church is a sacrament? 159
Christ the sacrament of God 159
The Church the sacrament of Christ 160
Church universal Sacrament of Salvation 162
Weaknesses of this model 163
Conclusion 164

5. The Church as Herald 164
   Strength of the model 166
   Weaknesses of the model 166
6. The Church as Servant 167
   Strength of this model 167
   Weaknesses of this model 168
Conclusion 169
Excursion: The meaning of the term "Church" in Vatican II. 170
   1. Church as "CATHOLIC CHURCH" 170
   2. Church as "LOCAL CONGREGATION" 171
   3. Church as "COMMUNITY OF THE BAPTIZED" 172
   4. Church refers to the "PEOPLE OF ISRAEL" 173
   5. The Church "FROM ABEL ON" 173
   6. The "HOUSE CHURCH" (Lumen Gentium 11) 174

Chapter Six: Two most relevant Models for the Future Church:
Basic Ecclesial Communities and Contrast Society 179

Introduction 179
I. Church as BASIC ECCLESIAL COMMUNITIES 185
   The New Testament background: "House Churches" 185
   The theological background: the council's view of the
      church as Local Church 187
   The concrete situation as the real origin of Basic Ecclesial
      Communities 187
   What are basic Ecclesial communities? 188
   A new ecclesiology 190
      Positive experiences: 190
      What kind of community do we have here? 192
      Problems these communities have to face 193
   Renewal of the Parish Church through SCC in Africa 194
   The first stage: The Provided-for Church 195
   The second stage: A Pastoral Council Church 195
   The third stage: The Awakening Church 195
   The fourth stage - The Task Group Church 195
   The fifth and final stage - The Communion of Communities 196
   How do ministries arise in these communities? 196
   Conclusion 197

II. The Church as a "CONTRAST SOCIETY" 200
　Biblical Basis 201
　The Early Church as "Contrast Society" 201
　The Church as Contrast Society today 203
　Globalization and Contrast society 205
　The internal challenge to a Church as Contrast Society 206
　The theological value of such a conception of Church 208
　Conclusion 209

Chapter Seven: Mission of the Church 215

　Introduction 215
　The Threefold Mission 216
　The two ways of mission 219
　The Church, the "Universal Sacrament of Salvation" as
　　mediator of the Kingdom 221
　Kingdom consciousness and the mission of the Church 224
　Conclusion 226

Epilogue 228
Selected Bibliography 229

Preface

My fascination in theology has always been the Kingdom of God, the symbol Jesus consistently used to explain his life and mission. Thus this book aims to present a vision of the Church that understands herself wholly from the Kingdom, finds her identity in the presence of the Kingdom now and sees her mission entirely in the service of the Kingdom.

The title, *Church: Community for the Kingdom*, indicates this purpose. First, the Church is the community where the Kingdom is now experienced and celebrated and where the future fulfilment of God's great design for creation already dawns. She is the community where the future life with the Triune God is already happening in hidden but real signs, for it is an icon of the Trinity. Second, the Church is for the Kingdom because her mission is totally geared to witness and proclaim it. As Jesus saw himself charged to proclaim the Kingdom and to bring it to all cities and towns (Lk 4:42), so the Church, following his footsteps, has to understand her very essence and mission in the service of the Kingdom as well. That is how Jesus instructed his disciples: "As the Father has sent me so I am sending you" (Jn 20:21).

There are many possible approaches to the mystery of the Church. The one presented here tries to capture Jesus' vision of the Kingdom, which he threw like fire into this world and which he wanted to see burning everywhere (Lk 12:49). This fire he entrusted to the community of his disciples who, after they had received it as the great gift of the Risen Lord on Easter (Jn 20:22) or on Pentecost (Ac 2:3-4), went out and preached what they themselves had received.

In our time the Church in Vatican II realized how necessary it was to go back once again and open herself to that fire of the Master so that the world may come to believe. The Council presented a vision of the Church that will remain a challenge for many years to come.

In the meantime the Church as a Pilgrim people has to move on. New challenges arise and new models of how to conceive church have to be sought and developed if she wants to remain faithful to her Master's message. As Jesus learnt the way of the Kingdom through circumstances into which he was put (Mk 7:25-29), so the Church will come to understand her very being and mission always anew if she remains open to the times and the Spirit of Jesus. Two big challenges face the Church today: How to make the Kingdom of God understood in the different cultures of the world and how to live Jesus' own life principle of justice and compassion in a world where the poor are getting poorer and a few are getting richer.

The approach to the Church in this book is accordingly presented: first, Jesus' message of the Kingdom and the Church; second, the vision of the Church herself as presented in Vatican II; and third, the challenges to the Church in the present world with an attempt to outline some models of Church in response to them.

This book is about the Church, her very being, purpose and goal today, written not from some neutral viewpoint but by people deeply engaged in her life. The answers that emerge affect our own life and self-understanding as priests, religious or lay people who belong to the community called Church. Far from some kind of purely "objective" discourse about Church, we speak as people who live in her, celebrate her and take part in her mission. To get a better understanding of Church therefore means to enter more deeply into our own identity. This is not just any topic that we discuss, investigate scientifically, observe critically, and propose to correct and resolve in view of today's pressing problems. Our investigation is not purely neutral or detached as if its outcome bears no consequences for our vocation as Christians. For us the Church is an object of faith because as believers we pray: "We believe in the one holy, catholic and apostolic Church." Accessing and understanding our topic requires, besides purely scientific methods, an engagement of faith. The Jewish philosopher, Martin Buber, was once asked by Ben Gurion, first prime minister of Israel: "Why do you believe in God at all?" Buber responded: "If God would be one about whom we could talk, I would certainly not be a believer. But since God is one with whom I can talk, I believe." Our talk about the Church will therefore be holistic. That means it must be, first, objective: scientific, rational and theological; second, pastoral: witnessing, creating and strengthening our faith; third, spiritual: nurturing, enhancing and vivifying our own faith. Our aim is an understanding of Church which will renew our reasons for being part of it and reanimate our joy and love for this Church that Jesus loved by laying down his life for her (Eph 5:25). More than ever before we must come to love what often seems a hopeless, overaged, and scandal-ridden Church. Otherwise we cannot live in her with the joy and enthusiasm needed to carry on our vocation to proclaim the joyful news of God's Kingdom in this age. Hans

Urs von Balthazar coined the phrase, "kneeling theology," which many theologians have since picked up. Balthasar regards it as "literally being one of the saddest chapters in the history of theology that at one point there came the change from a kneeling theology to a sitting theology." For him, good theology is always praying theology. Serious theology cannot be contented with just being a sitting theology; it must remain a kneeling theology. J. B. Metz puts it another way: "The talk about God originates from talk with God and theology originates from the language of prayer."

To fathom the Church we cannot just talk about her we must talk with her since we are part of her. Only in this way we can come to sense the divine mystery behind the phenomenon we call Church, a mystery which goes beyond all human comprehension.

My wish is that all who read this book will come to understand the Church a little better but ultimately that they come to love her in a new way based on an experience of her. This can only happen to those who have been touched by the fire that Jesus came to throw, the Holy Spirit who according to Luke will fall on those who ask the Father for Him (Lk 11:13).

Rome, Pentecost 2000

Fr. John Fuellenbach, SVD

Acknowledgment

The Kingdom of God has been a key part of courses on the Church I taught for many years to seminarians in the Philippines, Australia, and Germany, to participants of renewal courses for priests and catechetical institutes all over the world and in the Gregorian University's graduate program in Rome over the last 20 years. Two factors have shaped my view of the Church. The first is the central message of Jesus, the Kingdom of God. The second, and what determines my understanding of Church most deeply, is the experience of so many different local churches themselves that I have come to know in travels and exchanges with people most involved in them. I owe them a word of deep gratitude, particularly for their unwavering love for the Church despite many difficulties they have to face, often from the very Church they want to serve. I dedicate this book to them and to all who love the Church as she is, for they know this is not a mere human institution, some kind of club of like-minded people, but a mystery chosen and loved by Christ himself.

Finally, a special word of thanks goes to Fr. John Donaghey, SVD who with great dedication and skill read through the whole text and made the necessary corrections. To Sister Christel Daun, SSpS I owe more than one word of gratitude for all her help and so to Mike Blume who read and edited all the odd ends that had to be looked at more than once. Josie Sarmiento of the Logos Publication staff deserves a word of special thanks for all her effort and care to prepare the text for printing and to get it printed on time.

Introduction

Presuppositions

Every theological topic presupposes a "horizon of understanding" (*Verstehenshorizont*) against which it projects its findings and synthesizes them into a comprehensive view. Most of the time this background is taken for granted and not explicitly reflected upon. Explaining it permits easier understanding of the main thinking underlying the topic. The following presuppositions provide the background against which this course on the Church has been conceived.

The Distinction between individual salvation and the necessity of a Church

God wants the salvation of all people not only theoretically but effectively (1 Tim 2:4-5; Tim 2:11). Every human person — no matter what his/her faith and religion may be — can effectively be saved by following his/her own religion and conscience.

> Salvation must be held possible outside the Church. The Second Vatican Council (1962-65) has reaffirmed this doctrinal stand in unambiguous terms in its Dogmatic Constitution on the Church (Lumen Gentium, nn. 16-17), as well as in its declaration on the relationship of the Church to non-Christian religions (Nostra Aetate), its Decree on the Church's missionary activity (Ad Gentes), and its Pastoral Constitution on the Church in the Modern World (Gaudium et Spes). A celebrated passage of the last document, after stating how Christians come in contact with the paschal mystery of the death and Resurrection of Jesus Christ, affirms clearly that the same applies — 'in a way known to God' — for members of the other religious traditions. It says: 'All this holds true not for Christians only, but also for all men of goodwill in whose hearts grace is active invisibly. For since Christ died for all, and since all men are in fact called to one and the same destiny, which is divine, we must hold that the Holy Spirit offers to all the possibility of being made partners, in a way known to God, in the paschal mystery' (Gaudium et Spes 22).[1]

Several points need to be noted here.

First, the Council looks at God's universal salvific will not as an abstract possibility but as a concrete reality, actually operative among all people. God's ultimate aim with creation is the salvation of all people. This purpose was present in creation right from the beginning.

The Bible begins, not with the election of the people of God, but rather with the creation of the world. The first figure is not Abraham, but the *adam*, the human being, and in the first chapter of Genesis *adam* refers not to a particular individual, but to humanity as a whole. The Bible begins with humanity. The observation is of serious theological import, for it makes clear that everything the Bible goes on to describe is not only an action between God and God's people: it is aimed towards the nations, the world, the universe. God's concern is not first of all for Israel but for the whole world. God did not create religion but the world.

As universally as the Bible begins, so does it end. Its first image is the creation of the world out of chaos. The last great image is God's new world, God's new creation, in which all creation finds its goal and its perfection. This last image of the Bible spread before us is John's prophetic vision in Rev 21:1-22:5. John deliberately connected his great closing vision to the opening chapters of the Bible. The Scriptures opens with "In the beginning... God created the heavens and the earth" (Gen 1:1) and now closes with "Then I saw a new heaven and a new earth, for the first heaven and the first earth had passed away" (Rev 21:1).[2]

What is important here is the universality of God's plan of salvation, which embraces the entire human race and the whole of creation. This broad understanding of God's plan of salvation and of his loving concern for all people and every aspect of their lives enjoys a widespread acceptance today. Mission means, therefore, first and foremost God's turning towards the world in creative love, redemptive healing and transforming power. This turning takes place in ordinary history and it is not confined to the activity of the Church. The activity of the Holy Spirit is universal, not limited by space or time (RM 28). The Church is called to participate in a project that comes from God and belongs to God. In participating in God's plan, the Church never starts from scratch. The Church encounters human beings and a world in which God's Spirit is already operative.

Secondly, the concrete possibility of salvation available to all men and women of goodwill is salvation through Jesus Christ and his paschal mystery. The uniqueness and centrality of God incarnated in Jesus Christ remains the basic foundation of all salvation.

Thirdly, this salvation for all reaches out to everyone through the universal action of the Holy Spirit, released through the death and resurrection of Jesus Christ. His action "affects not only individuals but also society and history, people, cultures and religions" as Pope Paul II affirms in *Redemptoris Missio* 28.

Fourthly, the manner in which salvation in Jesus Christ is made available outside the Church through the working of the Holy Spirit remains for us mysterious. This last point does not amount to saying that the 'how' of salvation outside the Church lies altogether beyond the scope of theological investigation, but rather indicates that whatever theological explanation may be given would have to preserve the reference to Christ and his Spirit. God's saving grace or the faith that justifies has, even outside the Church, a Christological and pneumatological dimension.

If we hold to this conviction, we have to conclude that membership in the Church is not necessary for one's personal salvation.

Personal salvation, in other words, is not inextricably linked with one's membership or non-membership in the Church. It is existence within the Kingdom of God, not within the Church, that finally determines our relationship with God and our reception of salvation.[3]

But this view, commonly held today, does not mean the Church is not needed at all for the salvation of humankind. The issue is not anymore: "Outside the Church no salvation." The question is: Without the Church, could there be salvation for humanity at all?

An initial answer would be: The Church is necessary for the world at large as a sacrament, an efficacious sign and instrument of God's redemptive activity in Jesus Christ, leading towards the final Kingdom of God. For those who are called by God to profess the Lordship of Christ and to collaborate with him in the coming of the Kingdom for the salvation of all, the Church is definitely necessary for their personal salvation as well.

Salvation as bound to community - in contrast to a purely subjective and individualistic understanding of the Christian faith

God's saving action is historically bound up with a community rather than with a divine approach to persons individually, notwithstanding the community they may live in. Why did God choose Israel? The element of choice is underived and remains a mystery, much like the mystery as to why one falls in love with this particular person and not with some other person.

But the concept of election is always combined with a mandate. God's choice fell on Israel for the sake of the nations. God needs a witness in the world, a people in which God's salvation can be made visible. That is the reason why the burden of election rests on the people of Israel. Israel's being chosen is not a privilege or a preference *over others*, but existence *for others,* and hence the heaviest burden in history.

The idea of election is central and fundamental in Scripture but it is not a concept very much appreciated today. The concept crystallizes Israel's knowledge that God desires to liberate and change the entire world but for that purpose needs a beginning in the midst of the world, a visible place and living witnesses. This has nothing to do with preference, advantage, elitism, or being better-than, but it has a great deal to do with God's respect for human dignity and human freedom. God's omnipotence consists not in that he can do what he wants but in the fact that God's plan for the world will succeed. The problem here is human freedom. Human beings can oppose God's plan. They can refuse to be a people of God they can say: "I reject all of it."[4]

The message of Jesus, first of all, is not addressed to scattered individuals but to a community, in which individuals live and come to understand their salvation. Only on this basis can one grasp why a topic like 'The Church' is so urgent and not rightly left to subjective interpretations. To understand the Church, the communitarian aspect of salvation must be fully grasped and understood. Otherwise we see no need for a Church at all.

Christianity is not a religious supermarket where everyone picks up what he/she wants to buy. In that scenario all the Church would have to do is make sure the shelves are well stocked with the goods people want to find there.

Being a Christian as a call to mission

We should distinguish between being called into the Church through baptism and one's personal salvation. To "be called by God" means to be drawn into God's own plan and into the mission of his Son, which extends into the mission of the Church. Because of this call a person chosen by God is "holy, consecrated, set apart". But that happens for a specific purpose: to "be sent out" (Mk 3:13-15), to engage actively in God's mission, to become a co-worker with God for the salvation-transformation of the world into God's final design. Mission is, therefore, the ultimate aim of any call by God. We are not called to occupy a place of honor or accumulate personal gains. It means that we are on an assignment for God. To be a Christian means being called to mission by the sacrament of baptism. Baptism is not a passport to heaven or a ticket for entering eternal life; it is above all a call to mission. Most people will find eternal life without being baptized. The privilege of being a Christian consists precisely in having been called to participate in a special way in the mission of Christ, which continues in the Church and is meant for the salvation of all.

However, the correct understanding of what it means to be a Christian in terms of mission should not lead us to look at the Church in purely functional terms. The Church community itself is a sacramental anticipation of God's final plan with the whole of humanity. It is the celebration of God's plan of salvation initially already achieved in the here and now. This gives meaning and joy to those invited to share God's own mission for the world. The person called by Christ into his mission should perceive of him/herself as Paul did:

> *This mystery, as it is now revealed in the Spirit to his holy apostles and prophets, was unknown to humanity in previous generations... I, who am less than the least of all God's holy people, have been entrusted with this special grace, of proclaiming to the gentiles the unfathomable treasure of Christ and of throwing light on the inner workings of the mystery kept hidden through all the ages in God, the Creator of everything (Eph 3:3-11).[5]*

The meaning of "the keys of the Kingdom" given to Peter (Mt 16:18-19)

Jesus gave to Peter, upon whom he has built his Church, the "keys of the Kingdom of God" (Mt 16:18-19). Therefore the Church has an important role to play concerning the Kingdom now in history. In other words, the key lets the Church unlock the secrets of the Kingdom and proclaim God's terms. That does, however, not mean only those who join the Catholic Church will enter the Kingdom. Rather, the keys are entrusted to the Church so she can disclose to the people the conditions for entry into or exclusion from the Kingdom of God. The Church does not decide to whom the Kingdom will ultimately be granted nor who will ultimately be excluded. In this context the words of Jesus, *'Many will come from east and west and will take their places in the Kingdom of God while the presumed heirs of the Kingdom will be thrown out'* (Mt 8:11-12), are very significant for the members of the Church as well.

Essential Relationships: Jesus - Kingdom - Church - Israel

Jesus and the Kingdom

The central message of Jesus was the Kingdom of God which he came to "throw like fire into this world" (Lk 12:49). This 'fire' is not to be understood as an abstract idea or as a world-view but as a 'world-transforming power'. Its sole aim is to extend the life of the Trinity into the whole of creation, to draw all that exists into God's own communion and love. God's Kingdom is therefore meant for the salvation of all human beings who ever lived and will live.

The Kingdom of God is that final state of creation, in which God's being Abba will be the all-embracing and determining factor. All reality will be fully permeated by this love and fully respond to it. It is that state of creation which Scripture calls New Heaven and New Earth. Both realities, Kingdom and Father, though distinct and not simply interchangeable, complement each other. The Kingdom explains God's being Abba and the Fatherhood of God provides a basis for and an explanation of the Kingdom. Everything Jesus said and did was said and done in the light of the Kingdom of God that was coming with him and through him.[6]

> The reign of God is the key. Jesus without it is a disincarnated person, a person without a body. Separated from the reign of God, Jesus is a theological construct that does not correspond to reality. Only loosely connected with the reign of God, Jesus is a phantom that preoccupies the doctrinal interest of the religious authorities but haunts the hearts of people in the street. Without the reign of God Jesus is an incomplete Jesus, whose life and mission are not shaped by it, is not the way, the truth, and the life (John 14:6), to use that profound expression in John's Gospel. Jesus is the way because his is the way of God's reign. Jesus is the truth because his is the truth revealed by it. Jesus is the life because his is the life empowered by it.[7]

The two terms *Abba* and *Kingdom of God* embrace Jesus' vision, the vision for which he lived, suffered and died.

God's intention - his plan for the world

Jesus' vision has something to do with the ultimate meaning of every human being, the fulfillment of the deepest aspiration of every human heart, the plan God has for all of creation. It has something to do with what Saint Augustine expressed in this way: "Restless is our heart, O God, until it rests in you." Or, in the words of M. Gandhi: "Man's ultimate aim is the realization of God. I live and move and have my being in pursuit of this goal."

The deepest desire of every human heart is complete union with God, a union which includes union with all of God's family and harmony with the universe. It embraces God, all human beings and the world and nature as well. To the vexing question that has haunted millions of people, "Why did God create the universe and human beings?" there is a simple answer that could be phrased as follows: God, the Triune One, said, "We enjoy life so much that we want to share it with other beings whom we will create for that purpose." God created us with the sole purpose of bringing us to share his own life with him. But it is not only we humans that will participate in his life, it is the whole universe that God's love wants to lead into the fullness of life because God is a *"lover of life."*

> *Yes, you love all that exists, you hold nothing of what you have made in abhorrence, for had you hated anything, you would not have formed it. And how, had you not willed it, could a thing persist, how be conserved if not called forth by you? You spare all things because all things are yours, LORD, LOVER OF LIFE, you whose imperishable spirit is in all (Wis 11:24-26).*

Kingdom as belonging to this world

There is a danger of seeing the Kingdom as a totally transcendent, other-worldly reality that lies beyond this one as if it had nothing to do with the "labyrinth of this world." Such a view could be called the *"trampoline effect."* Whenever life begins to become oppressive and troublesome a person just leaps into the air with a bold kick and soars relieved and unencumbered into so-called eternal fields.

Jesus did not envision the Kingdom that he preached as something that belongs totally and exclusively to the world to come. His Kingdom-vision leaves room for interpreting it as belonging to this world as well as for proclaiming a future that cannot be deduced from the circumstances of present history. The future, as the Bible understands it, is something qualitatively new. It lies beyond human planning and capability, something we can only allow to be given to us. While this symbol takes the world and human effort in history seriously, it does not surrender openness to a transcendent future in the fullness of God. Only God can ultimately guarantee the fulfillment of humankind's deepest aspirations.

> Our engagement in this struggle (to make the kingdom hope come true) can be without illusions because we know by faith that no human program by itself will bring in the eschaton. Our engagement can also be without ultimate despair, because we believe that, no matter how great our self-created horror becomes, God is faithful to his promise and he will bring the kingdom which has already drawn near to us in his Son.[8]

The Kingdom of God is incarnated in history, in human society and in the world. Although it is not purely and simply identical with the world, it is "identifiable" in the world. We could also say that the Kingdom shows itself in society and is encountered in society, but this society is not the Kingdom.

> To discover the theme of the Reign of God is to discover the full dimension of the inevitable historical character of Christianity. Our God is the god of history, who has entered into history, has a purpose and a plan for history, and has shown these to us in Jesus. God's plan is the Reign of God. The Reign is the dream, the utopia God cherishes for history, God's overall design for the world, the arcane mystery hidden for centuries and now revealed fully in Jesus.[9]

The Dream of God for creation

Markus Borg described the Kingdom of God as God's dream for creation in these words: In a broad sense the Bible as a whole is the story of the dream of God, beginning in Genesis with paradise and ending with paradise restored in the great concluding vision of the Book of Revelation. The first paradise is two individuals in a garden, and the second paradise is communal and urban — the new Jerusalem, the city of God.

Yet the dream of God is not the whole of the biblical story, for the Bible also includes the nightmarish elements introduced by what happens in human history. The Bible speaks about the rejection of the dream as well as the dream itself. Thus in a narrower sense, the dream of God is a social and political vision of a world of justice and peace in which human beings do not hurt or destroy, oppress or exploit one another. It is the dream expressed with many images and by many voices in the Bible, for example in Micah 4:3-4.

> *He shall judge between many peoples, and shall arbitrate between strong nations far away; they shall beat their swords into plowshares, and their spears into pruning hooks; nation shall not lift up sword against nation, neither shall they learn war any more; but they shall all sit under their own vines and under their own fig trees, and no one shall make them afraid; for the mouth of the LORD of hosts has spoken.*

The dream of God is a vision of Shalom, a rich Hebrew word often translated as "peace" but meaning much more than the absence of war. It means well-being in a comprehensive sense. It includes freedom from negatives such as oppression, anxiety and fear, as well as the presence of positives such as health, prosperity and security. Shalom thus includes a social vision: the dream of a world in which such well-being belongs to everybody. As the story of the interaction between the dream of God and the rejection of the dream shows through what happens in history, the Bible is a tale of two kingdoms: the Kingdom of God and the kingdom of this world.[10]

This seems to have been the Kingdom message Jesus came to proclaim. It is a vision of God, the world, humankind and creation as a whole as well as of each individual human person. It is the most grandiose vision that the world has ever known. For this vision Jesus lived, labored, suffered and died. This is the vision he entrusted to his disciples: "As the Father has sent me, so I send you" (Jn 20:21).

The final goal of creation can therefore be envisioned as the great gathering of all human beings that have ever lived, live and will live together with all creatures of any kind celebrating an eternal feast, "the great banquet" envisioned by Isaiah. Here everyone will know everyone and know him/her intimately as an enrichment, a gift to be immensely enjoyed. The possibility of exclusion of some (hell) is possible and cannot be denied as a real possibility. However, if some will really be excluded from the banquet, it is not ours to know nor decide who they will be. Only God will make this decision. We will always have to remind ourselves of Jesus' own words: "What is impossible for human beings, God can still make it possible" (Mk 10:27).

Jesus and the Church

This joyful message of salvation for all, however, is intrinsically bound to the unique person Jesus of Nazareth. Jesus is the Kingdom Himself, and he remains the radiating center from which its world-transforming power will accomplish the task for which he came. The Kingdom cannot be separated from the person of Jesus of Nazareth if Christianity is to remain true to its very name.

> The proclamation and establishment of God's Kingdom are the purpose of Jesus' mission: "I was sent for this purpose" (Lk 4:43). But that is not all. Jesus himself is the "good news," as he declares at the very beginning of his mission in the synagogue of Nazareth when he applies to himself the words of Isaiah about the Anointed One sent by the Spirit of the Lord (cf. Lk 4:14-21). Since the "good news" is Christ, there is an identification between the message and the messenger, between saying, doing and being. His power, the secret of the effectiveness of his actions, lies in his total identification with the message he announces: He proclaims the "good news" not just by what he says or does, but by what he is.[11]

But Jesus is gone. Since his death and resurrection he has entered into the new creation that is not visible and tangible to us. How then will God's saving presence — intrinsically tied up with the one mediator Jesus

Christ — be available to us in space and time? How will that saving person remain present until the day of the final fulfillment of his promises? Who will make Christ present now in our age and time?

The answers given to these questions differ. The traditional response is that Jesus founded a Church that would make him and his message of the Kingdom present throughout the centuries. For the Catholic Church, therefore, it seems to be the visible and tangible community with its divinely willed hierarchy and magisterium that guarantees the presence of Christ through the centuries.

For many protestant Churches the enduring presence of Christ and through him the presence of God, who wants to save all, is guaranteed through the Word of God contained in Holy Scripture. God makes his saving presence tangible and concretely accessible wherever the Word of God is proclaimed. In the words of the Lausanne Covenant:

> Christ is universal in the sense that he is available to all who hear his people's proclamation of the Gospel, but effective only to those who believe.[12]

Therefore people ask: Is organized religion necessary or should Scripture not be enough to ensure the perpetual presence of Christ in history? Does he have to be tied to a particular group of people with a particular structure and way of making him present? Why Church at all? Do we need a Church? How necessary is the Church for salvation?

Should we not let the Word of God take care of itself? Can the Bible not vindicate its claim of possessing the absolute truth alone? As a Hindu once asked me: "If you Christians are so sure that only your Holy Books contain the full truth, why don't you let these books themselves prove it, instead of binding their truth to the interpretation of a magisterium and a hierarchical office?"

The answer to this pointed question is linked to the incarnation of God in Jesus Christ. Christ is the historically real and actual presence of the eschatologically victorious mercy of God (Rahner). He is God made visible and present to us with the aim and goal of communicating himself once and for all to us. God has bound himself to this person Jesus of Nazareth in a way and to a degree not done in any other religion. Only through him and in him is God's saving grace now available for all. In the words of K. Rahner:

> From the moment the Logos assumes this human nature from out of the unity of mankind, as a part of it, redemption cannot be arrested or canceled. The fate of the world has been finally decided, and in the sense of divine

mercy. Before Christ, the dialogue between God and humankind in the history of eternal welfare and loss was an open one... Everything was still unsettled.... But now in the Word of God, God's last word is uttered into the visible public history of humankind, a word of grace, reconciliation and eternal life: Jesus Christ. The grace of God no longer comes (when it does come) steeply down from on high, from God absolutely transcending the world, and in a manner that is without history, purely episodic, it is permanently in the world in tangible historical form, established in the flesh of Christ as part of the World, of humanity and of its very history.[13]

The question now is: How can this redemption accomplished in Jesus Christ become effectively present in time and space for every human being since Christ is not physically present in the world in the way he was when he walked this earth? Or, how can we come in contact with him in a manner that is certain and reaches into this our very world? Who represents him, "the historically real and actual presence of the saving love of God?" It is here that we have to locate the Church.

Jesus and Israel

Another related issue to consider before answering the above questions is that of 'Jesus and Israel'. Jesus understood his mission first and foremost in the context of Israel's mission. He saw himself as "being sent to the house of Israel" and not to the gentiles. His instructions to the disciples were: "Go nowhere among the gentiles and enter no town of the Samaritans but go rather to the lost sheep of the house of Israel" (Mt 10:5-6). He came to restore Israel to make it once and for all what it never managed to become, the true Covenant partner. The issue of Jesus and the Church can, therefore, be raised in a double context: that of Jesus' preaching of the Kingdom and also that of the way he understood Israel's mission in God's plan of salvation. The community that evolved after Easter has to be seen and evaluated in the context of Israel's election and mission as presented in the Old Testament since God's plan of salvation is one.[14]

Procedure

We will attempt to answer these questions in two ways. First, we go back to Jesus himself, as far as possible, and ask: Did Jesus envision a church establishing itself after his death and resurrection? What did Jesus himself intend with the group he gathered around him? Since Jesus understood his mission in the setting of the Old Covenant, were his disciples to become the true Covenant people as the messianic age had promised? What were they to be, once he would not be in their midst any longer? Did he foresee a church in an organized form that would go on preaching his message until the end of time?

Second, we will ask the present Church how it understands and evaluates itself. Since Vatican II was the Church's official contemporary self-evaluation, we will see how this assembly saw itself and how it understood and presented the essence and mission of the Church for today. Surely one cannot stay with Vatican II alone since new questions and problems, which the Council could not foresee, have arisen.

We will examine both aspects: Jesus' own foresight of a future community to proclaim and carry on his vision as well as the Church's self-understanding as it emerged in Vatican II.

Notes

1   Dupuis, J., "Religious plurality and the Christological debate" *Sedos Bulletin* 28 (1996) pp. 329-333 at p. 330.

2   Lohfink, G., *Does God Need the Church*, (Collegeville Minnesota: Glazier Book, 1999) p. 21.

3   McBrien, P., *Catholicism*, (London: Geoffrey Champman, 1981) p.772.

4   Lohfink, G., *Does God need the Church*, pp. 31-39.

5   Fuellenbach, J., *Throw Fire*, pp. 85-101.

6   Fuellenbach, J., *Throw Fire,* pp. 13-60.

7   Song, C. S., *Jesus & the Reign of God*, (Minneapolis: Fortress Press, 1993) pp. 8-9.

8   Viviano, B. T., *The Kingdom of God in History* (Wilmington, Delaware: Michael Glazier, 1988) pp. 28-29

9   Casaldáliga, P. & Vigil, J. Maria, *Political Holiness* (New York: Orbis Books, 1994) p. 82.

10 Borg, M., *The God we never knew*, (San Francisco: Harper, 1998) pp. 133-134.

11 John Paul II, *Redemptoris Missio* (Vatican City: Liberia Editrice Vaticana, 1991) No. 13.

12 as quoted in Ralph Covell, "Jesus Christ and World Religions" in T*he Good News of the Kingdom: Mission Theology for the Third Millennium*, eds. Charles Van Engen, Dean S. Gilliland, Paul Pierson (New York: Orbis Books, 1993) p. 163.

13 Rahner, K., *The Church and the Sacraments* (London: Burns & Oates, 1963) p. 15.

14 Lohfink, G., *Jesus and Community,* pp. 75-148.

Part 1

The Church in Scripture and in Vatican II

Chapter One

JESUS AND THE CHURCH

I. Return to the Jesus who walked over this earth

In dealing with our topic it is essential that we go back to the Jesus who walked on this earth, to have a fresh look at his vision. Only by returning to the Jesus who walked over the earth will we find anew a foundation for our self-understanding not only as individual Christians but also as Church. As Metz sees it, only the imagery of discipleship carries the capacity to call the Church back to its origins, authentic life, and mission:

> The Church... cannot solve the crisis of its historical identity and its societal legitimation in a purely interpretative or hermeneutical manner, but only by practical identification. The problem of her identity is fundamentally a theory-praxis problem. That praxis whose intelligible and identity-securing power cannot be replaced by interpretation is called discipleship. The Church's crisis is due to a deficit in discipleship and to difficulties in adapting to Jesus.[15]

The most salient sentence in this quotation is the last one concerning the crisis in the Church today. As early as 1968 the German Bishops Conference assessed the situation of the Church in Germany. Looking for an appropriate response to the then emerging faith crisis in the country, they proposed a solution that echoed the words of J. B. Metz: "The way out of the situation in which we find ourselves today can only be once again a way into fellowship with Jesus the Lord."

Today more than thirty years later the crisis has heightened and the response proposed at that time seems to be even more urgent now: "the way out ... can only be a way into following the Jesus who walked this earth."

Looking at their Churches, the bishops found it necessary to stress the following 'signposts' to discipleship: *the obedience of the cross, poverty, freedom and joy* — attitudes and behaviors that counted so high in Jesus' own life. The bishops then confess that their Churches portray a 'religion of prosperity' rather than a 'religion of the cross'; a 'rich Church' rather than a Church in solidarity with the poor and weak; a Church anxiously holding back from the risk of the freedom of the Gospel rather than going on the offensive; and finally a Church which looks anxiously inward rather than radiating the joy of the redeemed. They felt the urgent need to return to the root of our commitment, the Jesus who walked the earth and died for a vision the world today needs so badly.[16]

In the light of the image crisis of the Church today, Avery Dulles proposed a new conception of the Church which he calls *Community of Disciples*. Behind this image we find again an expression of the newly discovered realization that the basic vocation of any Christian is first and foremost to follow the Lord as he walked over this earth. The emphasis here is on following the Lord rather than following the Church, on being constantly on the road rather than having already reached the goal. The Church must be seen as the community of those who have made it their lives' profession to follow the Lord and as such to build a community called Church.[17]

Discipleship gives to the individual as well as to the Christian community a unique identity and purpose. But this should not lead it to a withdrawal into a cozy community. By itself it does not exclude the wider world. As a notion that refers Christian identity to the actions of Jesus, discipleship demands from Christians a commitment to mission in the world. Though disciples are separated from their cultural milieu by taking their cue for action only from following Jesus, they are not exempt from acting in or on behalf of the world. On the contrary, this very independence provides the Church with a basis for criticizing and challenging the false standards of the larger society. Being called to participate in God's own mission for the world demands the baptized not to withdraw but to vigorously engage in God's saving actions for humanity and in all human affairs.

II. Biblical findings concerning Israel, Kingdom, Church

The Exodus story: God's election of a "counter society"[18]

The Exodus story in the Old Testament explains to us most clearly what God has in mind for his creatures: he intends to lead all of humanity by choosing one particular people to be the sign and instrument to accomplish this goal. To understand the purpose and mission of the Church as the newly chosen people of God, it is of tantamount importance not to lose sight of this foundational story of God's saving intervention in history.

The oldest historical summary of the faith that we have from Israel is Numbers 20:15

Our forefathers went down into Egypt, and we lived there many years. The Egyptians mistreated us and our fathers, then we cried to Yahweh and he heard our cry. He sent an angel who brought us forth out of Egypt.

But the official creed became: Deuteronomy 26:5-9

Then you shall declare before the LORD your God: "My father was a wandering Aramean, and he went down into Egypt with a few people and lived there and became a great nation, powerful and numerous. {6} But the Egyptians mistreated us and made us suffer, putting us to hard labor. {7} Then we cried out to the LORD, the God of our fathers, and the LORD heard our voice and saw our misery, toil and oppression. {8} So the LORD brought us out of Egypt with a mighty hand and an outstretched arm, with great terror and with miraculous signs and wonders. {9} He brought us to this place and gave us this land, a land flowing with milk and honey;

This text is the quintessence of Israel's faith, and it is neither accident nor exaggeration that it is entirely subsumed under the theme of liberation.

This central Old Testament text alone should silence anyone who finds it embarrassing for Christian Churches to speak of an "option for the poor" and for a theology to call itself "liberation theology." This credo is above all a confession of God who led the poor into freedom. If the credo of the New Testament adds new dimensions, it certainly never falls short of this credo.[19]

This creed has the following scheme of action:

1. People are in distress.
2. They cry out to God.
3. God hears their cry and sees their distress.
4. God intervenes and alleviates the distress.

Israel shares these points with other religions around it. In these as well the gods are concerned with the poor and listen to their cry. But what is the difference between these gods and the God of Israel?

1. In the Near East poor people would pray to their gods and experience help from them as individuals or as small groups. The social system, however, in which they lived and which might have been the source of their poverty, was not expected to be changed by the

gods in favor of the poor. It would remain the same. There was never a large group in a given population that was recognized as a group of poor and oppressed people and then rescued by a god from their poverty and oppression. In the word of Deuteronomy 4:34:

> *Or has any god ever attempted to go to a nation and take it himself from the midst of another nation, by trials, by signs, by wonders, and by war, by mighty hand and an outstretched arm, and by great terror, according to all that Yahweh, your God, did for you in Egypt before your eyes?*

The Israelites were the Egyptian lower class, the bottom line of Pharaoh's society, with no class lower being mentioned, much like the underclass found in every major society. Poor as a large group within a larger society, they exceeded the dimensions normally envisioned in the lament and thanksgiving prayers of poor people. In these only individuals or very small groups direct themselves to the gods, be it in lament, expressing their distress and asking for help, or giving thanks for received help.

2. The misery of these poor is clearly explained in the Credo of Dt 26 as resulting from economic exploitation and social degradation. Poverty is recognized as the product of human action. It is not fate or the will of God or something deserved because of personal fault. It was created by the social system represented by Pharaoh.

3. Yahweh does not intervene to lighten the suffering only to leave the system intact or even helping it to get reestablished by integrating the poor again into society. Instead the poor are removed from the impoverished situation. This is a previously unheard-of message: God physically removes the poor from the world of oppression. He takes them completely outside the Egyptian system.

Different attempts to aid the exploited Hebrews are made.

   – Pharaoh's daughter rescues Moses, a well known example of royal concern for an individual poor person. But what do these individual acts of charity do for the other poor in society?

   – Moses tries to be a liberator himself through counter-terror when he kills an especially brutal oppressor. But the system is too powerful and the structures of fear have already been so interiorized by the oppressed that they do not want to have anything to do with him. He acts like a terrorist who, to become the leader of the oppressed, behaves exactly like the oppressors themselves.

– Moses and Aaron constantly attempt to achieve an amelioration of the condition of the oppressed people within the system through negotiations with the Pharaoh. One could call this a "reformist or revisionist" method. But it did not work either. The system that despises and exploits people creates its own downfall. God seems to prepare his plan in showing that nothing will work along the line of reform and negotiation except a total withdrawal of the oppressed from the oppressing society.

– Yahweh has another plan for dealing with the situation. He leads people out of the system. The victims, once freed, can at times not cope with their new situation. They want to go back into slavery. They start complaining in the desert and yearn for the fleshpots of Egypt (Ex 14:10-12).

 – The removal of the poor from the system that enslaves them is entirely the work of Yahweh, "with mighty hand and outstretched arm, great terror, signs and wonders." It breaks all laws of nature.

 – Something new is to be created. The departure from the corrupt and therefore impoverished world of Egypt would not have been a divine miracle, a new work of creation, if it had not at the same time marked the beginning of something new and greater: It is the departure from an old society to a new society. It marks the entrance into a "land flowing with milk and honey". Milk and honey are regarded in the ancient world as the Elysian food of the gods. This is an image of the plenitude of paradise.

At Mount Sinai Israel was made into a new society on its way through the desert. So changed, they will now enter the promised land flowing with milk and honey to celebrate a "feast for Yahweh." The aim of the Exodus is to create a new people that will for ever celebrate its God in a new society.

The point of this is that the departure from the impoverished society was not a genuine removal unless it led to the constitution of a new society that does not know poverty anymore and in whose midst Yahweh their God is celebrated in an everlasting feast. Yahweh intends to create a society of brothers and sisters where there will be no poor anymore. The poor of Egypt are to become, through the Exodus, a kind of divinely-willed CONTRAST-SOCIETY.

This new society stands in contrast not only with the society they just left but with all other existing societies in their world. It is meant for the good of all humanity. Israel's laws and statutes aim at making them into such a contrast society that others will marvel at what a wise and understanding people they are.

> *You shall keep them and do them; for that will be your wisdom and understanding, which the nations seek. When anyone reads these laws to them, they will cry: "Surely this great nation is a wise and understanding people!" For what great nation is there that has gods so near to it as Yahweh our God was to us, whenever we have called on him for help? And what great nation is there, that has statutes and ordinances so righteous as all this social order which I set before you this day? (Dt 4:6-8)*

Walter Brueggemann shares this view with Lohfink in almost all aspects. He comments:

> The call of Israel can only be understood as a new call of God to create an alternative social reality. The break of Moses and Israel from imperial reality is a break from both the religion of static triumphalism and the politics of oppression and exploitation. What emerges is an alternative religion of the freedom of God, and the politics of oppression and exploitation is met with a politics of justice and compassion. What emerges is a new social community that matches the vision of God's freedom.[20]

The intervention of God into the history of humankind on behalf of Israel aims at creating an alternative social vision to the social vision which regarded oppression and dependence as part of human society. The Exodus opens up a new vision of what it means to be human in the eyes of God. The Covenant with his people is God's view of how he envisions a society in which human beings will live as his children in justice and peace with each other. They are to form a *contrast society* in opposition to the *Pharaoh society* in which they had experiences oppression and injustice. On this presupposition rested Israel's very reason of existence. In being such a society, the Covenant people revealed already what God had in store for all of humanity.

If this held true for Israel of old, how much more would the eschatological community mirror this ultimate plan of God. Israel was to witness to this plan, but its history showed clearly how the people failed constantly to the degree that the Old Testament Covenant has been looked upon as the *history of a broken Covenant.* The leaders of the people always managed to return to the same *Pharaoh society* from which Yahweh had rescued them.

Jesus' main mission must be seen in this context of a broken Covenant. He understood his mission as being sent to restore the Covenant to its original intention and meaning. But the social vision of society in his days had once again acquired all the features of a *Pharaoh society* even though names and certain traits had changed.

The dominant social vision of his time was centered on *holiness* and *purity* which in practice had ostracized almost half of the population. In protest and in opposition to this reality, Jesus once again offered an alternative vision based on the ideal of the Covenant that Yahweh had offered. Jesus' social vision focused on *justice* and *compassion* as the prophets had already demanded from people in their time. What should rule the life of a community was not holiness, which means separation and withdrawal leading to marginalization and oppression, but compassion which calls for creating a community that is inclusive and tears down what separates and divides people. He understood his community to be a place where all people would be brothers and sisters, where justice and compassion would reign under the one Fatherhood of God.[21]

From this vision of God's Covenant with his people as a "contrast society" and Jesus' ultimate intention of restoring this vision and leading to completion, it becomes obvious that a correct understanding of Church cannot be attained without taking the whole of salvation history into account as it unfolded in the Old Testament.

Kingdom and Church in the Gospels

Since Jesus' central message was the Kingdom, the first question to be dealt with is: What exactly is the relationship between the Kingdom that Jesus preached and the Church he intended? The only biblical text where Church and Kingdom appear side by side in the teaching of Jesus is Matthew 16:18-19.

> *You are Peter and on this rock I will build my Church... I will give you the keys of the Kingdom of Heaven: whatever you bind on earth will be bound in heaven; whatever you loose on earth will be loosed in heaven.*

Traditional apologetics look at this text as a "Church-founding" logion of the earthly-historical Jesus. Here Jesus declares, clearly and without any doubt, Peter as the head and foundation stone of His coming Church community, and to him he entrusts the keys to God's Kingdom. A fundamentalistic interpretation of this text will not do. Jesus and the Church cannot be explained from this text alone. Today most exegetes hold that this saying points back to a post-Easter evaluation of Peter's role in the

Church at that time. The text as found in Matthew 16:18 is an enlargement in contrast to Mark's story of Peter's confession of Jesus as the Christ (Mk 8:27-30). Matthew added the so-called Petrine text to Mark's basic text to portray the head of the apostolic college as the prototype and example of faith in Christ. Peter, who was the first witness of Jesus' resurrection, became the basis of the resurrection faith and was, accordingly, regarded as the leader of the first community in Jerusalem. Matthew's version is regarded as "Gemeindebildung".[22] It is, therefore, not wise to put too much weight on this text though, at first sight, it may appear clear and convincing.

The word 'Church' itself is found only twice on the lips of Jesus (Mt 16:18 and 18:17), while the phrase Kingdom of God can be found 92 times in Jesus' own words. (In comparison, the Kingdom of God appears only 75 times in all the documents of Vatican II, while the word Church appears approximately 2000 times. If we limit our search to the two main Vatican II documents on the Church, *Lumen Gentium* and *Gaudium et Spes*, we find the symbol Kingdom 48 times and the word Church around 400 times.)

All together the term 'ecclesia' appears 114 times in the New Testament: 65 times in Paul, 23 times in Acts, 20 times in Revelation, and twice in Matthew (it is not used in Mark, Luke or John). It can signify the whole Church (cf. Eph 1,22f; Col 1,18; Gal 1,13; I Cor 15,9), as well as local Churches (cf. the beginnings of epistles, 1Cor 1,2; Rev 2,1.8,12, etc.) and particular house-Churches (Phlm 1,2). The word did not have this meaning in its original Greek form, where it simply means "public gathering." It was borrowed from the Septuagint, where it is used about a hundred times and most often signifies the cultic community, the gahal Jahweh (this is also the meaning of synagogue).[23]

Considering the rare use of the word *Church* on the lips of Jesus (twice in only one Gospel), can we conclude that the central teaching of Jesus was the Kingdom while the Church occupied no significant place in Jesus' own thought? Did the early Church substitute the Kingdom for the Church because the parousia did not come? It would be dangerous for theology to measure everything by the range of the names applied to it. The word Church may not appear often in Jesus' teaching. Nevertheless the concept of the messianic community, intrinsically bound up with the Kingdom, implies what is meant by the concept Church. It is therefore correct to say:

> The Kingdom of God and the Church are two key New Testament concepts, both are crucial for the understanding of God's plan for humanity. They are central to the fulfillment of his redemptive purpose. While the Church can-

not be identified with the Kingdom, for the latter is a larger and more comprehensive term, the two are nevertheless in such close correlation that they cannot be separated either.[24]

Most moderate theologians agree that the Kingdom of God and the Church as the messianic community are intrinsically connected and cannot be separated from each other. This holds true not only for the final fulfillment of the Kingdom but already for the 'Kingdom now'. The Kingdom present in history and the Church here on earth are two closely interrelated realities. The difficulty we encounter is how to explain their relatedness without doing violence to either one. Is it the Kingdom that explains the Church? or is it the Church that explains the Kingdom? Does the Kingdom need a Church to remain present in the world? Does the Church need the Kingdom to be understood at all? The answers to these questions will be taken up later.

The other issue related to the question of Jesus and the Church is the relationship between Jesus and Israel. For some exegetes, like Lohfink, the question whether or not Jesus founded a Church is superfluous. Jesus did not have to found a Church; it existed already for many centuries as the people of Israel. For this reason Jesus addressed himself exclusively to the Jewish nation. Israel would constitute the definite people of God that was to come to power soon. Jesus' intention was to reassemble his people in the light of the imminent Kingdom by making them into the true people of God, faithful to the real intentions of their Covenant with God.

The question of the origin of the Church is intimately linked with Jesus' preaching and practice of the Kingdom and with Israel's response or failure to respond to Jesus' message. The early Christian community understood itself in the context of Israel and had no intention of separating itself from the Covenant people. Only the resistance and rejection of the Jewish people forced the followers of Jesus to go to the pagans in the power of the Risen One's Spirit.[25]

The Kingdom vision mediated through the Church

We described the Kingdom as the vision of reality, of creation, of God and of humankind which Jesus came to communicate.

Jesus entrusted this vision to the community of his disciples. We in turn received the Kingdom vision of Jesus not like a sudden bolt of lightening but through the faith community into which we were born, the Church. This community in turn has given to this vision of the Kingdom its own framework and shape and communicated all this to us. In short, the vision came to us in the understanding and form it has taken in the long tradition of the Church community herself. As members we have to ask how this community, called Church, understands herself now vis-a-vis Jesus and his Kingdom.

Jesus' vision is always communicated in some concrete shape, in this case through the preaching and teaching of the Church. Thus the basic question is: What image do we have of the Church as the true bearer of Jesus' own vision?

Do we find in the Church's vision of reality Jesus' own vision of the Kingdom? One may object and insist that there is no other vision of Jesus' Kingdom accessible to us than the one the Church offers us. This might be true but it is equally true that the Church while containing Jesus' Kingdom vision might have turned the focus on secondary concerns and in so doing might have notably obscured the center. Because of this many find it difficult to discover in her easily and spontaneously the vision Jesus came to *throw like fire* into this world. For them the fire seems to have gone out, or at least, it seems to have been dimmed considerably.

The question is ultimately one concerning the *image* of the Church. The crisis of faith today is widely a crisis of image. Images are powerful since they speak to us existentially and find an echo in the depth of our being. They have an evocative power. They convey a meaning that is apprehended in a non-conceptual way. In the words of A. Dulles:

> Symbols transform the horizons of man's life, integrate his perception of reality, alter his scale of values, reorient his loyalties, attachments, and aspirations in a manner far exceeding the powers of abstract conceptual thoughts.[26]

Do we have an image of the Church today that can inspire people and supply an ideal they can identify with and commit themselves to with enthusiasm and lasting zeal? For this we need a vision that does several things:

- explain the *raison d'être* of the Church
- clearly indicate the goal towards which she is moving
- correspond to the faith experience of the individual member as well as the community,
- present a set of values and priorities
- explain the relationship between the Church to which we belong and the world in which we live today
- act as a guiding star, and yet not out of our reach, so that it can give us a clear mandate for action.

Do we have such a vision and, if not, can we provide one? Some scholars claim that the ineffectiveness of the Church in many sectors of her apostolate today is due to the fact that we have no adequate image of the Church "into which people can plausibly fit what they think they ought to be doing." They claim that,

> If we could fashion an inspiring and realistic image of the Church, we might be able to act confidently, and in such a way that our self-understanding would be reinforced by feedback from others.[27]

The present prevailing image of the Church in many parts of the world is still that of organized religion with laws, rules and structures. The Church is seen as an institution in society that fulfills expected functions side by side with other entities like business, government, labor and entertainment. Society has allotted a role to religion and expects it to be fulfilled without interference in the functions of other agencies. In letting herself be integrated totally into society, the Church loses her world-transforming power. Jesus gave the key to the Kingdom to his Church, but to many today it appears that the Church has lost the key. The result is the constantly heard refrain, "Jesus Yes, Church No." The need for a prophetic ministry that could enkindle once again the fire that Jesus came to throw into the world is obvious.

> The time may be ripe in the Church for serious consideration of prophecy as a crucial element in ministry.[28]

What Walter Brueggemann is asking for is the exercise of a prophetic ministry that can create a new consciousness in the Church. Its task is to evoke an alternative to the consciousness and perception of the dominant culture around us with its overpowering ethos of consumerism. This alternative would engage in the dismantling of the way the present order of things is legitimized by the dominant mentality. But criticism alone is not enough. The new alternative must at the same time energize the faithful and the communities through its promise that there are other ways of living Christian community, different from the ones contemporary society offers. It must lead the Church to form or reform herself into another kind of community in order "to live (once again) in fervent anticipation of the newness that God has promised and will surely give."[29]

It has become a common-place truth to declare that the Church of today is 'sick' and needs serious attention. The cure, of course, depends largely on the right diagnosis. Many experts diagnose her sickness precisely as the lack of a comprehensive vision. Could a return to the fundamental vision of Jesus, the Kingdom of God, be the best starting point for

the necessary cure? There is no better way to start than to go back and to
reclaim for ourselves the memory of that vision that Jesus came to throw
like fire into this world (Lk 12:49).

> The Church will not have power to act or believe until it recovers its tradi-
> tion of faith and permits that tradition to be the primal way out of
> inculturation. This is not a cry for traditionalism but rather a judgement that
> the Church has no business more pressing than the re-appropriation of its
> memory in its full power and authenticity.[30]

According to the Gospel of Matthew, Christ entrusted the keys of the
Kingdom to his Church (16:18). In doing so, he gave her not only the
medicine for the whole world but also the medicine for her own sicknesses.
The cure for the Church is the return to the Kingdom vision of Jesus. People
looking at the Church today might say: Physician heal yourself first before
you offer your medicine to us. The symbol, Kingdom of God, offers the
Church a horizon of transcendence that will save her from again and again
closing herself up in stifling structures. Only this has the dynamic power to
create new images and visions of what the Church is to be and has to do in the
concrete situations of human history on its way towards its final goal.

Conclusion

We have seen that the word Church appears only twice on the lips of
Jesus. Since Matthew 18:17 clearly refers to the local community, only
once is Jesus remembered to have spoken about the Church in the wider
sense: "Upon this rock I will build my Church" (Mt 16:18). Both texts,
however, are generally regarded as "Gemeindebildung", meaning they were
formulated by the evangelist and put into the mouth of the earthly-historical Jesus. These words nevertheless remain important, for by means of
these ecclesial Jesus-words the early Church expressed her self-understanding and structured her ministries and offices.[31] Dulles insists that this text,
from a theological point of view, not only binds the Church to the Kingdom but also the Kingdom to the Church. He writes:

> So far as I am aware, there is only one text in which Church and kingdom
> are mentioned together: "And so I say to you, you are Peter, and upon this
> rock I will build my Church, and the gates of the netherworld shall not pre-
> vail against it. I will give you the keys of the kingdom of heaven. Whatever
> you bind on earth shall be bound in heaven; and whatever you loose on earth
> shall be loosed in heaven" (Mt 16:18-19). Peter, by the same act, is made
> the foundation of the Church of Christ and the keeper of the keys of the
> kingdom of heaven. The metaphor of binding and loosing reappears in Mat-

thew 18:18: "Whatever you bind on earth shall be bound in heaven, and whatever you loose on earth shall be loosed in heaven." "Heaven" in the second quotation may be equivalent to the "kingdom of Heaven" in the first. In both texts the correct interpretation may well be that decisions made in the Church on earth have validity for a person's definitive participation in the ultimate kingdom.[32]

Although Jesus may never have used the word Church, it is amazing to see with how much ease the early Christian communities right away linked Jesus to the Church and the Church to the Kingdom and Israel of Old. Referring to the minimal use of the word Church by Jesus R. Brown writes:

> In spite of this slender terminological basis in Jesus' recorded ministry, within a half century Ephesians 5:25 claims: "Christ loved the Church and gave himself up for her." It is remarkable how quickly the Christians became community-minded even though Jesus showed little interest in a formally distinct society. The ritual of baptism — absent from Jesus' own ministry — seems to have become very soon the standard feature of Christian life as Matthew, Acts, Paul, and John indicate. The baptized were designated as those who "belonged" to the KOINONIA, the community, a name that seems to have been one of the first names the "followers of the way" assumed for themselves.[33]

III. Jesus and the foundation of the Church

If we start with Jesus' own message to recapture his vision and furnish the Church with a viable image, our first question will be: Did Jesus intend a Church? What connection, if any, can we establish between the Church's evaluation of herself and Jesus' evaluation of the Church? The relationship between the historical Jesus and the Church has remained one of the greatest problems in Christian theology. So far, a unified solution has not been found.[34]

Many answers have been given to this question. One extreme posits a direct, explicit and deliberate act, by which Jesus established a new religious organization with all its structures, seven sacraments and hierarchy firmly in place and outlined in detail. The other extreme claims that Jesus came to proclaim the Kingdom of God and had no intention whatsoever of founding a Church. He came to teach us a way of life centered on love and based on freedom from any institutional oppression. The fact is that Jesus showed little interest in structural and foundational issues. His interest was the renewal of Israel, which already had established forms of worship, priests, sacrifices — Jesus did not need to plan such structures.

1. The most common positions today

The most commonly held views in Catholic theology today are expressed by authors like H. Küng, K. Rahner, and G. Lohfink. Those who follow Küng maintain that Jesus neither founded nor instituted a church, that the Church's origins are to be traced to the faith confession — the Easter faith — of the post-paschal community of Jesus Christ. According to this view, the actual foundation and institution of the Church is to be situated in the resurrection faith of the first Church. Hans Küng expressed this view in *Die Kirche* (1967) and, more markedly still, in *Christ Sein* (1974). For Küng the Church does represent the continuation of Jesus' mission and his activity, but she nevertheless is a post-paschal phenomenon.

R. Michiels holds that the best starting-point for answering the question of Jesus and the Church is Küng's position. He writes:

> Our point of departure will be the position of Hans Küng, which one can formulate either positively or negatively.
>
> Formulated negatively, one can only admit that the life of the earthly-historical Jesus contains neither a specific moment or instance, nor a word or deed which, strictly speaking, can claim to represent the distinct institution of the Church. Such an admission does justice to the first position, i.e., that position which maintains that the historical Jesus did not found a Church, and that Jesus' institution of the Church has its foundations in the resurrection faith of the first Church.
>
> Formulated positively, this first position consists in the affirmation that the Church has only existed since the disciples believed in the resurrection of Jesus, that, therefore, she only exists by the grace of the risen and glorified Christ or in the power of his Spirit. Accordingly, the Church was born or came to be on Pentecost, 'instituted' as the harvest of Easter. Almost no one would now maintain that the concrete development or organization of the Church, including her liturgies and offices (excepting, of course, the apostolic office, understood as 'being sent by Jesus'), derives from Jesus himself. This organization and its accompanying structures are the result of a complex historical process, necessitated by the fact that God has placed his Church firmly in history with all that attends on such a placement. One can give the ideological-ecclesiological expression to the fact that the earthly-historical Jesus did not found or institute the Church by saying (first negatively, then positively) that the Church is not so much the continuation of Jesus' humanity or the perpetuation of the incarnation of the Word, but rather the continuing mission of Jesus' Spirit, the perpetuation of his action in God's Spirit. The underlying truth in Küng's vision of the non-institution of the Church by Jesus consists then in the ecclesiological perception that it is the Spirit which effects the actual and complete foundation and institution of the Church from Pentecost onwards.[35]

Küng insists that we should not speak of Church unless we start from the resurrection of Christ and from the event called Pentecost. Surely there was a community of disciples before Easter gathered around Jesus. He himself must have seen a connection between this group and the coming about of the eschatological community to which all of Israel was called. But for him it is not possible to give the title Church to the group of those who responded to Jesus' proclamation of the Kingdom. Whatever connection there may be between those who followed the Lord when he walked this earth and the community that emerged after Easter, one should not call it Church. Küng correctly makes the point that without the Easter faith and Pentecost we could hardly talk about Church in the proper sense of the word.

Others like K. Rahner insist that the earthly and historical Jesus did indeed lay the foundation for a Church. In this view the foundation of the Church is to be situated in the life of Jesus himself. Rahner uses the word 'foundation,' which does not mean the same as saying that Jesus 'instituted' the Church. 'Institution' would express a juridical act on Jesus' part, which had the establishment of a new religious organization as its goal.

A third approach to the question of Jesus' relationship to the Church was developed by Gerhard Lohfink in *Hat Jesus eine Kirche gestiftet?* (1981) and *Wie hat Jesus Gemeinde gewollt?* (1982,1987). He insists that Jesus never intended to institute a new religion or a new religious grouping or a Church, and certainly not a personal or distinct community within Israel itself. The Church that Jesus wanted had long existed — Israel, the people of God. Accordingly the beginning or coming of the Church should not be situated in a special institutive act or plan of the historical Jesus or in some last will and testament of the crucified but divinely Risen Lord. On the contrary the origin of the Church is a process, intimately connected with Jesus' preaching and praxis of the Kingdom of God and with Israel's response to it. This entire process is the work of God, God's way with His people.

This view of the Church begins with the Old Testament. It includes Jesus, who sought to reassemble his people but, having met with resistance, was thus obliged to concentrate on his own followers and the Twelve in particular. The latter represented the whole of Israel, to whom in turn they were sent. This perspective continues in the post-paschal community of Jesus' followers, who themselves met Jewish resistance and, therefore, in the power of the Risen One's Spirit, chose to go the way that brought them to the pagans. In short, Lohfink sees the foundation of the Church in the existence of Israel as such.

2. Four representatives of the common positions

Since none of the extremes can substantiate its claims from the sources themselves, we will briefly introduce four Catholic scholars from different cultural backgrounds, who present the common positions generally held in the Catholic Church today.

Richard McBrien: Catholicism[36]

McBrien, following Rahner's lead, distinguishes between the Church having its origin in Jesus and having been founded by Jesus. To the first he says "Yes," to the second, no. Jesus never addressed his message to a selected group but intended it for Israel as a whole. The election of the Twelve has to be seen in this light. They were meant to represent Israel as a whole. Salvation of the individual was not conditioned by a specific rule of life nor was membership in the company of his disciples required. However, Jesus did lay the foundations for a church.

Firstly he did gather disciples around himself. They are the ones who accepted his message and to whom he gave a share in his ministry by sending them out to preach (Mt 10:1-16).

Secondly, Jesus anticipated an INTERIM PERIOD between his death and the Parousia. He could foresee that Israel as a whole would reject him and that the gentiles would take the place of the Jewish people and thus become the new eschatological people.

Thirdly, the group of the disciples did stay together after the rejection of Jesus. From this perspective the Last Supper becomes decisive with its injunction: "Do this in remembrance of me." Likewise the word to Peter suggests that Jesus intended his disciples to stay together: "I have prayed for you, Simon, ...and once you have recovered, you in turn must strengthen your brothers" (Lk 22:31-32. See Mt 16:13-19: "You are Peter and on this rock I will build my Church"). In that sense there was never a churchless period in the New Testament.

Gerhard Lohfink: Did Jesus found a Church?[37]

Lohfink summarizes his view under seven points:

1. Jesus never wanted to found a new religious body distinct from Israel. He saw and understood his mission in the confines of Israel.

2. Jesus did not intend to found a distinct community, a holy remnant WITHIN Israel, like the Essenes.

3. Jesus' concern was for ALL Israel; he wanted to gather and renew the whole people for the in-breaking of the final Kingdom. The election of the Twelve is a clear sign of this intention. There were only two-and-one-half tribes left: Judah, Benjamin, and half of Levi. The complete restoration of the twelve-tribe people was expected for the eschatological time of salvation (see Ez 37; 39:23-29; 40-48).

4. The early community saw itself as God's eschatological people who, by faith in the risen Christ and his message, were to gather all Israel.

5. The fact that the majority of Israel rejected Jesus had a decisive influence on the phenomenon we call Church.

6. It is hard to fix a point for the Church's origin. It was rather a 'process' that gradually brought forth what we now mean by Church.

7. The establishment of the Church is the work of God, who through Christ and the Spirit created his end-time people.

Walter Kirchschläger: his common points can be summarized as follows:[38]

1. The most fundamental basis for the emergence of the Church is Jesus' proclamation of the Kingdom of God. This proclamation is directed to all, namely to the community of those who are ready to convert and to accept God's offer of salvation present now in Jesus. The presence of God's Kingdom now is intrinsically connected with the person of Jesus. Fellowship with Jesus becomes, therefore, a fundamental concept regarding any definition or concept of Church. The final revelation of God's message of salvation is only accessible through an orientation towards Jesus.

2. Jesus called disciples, men and women (Lk 8:1-3), and binds them to his person. Two aspects are clearly distinct in the vocation stories of the Gospel (Mk 3:13-15): those who are called enter into a deep communion with Jesus and are then sent out to proliferate the message of Jesus. This clearly indicates that Jesus intended to multiply his activity and to ensure the permanence of his proclamation of the Kingdom through those whom he called. Through the election of the twelve Jesus made it clear that he wanted to create a new people of God that would, of course, include Israel, but an Israel restored and renewed.

3. The community that followed Jesus is structured from the start and shows an initial ordering. There are the Twelve, who form a core-group around

Jesus. There are those who form a wider circle of disciples including men and women who follow him permanently on the road. Finally, there are others who follow him only occasionally. Yet what is common to them all is: they follow Jesus, although this following might have taken different forms and the life shared with him might have known different degrees of intimacy and intensity. In this connection, it is important to point out the special role Peter seems to have played. The name Jesus gave him "Cephas" (Jn 1:42) indicated that Jesus had in mind a permanent group among which Peter would have a special mission to perform.

4. Jesus gathered disciples, both men and women, into a personal communion with himself. The purpose of such a gathering is missionary. His message should not be limited to those gathered around him but it must be spread through all the earth (Mk 6:7-13). The final revelation of God's saving love for all now made irrevocably present through Jesus of Nazareth, is the most fundamental fact on which the Church is founded.

5. The institution of the last supper makes it clear that Jesus reckoned with the certainty that his disciples would continue to proclaim his message of salvation now sealed through his immediate death for the many. Jesus' death becomes the ultimate yes of God for the salvation of the world irrevocably sealed on the cross. Here Jesus laid the foundation for the *New Covenant in his blood* which created the new Community of salvation. This Covenant will be made present always anew wherever his disciples will celebrate this last supper and doing it *"in memory of me."*

Leonardo Boff: Church, Charisma and Power[39]

Jesus' concern was the Kingdom of God, not the Church as such. For him the Kingdom contained the global transformation of the old world. It would become the new world without sin, sickness, hatred, and all alienating forces that affect both human life and the entire cosmos.

In his preaching Jesus introduced elements, such as the gathering of the twelve apostles and the institution of the last supper, which later would form the basis of the Church. But these elements do not constitute the entire reality of the Church. The Church exists only because the Kingdom was not accepted by the Jewish people and Jesus was rejected by them. Therefore, the Church substitutes for the Kingdom and must be seen as an instrument for the full realization of the Kingdom and as a sign of a true yet still imperfect realization of this Kingdom in the world. We could also say: the Church is the presence of the Kingdom in history insofar as the

Risen Christ is present in this community of believers. But she is not the Kingdom insofar as the Kingdom is still to be realized eschatologically in its universal dimension. The Church must see itself totally in the service of the Kingdom. She is the sacrament of the Kingdom in the sense that she is a sign and instrument of the Kingdom's appearance and realization in history.[40]

The apostles went out to preach the Kingdom to Israel as Jesus had done and awaited the imminent eruption of the Kingdom with the glorious and definite coming of the risen Lord. Since Israel refused their message as it had refused to listen to Jesus himself, they were prompted by the Holy Spirit to turn to the pagans. This turning to the pagans became the decisive step towards the foundation of a church. By taking the elements introduced by the historical Jesus — his message, his summoning of the Twelve, Baptism and the Eucharist — the apostles founded the Church. In her concrete historical form, the Church is based on the essential elements given by Christ and the decision of the apostles inspired by the Holy Spirit. The Church as an institution in space and time arose from a historical decision by the apostles, enlightened by the Holy Spirit. For Boff, then, the Church will continue to exist only if people of faith in the Risen Christ and his Spirit continually renew this decision and incarnate the Church in ever new situations.

Conclusion

We have looked at a wide spectrum of what Catholic theologians hold today. McBrien sums up a whole generation of theologians like K. Rahner, Vögtle, Semmelroth, Ratzinger, etc. For them the Church is a post-Easter reality brought about through the outpouring of the Holy Spirit but having its origin in the historical Jesus. Lohfink as an exegete is already more critical. For him the Church is based on a whole string of elements out of which she gradually emerged. It is not possible to fix one particular event and regard it as the decisive act that created the Church. In his concern for flexible structures, Boff sees the *concrete historical form* of the Church — while not denying its divine origin — first and foremost as a result of the decision made by the apostles and their successors after them. While the Church is based on Jesus and his Spirit, the existence of the Church as a historical reality also depends on the willingness of the faithful to go on 're-inventing' the Church in ever new situations. Boff's ecclesiology is very much concerned with showing that the basic ecclesial communities are the ones that, so to speak, *re-invent* the Church today in new situations, which demand new forms of structures under the guidance of the same Spirit whom Jesus had promised to his apostles and their successors.

In conclusion we could say with Michiels:

As far as the institution of the Church by Jesus Himself is concerned, what are involved are not so much Church-foundational movements or words but the continuation of Jesus' mission in and through the mission of the first Church.[41]

Vatican II had this to say about Jesus and the Church:

The mystery of the holy Church is manifested in her very foundation, for the Lord Jesus inaugurated her by preaching the good news, that is, the coming of God's Kingdom.... When Jesus rose up again... he poured out on His disciples the Spirit promised by the Father. The Church, consequently, equipped with the gifts of her founder... received the mission to proclaim and to establish among all peoples the Kingdom of Christ and of God. She becomes on earth the initial budding forth of that Kingdom (Lumen Gentium 5).

The Council seems to agree that the empowerment to continue the mission of Christ by bringing God's Kingdom to the end of the earth is the most essential aspect about the foundation of the Church by Jesus himself. It is the decision to carry on the mission of Jesus' Kingdom that remains the basis of the Church. This decision flows from the desire to follow the Lord, who had called the disciples precisely for that purpose and promised them his continuing presence in the Holy Spirit. Thus the Church is, first of all, not a question of holding on to particular structural elements. It involves obedience to fulfil faithfully the mission entrusted to her, i.e., carrying on the message of the Kingdom as Jesus brought it.[42]

While the different authors may stress particular aspects, the common points that emerge from these different views can be summarized as follows:

1. Jesus preached the Kingdom as God's final coming to save his people. To this proclamation of the end-time belongs the *eschatological community* to which the Kingdom will belong. This community was expected to be Israel gathered and restored. Only then would the nations be taken into God's saving activity.

2. The gathering of Israel began in Jesus' ministry to the disciples, whom he invited to follow him and participate in his mission (see Mt 10:5-6). They were the first fruits to which all of Israel would soon be joined.

3. Jesus' death for his people and his resurrection changed the whole situation. His death is now preached as the basis of the possibility of new repentance on Israel's part. Salvation is again offered first to Israel, but now it includes the demand to accept it as accomplished through the death and resurrection of Jesus. One can enter the new eschatological community only through baptism in the name of Jesus.

4. Israel's refusal to accept the Kingdom of God, originating in Jesus' death and resurrection, leads the disciples to go to the gentiles. The NO to Jesus creates a new situation. The insight then starts emerging that God was now calling into existence a "New People" made up of many nations. This new perception comes through the concrete events in which the Spirit of Jesus reveals the direction the community has to take.

5. While remaining rooted in the Old People of God ("grafted into the olive tree of Israel" Rm 11:17), this new People of God will be the new agent and carrier of God's universal will of salvation for all. They will continue the mission of Jesus by being sent by the crucified and risen Lord. The content of their mission will remain the Kingdom of God as it has been realized through Jesus' death and resurrection.

Notes

[15] Metz, J. B., "For a Renewed Church before a New Council: A Concept in Four Theses," in _Towards Vatican III: The Work that Needs to Be Done, ed. David Tracy_ (New York: Seabury, 1978) p. 139.

[16] "Unsere Hoffnung. Ein Bekenntnis zum Glauben in dieser Zeit," _Herder Korruderespondez_ 30 (1976) 200-211 at pp. 208-209.

[17] Dulles, A., _A Church to Believe In. Discipleship and the Dynamics of Freedom_ (New York: Crossroad, 1982) pp. 1-18.

[18] Lohfink, N. F., _Option for the poor_ (Berkeley, California: Bibal Press 1987. The concept "Contrast Society" for the Church was coined by the two brothers Norbert and Gehard Lohfink. They developed this concept in various writings and against a host of critics.

[19] Lofink, N., _Option for the Poor_, pp. 35-36.

[20] Brueggemann, W., _Prophetic Imagination_, p. 16.

[21] Fuellenbach, J., _Throw Fire,_ "Definition of the Kingdom", pp. 193-218.

[22] Michiels, R., "Church of Jesus Christ, An Exegetical-Ecclesiological Consideration" _Louvain Studies_ 18 (1993) 297-317, at p. 314-315.   The term, _Gemeindebildung,_ means the text was formulated by the evangelist and put into the mouth of the earthly-historical Jesus.

[23] Auer, J. Ratzinger, J., _Dogmatic Theology 8; The Church: The Universal Sacrament of Salvation_ (Washington, D.C.: The Catholic University Press, 1993) p. 25. See also G. Lohfink, Jesus as Community, p. 77.

[24] Kuzmic, P., "The Church and the Kingdom of God: A Theological Reflection" in _The Church. God's Agent for Change._ Edited by Bruce J. Nicholls (Flemington Markets, Australia: Paternoster Press, 1986) p. 49.

25 Lohfink. G., *Jesus and Community*, pp. 75-81.

26 Dulles, A., *Models of the Church. Expanded Edition* (New York: Image Book Doubleday, 1987) p. 20.

27 Dulles, A., *A Church to Believe In. Discipleship and the Dynamics of Freedom* (New York: Crossroad, 1982) pp. 1-18.

28 Brueggemann, W., *Prophetic Imagination* (London: SCM Press, 1992) p. 9.

29 Brueggemann, W., *Prophetic Imagination*, pp. 11-14.

30 Brueggemann, W., *Prophetic Imagination*, p. 12. He means by inculturation here the way the Church has wrongly succumbed to the ethos of consumerism.

31 Michiels, "Church of Jesus Christ", pp. 313-317.

32 Dulles, "The Church and Kingdom", p. 15.

33 Brown, "Early Church", pp.1-2.

34 Schüssler Fiorenza, E., *Foundational Theology: Jesus and the Church* (New York: 1984) p. 59.

35 Michiels, "Church and Christ", pp. 300-302.

36 McBrien, R. P., *Catholicism* (London: G. Chapman, 1981) pp. 571-577.

37 Lohfink, G., "Did Jesus found a Church?", *Theology Digest* 30 (1982) pp. 231-235.

38 Kirchschläger, W., *Die Anfänge der Kirche: Eine Biblische Rückbesinnung*, (Graz: Styria Verlag 1990) 23-24.

39 Boff, L., *Church Charisma and Power. Liberation Theology and the Institutional Church* (London: SCM Press, 1985)

40 Boff, L., *Ecclesiogenesis. The Base Communities Reinvent the Church* (New York: Orbis Books, 1989) p. 55.

41 Michiels, "Church of Jesus Christ", p. 300, footnote 8.

42 Werbick, J., *Kirche, Ein Ekklesiologischer Entwurf für Studium und Praxis* (Freiburg: Herder 1994) pp. 76-80.

Chapter Two

The Church in Vatican II

I. The Council's vision of the Church

In our century we have seen an enormous interest in the Church, particularly in the years prior to Vatican II. The climax of this ecclesial interest was the Council itself with two important documents: *Lumen Gentium and Gaudium et Spes.* One should also include the encyclical of Pope Paul VI, *Ecclesiam Suam.* The Council was very much concerned with presenting to us an image of the Church as a reference point to grasp her identity and her mission in the world today. It wanted to express a vision of the Church that would generate new enthusiasm among the faithful and offer an alternative to the way the world perceived reality. What was this vision? and did the Council succeed?

The Council did not define the Church in clear concepts. The Council Fathers, however, were very concerned with correcting a Church image that was generally considered as being too rigid and in many ways out of touch with contemporary reality. Their first concern was to go beyond any purely apologetical approach to a self-understanding of the Church, so common in the time after the Reformation and in the wake of the Enlightenment.

As a result, we find in the documents on the Church a refreshing return to the biblical understanding of Church and the rich heritage of the Fathers, particularly that of St. Augustine. In addition, the theological and spiritual insights of our century are considered seriously when the Council elaborated a new self-understanding of the Church. The liturgical and biblical movements, prior to Vatican II, deserve a special mention. So does the return to a more universal view of salvation, as found in the Greek Fathers, and the awakening awareness of the mission Churches. All these aspects were employed to develop an image of Church that would be more credible for our age and time.[1]

Being fully aware of the mystery of the Church, the Council shunned definitions and fixed concepts. Biblical images and symbols from Patristic literature were used to portray the mystery and the mission of the Church.

(LG 6, footnote 12 lists a whole range of images found in Scripture) The Bible itself makes use of ninety-five images and symbols that refer to what we call Church.[2]

Vatican II took some of these images as a kind of reference point to indicate the perspective from which we should look at the Church in order to recognize her identity and mission in the world today.

Knowing how ecclesial documents want to express their main concern and thrust in their first words, we can already sense how the Council wanted to define and see the Church for today by just reading the opening phrases of the two main Council documents on the Church. *Lumen Gentium*, meaning "Light for the Nations," defines the Church as being light to all nations (although the term "light" refers first and foremost to Christ). Here the Church could be compared to a ship equipped with powerful lights, moving through the ocean of centuries and indicating to other ships the way they should move to reach the shores of salvation. If we compare this picture with the older one, there is indeed a change of how the Church is perceived. The older ecclesiology took the scriptural image of the dragnet, which Jesus used in his Kingdom parables, and applied it to the Church as a ship. But in this case it was a ship moving through the centuries, dragging behind it an enormous net and trying to catch as many fish as possible — all in the firm belief that only those actually caught in this net will be saved. Today we would say there are as many ships as there are religions that can carry people to salvation. The Church's mission is viewed here not as taking the people from their ship into the "bark of Peter" but rather as indicating to them which way to steer their boats. Or to use an other image presented by a research seminar in India. In their conclusion on the Church's mission today they state:

> Today we realize that the welfare of the whole creation is the object of the Christian mission. It is not a project for the construction of Noah's ark to rescue the 'Christian remnant' from the irredeemable rest. Instead, the Church is like the leaven that is meant to facilitate the transformation of the word.[3]

The document *Gaudium et Spes* (joy and hope) sets out to define the Church's relationship to the world. It basically describes the Church as a community whose mission is to give joy and hope to a world that often looks so gloomy and desperate, without real joy and knowledge of the way to move and the direction to take. In these two images the Council provided us with a vision of the Church for our age and time, something that can instil enthusiasm and renewed commitment, something one can live for, work for, suffer for and, if necessary, die for. What is proposed here is a true vision of the Church. But the question remains: Did the Council succeed with its vision? Did the renewed Church become a "light for the nations" and a community that radiates "hope and joy" into the world today?

In the encyclical *Ecclesiam Suam* (His Church), Paul VI wanted to show the real origin of the Church, her Trinitarian dimension. She is not merely a human reality but a divine mystery that ultimately escapes definition. Without the realization of this element we would despair because of her all too human appearance and sinfulness down through the ages.

The best way to start describing the Church theologically is to envision her as the community of the end time in the 'here and now', as the fulfilment of the eschatological Kingdom anticipated in space and history. She is the historical anticipation or the historical concretization of God's ultimate plan with humankind and creation as a whole. She is the 'already of the not yet', meant to be the concrete realization of God's Kingdom now and sent to witness the Kingdom present and proclaim it to the whole world. Wherever a Christian community emerges, its ultimate mission is to be a "light for the people" and to give "joy and hope" in the midst of an often hopeless situation. It can do this only because right in its midst the community experiences 'already' the vision that God intended to come true for all the world at the proper time.

II. Images of the Church in Vatican II

In concretizing this vision, the Council chose the following images from the ninety-five images and symbols, which in Scripture refer to the entity called Church, and regarded them as basic for our time:

Church as THE NEW PEOPLE OF GOD;
Church as BODY OF CHRIST
Church as TEMPLE OF THE HOLY SPIRIT

These three images seem to have been chosen because of their central importance in the New Testament and because of their significance of the Trinitarian dimensions of the Church.

Theologically, these images may adequately describe the essence and function of the Church and, as such, will always remain important points of reference when we are looking for an image of the Church. Nevertheless the question remains: How adequate are these images if we want to focus our vision of the Church in a way that expresses our own faith experience with conviction and enthusiasm for today?

1. THE NEW PEOPLE OF GOD

The favorite image the Council employed was St. Paul's vision of the Church as the New People of God. In taking the Jewish idea of Israel as the people of God, Paul sees the Christian community as the "new People of God" but profoundly linked with the Old Testament. For him, the history of salvation is one (Rm 9-11).The berit (covenant formula), "You are my people and I am your God" (Dt 6:6), finds its eschatological fulfilment in the new berit, in Christ's blood. The Church is grafted into the tree of Israel and lives from the power of the ancient olive tree (Rm 11:17). God has not rejected his people, for they remain the beloved of Yahweh. The privileges of Israel have been granted now to all who believe in Christ. Israel of old may have rejected Christ for the time being; nevertheless, the history of the new community in Christ remains inseparably bound to the history of non-believing Israel. It is precisely because of the failure of Israel that salvation has come to the Gentiles.[4]

The New Covenant, therefore, can be understood and explained only in terms of its origin: the Old Covenant.

> Although the Church, as a community founded by Jesus Christ, appears only in the New Testament, it can be understood only in connection with the history of the people of God in the Old Testament... There are at least two basic notions of the cultic community of the Old Testament which have become important for the Church: the idea of the covenant with God, and the idea of the people of God.[5]

However, the "new people of God" formed by Christians is the community of the "true descendants of Abraham," built upon the twelve forefathers of the new people of God in the Holy Spirit, the apostles. Christ is the new primogenitor of this new people of God. He is the head of his people and the ever living mediator of the New Covenant. For this reason Paul frequently replaces the notion "people of God" with the term, "Church of God."[6]

We have to realize that, from an historical perspective, the metaphor "people of God" did not play a dominant role in the tradition of the Church.

This was basically due to a negative view of the Old Testament people who failed to keep their part of the Covenant. Only in this century was the metaphor newly discovered in connection with the theology known as "salvation history" as Auer and Ratzinger observe:

> Especially since the 40s, exegetical research has led to a new understanding of this historical people of God. Through a clearer grasp of the term "eschatological," among Catholics as well, the bases were created for a concept of the people of God based upon the history of salvation. It was this concept which became the basis of Vatican II's Constitution on the Church.[7]

By stating that the Church is the People of God, the Council affirmed some important aspects:

A gratuitous election by God.

The New Testament Church is seen as the people of God created and constituted through the revelation of God in Jesus Christ. This view stresses the *gratuitous election and mission of the new people of God* in line with God's election of individual persons in the Old Testament. In his plan for salvation God "elects" people not on the basis of any merits but only out of a preferential love with the sole purpose of drawing them closer into the accomplishment of his salvific plan for all.

The idea of "election" or of "chosen" people for the Church is often offensive and has been the subject of much theological controversy. Most biblical references to "election by God" have to do with the choice of a group. It means a corporate election. God chose Abraham and all who are in him, that is, his descendants. God chose David in a similar way. But election of one does not mean "rejection" of the other. The words "I have loved Jacob but I have hated Esau" can only be understood from the Hebrew usage. "To love" is to choose; "to hate" is not to choose. These words are not about emotions but are acts of the will. Love in the biblical language involves choice.[8]

But the choice of a group in the Old Testament did not guarantee the inclusion of all individuals in that group in the blessings for which they were chosen. There was often a progressive narrowing down of God's choice. This narrowing down has been described as an hourglass. Christ is seen as the center of this hourglass through which the sand flows. God's saving action starts with creation: from there it narrows down to humanity,

Israel, the remnant, then to the center: CHRIST. Then it broadens out again from Christ to the twelve, the Church, humanity, the new creation.[9]

God's choice within Israel finally focused on the one person, Christ, the "Chosen One". This title was given to him on the Mount of Transfiguration (Lk 9:35). Therefore, we can say:

> All who are in Christ are included in this election. God chose Abraham (and all in him); God chose Jacob (and all in him); God chose David (and his descendants); God chose Christ (and all in him). Just as all who are "in" Abraham, Israel, or David were included in their election, so it is with Christ. The election in Christ entails the election of those in Christ.[10]

The new election of the community called Church is, therefore, related to Christ. The elected people are those chosen in Christ. The corporate nature of the election emphasizes the importance of the Church. This makes it also clear that "election by God" does not say that the people involved are better than others and nor should it give them a sense of superiority (Dt 7:7). Christians are the elect because they have been called by God through an act of infinite love and mercy.

> *You are a chosen race, a royal priesthood, a consecrated nation, a people set apart to sing the praises of God who called you out of darkness into his wonderful light (1 Peter 2:9).*

Election is for service. It means to be called to participate more actively in God's plan of salvation meant for the whole of creation. Of course, this carries with it a special closeness to God, joy in his friendship and love in a conscious and intensive way.

This view clarifies the historicity of the Church and its place in the realm of earthly history. The future and the mission of the Church are seen together with those of Israel of old: chosen for a purpose and not for personal gain. The saving function of the people of God for the whole of humanity is enjoined now on both: Israel and the Church as Auer-Ratzinger summarize it:

> The most important element in this model of the Church is historicity in the variety of its relations: back to the past of the Old Testament people of God with which the New Testament people of God will be judged and fulfilled in the coming end times; as a transformation in the present, in the conversion of the individual and the Church in the spirit of the call, through immersion in historical revelation and sanctification by the ever-active Spirit of God in the Church. The invisible in the visible, the past and future in the present,

salvation in sinfulness, eternal election in the course of history, the individual and the community, all of these polarities in their dialogical unity in
earthly history are expressed in the image of the people of God.[11]

The communitarian aspect

Prior to all individuality and every individual calling, the Church is
seen as a people founded by divine calling, into which the individual is
incorporated. *The communitarian aspect of salvation takes priority over
the individual-personal one.* The individual's relationship to God is not
private, independent of all socialization; rather the divine calling is aimed
at constituting humanity as a people by reason of its common eschatological
destiny, the Kingdom.[12]

Although the idea of the "People of God" reminds us that God has
bound his offer of salvation to a concrete community in history, we cannot
overlook that God is not necessarily bound to just one people. He can
choose other people besides Israel as Jesus says in Matthew 21:43, "The
Kingdom of God will be taken from you and given to a people who will
produce its fruits." This is a stern warning for the new people of God as
well. There is no place for arrogance. The question always remains: how
faithful does the Church live out its mission. God will not reject his Church,
as he has never rejected Israel, his chosen people, but he may have - so to
speak - to graft onto the tree of his Church another branch that will bring
"fruit in due season."

A people of equals

By choosing the image, people of God, for the Church, the Council
wanted consciously to *counter-balance a too hierarchically perceived image of the Church.* It was to restore to the people of God their legitimate
right to participate in the governing power of the Church since all are equal
before God. The image was thought to break with an in-egalitarian and
anti-democratic ideology of the earlier ecclesiology. Prior to dealing with
structure and order and deciding who exercises particular ministries and
functions in the Church, we must give precedence to the basic reality of
the ecclesial community: all are first and foremost brothers and sisters
united into one in Jesus Christ. All ordering into higher or lower offices and
functions in the community are of secondary importance and can never be
overruled by any position or rank one may occupy in the assembly.

The Council precisely aimed at undoing the wrongly chosen way of defining the Church from her office holders down by assigning rank and honors to particular members in the Church according to their position in the community and so allocating the people of God to the bottom of the barrel. The most appropriate image of the Church in this configuration was the *pyramid*, where one starts with the top pick (to be the Pope) and moving down to the base of the pyramid (the ordinary faithful). We can rightly say that the Council replaced the pyramid metaphor with that of the *circle* within whose embrace all are deemed equal and no one can claim to have special rights to lord it over others. In the words of Jesus the Council wanted to say: Among you it should be different. Whoever wants to be first should be last (Mk 9:35-36; 10:41-45).

A pilgrim people

This metaphor, *people of God*, sees the Church as a *pilgrim people*, a people on the road towards its final goal, the fullness of the Kingdom to come. By using this image for the Church, the Council further wanted to stress that the Church has to be seen as a growing community involved in history and, therefore, affected by the weaknesses and infidelities of its members who constantly stand in need of God's mercy and forgiveness.

This notion serves as a corrective and a warning against all triumphalism. It reveals the humanness of the Church, a community composed of people who, like the Old Testament people, are imperfect and unfaithful; a murmuring people who feel the heat of the sun on their march through the desert of this world. They cry out to God for help and relief and want to see an end to their journey. So they fervently pray and wait for the Lord to return. This brings out the eschatological and provisional character of the Church. As such, she should never settle in this world nor live in well-established structures and houses but rather in tents and booths: she knows her home lies in the world to come and not here in this world. This view could serve as a critique for a Church that has too comfortably settled into a culture and lost the sense of constant longing for the day of the Lord, as the early Church constantly cried: "Lord Jesus come". J. B. Metz might be right when he observes that the Second Coming of the Lord does not seem to occur since no one in the Church seriously longs for his Second Coming.

Conclusion

For some time after the Council, this image of People of God was in vogue and is still used, but its popularity is limited. It seems the faithful in many parts of the world cannot see themselves so easily as "people" in an Old Testament sense. This is because religious affiliation today is not congruent with one's ethnic and political identity as in the case of Israel. However, the image continues to appeal to marginalized groups in the Church who experience situations comparable to those of Israel: oppressed and dependent, struggling for identity and freedom. This is also the case where Church communities see themselves as tiny minorities whose views and values contrast to commonly held views. These minorities find in this image the vision that could lead and guide them in their struggle and search. However, in the Church as a large scale institution it can be said that the image People of God did not become the image of the Church that could provide an inspiring vision to lead to the desired reform of the Church. The immense potential of the image carries, however, an explosive power. It contains a 'dangerous memory' for any Church that envisages itself too easily in terms of hierarchy and order and forgets that the basic root metaphor for the Church will always have to remain the community that God chose in the beginning, a community in which there are no rulers or ruled but only equals who serve each other as brothers and sisters in a community where compassion and justice are the lens for seeing and the core value of an alternative way of thinking about society.

2. THE CHURCH AS BODY OF CHRIST

The image as used in the Council

To complement the image, People of God, the Council felt obliged to use another biblical image for the Church: the Body of Christ. This metaphor has been applied to the Church through the centuries and is most probably the one most theologians would agree upon.[13] Pius XII gave it a magisterial approval in his famous encyclical *Mystici Corporis* (1943). With this document he wanted to provide a balance to the highly one-sided ecclesiology of Vatican I, which so heavily stressed the institutional element of the Church that her inner, divine dimension was hardly recognizable anymore. From then on this metaphor became the image of the Church in most textbooks on ecclesiology. Strangely enough, although it was meant to balance the hierarchical aspect in the Church, in fact it made the hierar-

chical structure even more untouchable. Supporters of this view implicitly reason that, because the structures of the Church belong to the Body of
Christ, they are, therefore, divine and immutable. A further drawback was
that the encyclical identified the Church with the Roman Catholic Church
by stating that the Body of Christ exists only in the Roman Catholic Church.
This view then gave little opening for ecumenical dialogue.

Yet the Council did pick up the metaphor again and applied it to the
Church though in a more nuanced way than in *Mystici Corporis*.[14] The
Council felt that the notion People of God could not adequately express
the overwhelming change brought about by Christ. Body of Christ, on the
other hand, expresses the intimate union of the Church with the risen and
glorified Lord as his continuing presence in the world. It reveals the in-
nermost heart of the Church, namely dependence on and union with Christ.
Some hold this understanding of the Church as the most mature result of
the New Testament thinking of the Church. It certainly is the most important New Testament image for the Church employed by Paul. Vatican II
summarizes the wealth of this image in *Lumen Gentium 7*.

The origin of the "Body of Christ" symbol in St. Paul

The idea of the Body of Christ is definitely linked to the idea of "corporate personality" or "extended personality." The content fits well into
the Jewish way of thinking by which a group derived its identity from their
identity in one person. As Israel was both the forefather of the people and
the whole people itself and as Adam was both a person and humanity, so
Jesus includes all believers in himself. Paul lived in this pattern of Old
Testament thinking and developed his understanding of the symbol *Body
of Christ* along these lines.

This symbol applied to the Church is basically a term introduced by
Paul. As has been shown, Paul unfolds this concept in connection with the
word used in the Eucharist: *"My Body given for you."*[15] Since the Hebrew
language has no equivalent for the Greek word "body" (*soma*), Paul links
it with the Hebrew idea of "flesh" (*basar*). In the process a new understanding of "body" emerged which best served what he saw behind the
idea of the Church as "Body of Christ."

While the Greek differentiation between, "flesh" (*sarx*) and "body"
(*soma*) enabled the apostle to see in the body that side of human existence
which certainly has its weakness and reminded him of his total depen-

dence on God, it primarily provided him with the means to glorify God in serving one's fellow human beings. This he took from the Hebrew idea of *basar*. Listening to the Eucharistic words "This is my body given for you," the early Christians learned from their master to see the body as the means of rendering service to others. The understanding of body as the means of communication, even of service to others, became predominant in the New Testament Church, since it confessed that its life was completely dependent on Christ's giving up his body for their sake.

From this understanding Paul develops the three most important aspects regarding the body concept: first, the total dependence of the Church on Christ; secondly, based on the Hebrew background, the idea of bodily service for one's fellow human beings in the footsteps and in union with the Lord: thirdly the idea of unity and harmony of the whole body based on the Greek understanding of the term "*soma*".

First, the Church is totally dependent on the crucified and risen body of Christ, i.e., on the saving event which took place at a specific time in a specific place within our human history. This dependence on God's act is underlined by the fact that it is primarily in the Eucharist that this character of the "body of Christ" is given to the Church.

> "The church is the body of Christ, because it lives by all that has been done by Jesus Christ for its sake. It is united with him by the fact that his history, namely his life and death and resurrection, is the foundation of the church's life, without which it would not exist at all. The church exists in the body of Christ through the body of Christ crucified and risen for the sake of the world, still present in its blessing and challenge, for instance when the Eucharist is celebrated. Outside this body of Christ, for its sake, the church does not exist. The saying in 1 Co 12:27: "You are the body of Christ," and the surprising end of verse 12 in the same chapter: "...just as the body is one and has many members... so it is with Christ," are possible because the idea that a whole tribe is included in its ancestor is familiar to Paul. Hence these sayings describe the total dependence of the church on its founder, on Jesus Christ, in a most impressive way."[16]

For Paul the Body of Christ means the crucified body in its *for-our-sake-ness*. The crucified body of Jesus is the place in which the human person finds meaning for life, because the crucified Jesus becomes the token of God's incredible love and the challenge to service which makes his life meaningful. The Body of Christ is something like a sphere, a reality into which person has to go or to be put in order to find life. Or, to say it in another way, it is the Church, understood as the place, the realm, the sphere, in which Jesus, crucified but raised two thousand years ago, is still telling us of God's love, and is still challenging us and calling us under his Lordship.[17]

Secondly, being the body of Christ is not a mysterious experience but is lived daily in "bodily" manifestations of the Church's faith, namely in the concrete brotherhood and sisterhood in which obedience to the Lord is manifested in love for the brothers and sisters. The Church as Body of Christ is to be understood in such a way that it could be seen primarily in its openness for others and for the world or, therefore, in its mission to the nations and its self-sacrifice for those who are outside of it. Schweizer concludes his investigation by saying:

> This means that the last result of this investigation is the insight that the church can be body of Christ only if it is willing to suffer and thereby to be the body of its Lord who, in his body, goes into the world, serving all humankind. If the church is willing to live in this way as Christ's body, often suffering and dying, it will experience time and again that he himself creates in it that obedience and that readiness for self-sacrifice, in which he as its Lord encounters the world and converts Gentiles into members of his body.[18]

The community which unites itself with the Lord in the Eucharist by eating his body and drinking his blood becomes so united with the Lord that it takes on Christ's Eucharistic existence which is totally determined by the symbolism of the Eucharist: *bread to be broken and wine to be poured.* The community's whole being is now determined by the existence of the Lord. It becomes Body of Christ and takes over the mission of the Lord: to give oneself away in order to carry on this mission of Christ by being the means through which others are brought into unity with Christ and with each other. The members of the Church are to the world what the body of Christ is for them. The Eucharist should determine the life of any Christian worth her or his name.

It is now through the community's body that Christ remains present. He continues to "lay down his life" in his chosen body, the Church, in order to fulfill his mission on earth until he comes again. Christ, who is gone, needs human bodies in order to make himself present in this world and to carry on his world-redeeming mission.

The participation in the body of Christ in the Eucharistic celebration not only leads the Christian into deep union with Christ; it is at the same time a mission. After having been united with the Lord in the Eucharist, having being re-molded into the shape of the master, the disciple is now sent out to continue the Lord's mission by serving in the way the Lord served when he walked this earth. Of course, no one can take on such a mission solely on his or her own volition. It is precisely because we are in the "new ancestor", are his descendants that we have to "reproduce the pattern of his life" in our own lives. Seen from such a perspective, the Eucharist could be regarded as a sacrament of mission for Christians. The Faith and order Commission has this to say:

> The Eucharistic celebration demands reconciliation and sharing among all those regarded as brothers and sisters in the one family of God and is a constant challenge in the search for appropriate relationship in social, economic and political life (Mt 5:23ff; 1Cor 10:14; 1Cor 11:20-22). Because Holy Communion is the sacrament which builds up community, all kinds of injustice, racism, estrangement, and lack of freedom are radically challenged when we share in the body and blood of Christ. ... As participants in the Eucharist, therefore, we prove inconsistent if we are not actively participating in the ongoing restoration of the world's situation and the human condition. Holy Communion shows us that our behavior is inconsistent in the face of the reconciling presence of God in human history: we are placed under continued judgement by the persistence of unjust relationship of all kinds in our society, manifold divisions on account of human pride, material interest and power politics and, above all, the obstinacy of unjustifiable confessional oppositions within the body of Christ.[19]

Thirdly, one of the main concerns for Paul was the unity of the Church. This idea he unfolds against the background of those in the Corinthian community who had a rather anti-body view of things. Here the concept body is understood as in Greek philosophy, namely as being a unifying whole consisting of many parts and organs but making up one whole being. Unity can only be served if all parts play their role and function in harmony with the whole body. Paul developed here his idea of the Church as a charismatic entity (1 Co 12).

The Body of the Risen Christ and not the physical body of Jesus

One difficulty felt by Vatican II was that the physical body of Christ has been the comparative model for the Church. The physical human body is limited and well-defined. The Church, as the body of Christ, is also well-defined and limited. Thus members are clearly defined and so are the institutions that must maintain the Church's unity and strength in the world. It is argued that just as the body has various members and diverse func-

tions, so also does the Church have many members with diverse functions
The point of comparison is always the physical body of Christ. The metaphor is taken literally. In the view of Wehrbik:

> The conflictual character of metaphor "the Body of Christ" rests in its ten-
> dency towards identification: the Church which identifies herself with the
> "Body of Christ" identifies herself rather quickly with the head that unites
> the Body of Christ. And those in the Church who represent the "head" too
> readily identify with the head itself and act as well as decide on behalf of the
> head which they represent. This tendency towards identification implies —
> more or less explicitly — a monopoly or a set of boundaries: she lays claim
> to the "head" for this visible Catholic Church and denies the being "Body of
> Christ" to other churches, because there can be only *one* body. She focuses
> very much on the close relationship between head and body, sees in it the
> only meaning for being Church and tends so easily to overlook that the Church
> is called to live its "being the Body of Christ" for others, for the world — as
> a living witness. In this way the "Body of Christ" metaphor can favor an
> ecclesial introversion.[20]

Thus arises the danger of defining the Church too narrowly, because
the Church is not the physical body of Christ. Through the resurrection,
the body of Jesus Christ was not simply brought back to life. It was completely liberated from every temporal and spatial limitation. Christ was no
longer simply a carnal body, that is, a body subject to an earthly condition,
a prisoner to the conditions of space and time, in need of food and drink,
and subject to the limitations and ambiguous communication through word
and gesture. The resurrection transformed Jesus' carnal body into a spiritual body (see 1 Cor 14:44f). A spiritual body is the new reality of the
risen Jesus, now free from limitations of earthly existence, enthroned in
eternity and in the limitless arena of divine life, liberated from space and
time. Through the resurrection the limits of the carnal Jesus fell away and
were replaced by his global relationship with all of reality. The risen Jesus
became the cosmic Christ of Paul's letters to the Ephesians and Colossians,
the Prologue to the Fourth Gospel, and the Letter to the Hebrews. The
Body of the risen and pneumatic Christ can no longer be considered a physically definable entity from which we can deduce the limits of the Church
as the Body of Christ. Therefore the concept of the Church as the body of
Christ must be carefully defined.[21]

Yet the image clearly does express the divine dimension of the Church
in spite of all its faults. The Church is not a club of like-minded people
who pursue a common interest. Without the divine dimension one would
have to despair of the Church. Body of Christ best expresses theologi-

cally why the risen Lord will stay with his Church. She is his chosen partner or, as Scripture has it, his "bride," in spite of all her fault and infidelities.

An identification of the ecclesial Body of Christ with the body and
life of the incarnate Logos, which would make the Church appear as a
continuous incarnation, however, would divinize structures that are far too
human, would make it untouchable and unchangeable and would even
present it as undiscriminatingly significant for salvation. Already the Reformation protested against such a presumption. However, this protest probably went one step too far by presenting the visible Church, the Church as
institution and corporate body, as a merely human establishment, which
would seek its bearings as founded by Christ only in as far as it "would
preach the Gospel in as pure a manner as possible and administer the sacraments according to the Gospel" (Confession Augustana article 7).

Concerning the mission of Jesus which is continued in the Church,
and in this aspect the Catholic tradition is correct, the Church as a whole
should make Christ visible in all its lived expressions and forms as well as
in its institutional shape. Still she cannot presume that she is the authentic
incarnation of this Spirit in the way she concretely appears. The exact
opposite is true: in all her lived expressions she is constantly challenged
by God's Word and Christ's Spirit to witness to this Word and this Spirit,
to become an instrument of God's actions, and so make it possible for
people to experience God's grace. Where she is not sufficiently open to
the Spirit of Christ, there the Spirit is reduced to insignificance and she
loses sight of following in the footsteps of Jesus Christ (1 Peter 2:21). But
the Church can never really 'lose the Spirit': she has been promised never
to completely lose the right path. Concerning the sacraments, she has been
assured that the Risen Christ can be encountered in these wherever they
are preformed in his name.

But this mere "residual presence" of the Spirit would be at the same
time the judgment of an ecclesial organization which has become 'spirit-
less' and fossilized in the routine of its religious cults and should not be
surprised that it is being shunned by people. The ecclesial body is not
always nor automatically filled with the Spirit of Christ and alert to the
presence of Christ witnessed by its members. Unfortunately, she can even
be resistant to the Spirit's breath; she may atrophy by assertively and stub-
bornly focusing on the institution and the individual. The metaphor "Body
of Christ" is not simply a state but expresses a tension: the essence of

being Church is to incarnate the Spirit of Jesus Christ, to witness to it. However, there is no guarantee that she will always and everywhere live up to this essential calling. She is constantly in danger of betraying her very self and of becoming insignificant.

The ecclesial metaphor of the Body of Christ has been abused and overused again and again as a formula to legitimize its existence or else has been misinterpreted. Originally, in the authentic Letters of Paul, her task was to describe and call for the unity of the various "members" of this body in the spirit of Christ: the Church is a creation of the Spirit in so far as the members use their spiritual gifts (charisms) for the building up of the community, in so far as they practice solidarity with the weak and the suffering. Where the Spirit unites the members of the Body of Christ, where it breathes through this body and vivifies it, there the body is a visible manifestation of Christ in the witness of those who walk his way and live communion in his spirit.

The visibility of the ecclesial Body of Christ is very important. It is not sufficient to appeal to God's (Christ's) Spirit. The Spirit of Christ wants to be made present in those and through those who allow their lives and the life of their communion to be determined by the Spirit. Perhaps it is this experience of the Spirit, wanting to be made visible, which became for Paul the deepest motivation to repeatedly use the metaphor of the body. The exegete Hermann-Josef Venetz describes it in this way:

> This is what Paul experienced: Jesus and his mission were present and tangible in the early Christian community. Here he saw how the poor are included and true solidarity is being practiced. Here he discovered new and alternative ways to live. Here God's entering into the world became a tangible reality. Paul experienced the early Church as the place where faith in Jesus, the Christ, was incarnate. In the early congregations of the faithful the apostle encountered the living Christ....here he was visible, tangible and could be experienced. How? Because in its words and actions the community put its faith into practice. Jesus Christ was the motive for all its activities and the source of its life.[22]

Paul probably had this experience in mind but he also had noticed how the Body of Christ was endangered by selfishness and claims to power. This negative experience explains his warning words to the community of Corinth. This experience of tension within the Body of Christ is probably still having its effect on our present experience of the Church: the community, the Church, can be a visible experience of Christ; the community of authentic disciples; it is all the more painful if this is either not the case or hardly so. The community of the faithful can be "a place where I can begin anew again and again, because the community accepts me just as I am: a sinner, a failure, someone who did not make it." The community provides this visible experience of Christ in that moment when this acceptance is not merely a theory but a true experience: a helping hand is offered, someone sees to it that I have a roof over my head and work to do; I am trusted. Again, it is the Kingdom already present that is experienced in such instances mediated through the community that makes up the Church.

But today who will experience community or Church as the tangible Christ? Do people see and feel in our communities today the Spirit of Christ? or is it rather the spirit of 'territorial rights and power', of dogmatism and fear of life?

We are not talking about a way-out community romanticism, but we are asking whether communities consider it their essential vocation, not just to talk about the Spirit of Jesus, but to go beyond such words and witness to it with their lives. This witness means that they allow themselves to become servants of Christ in his body the Church. The central issue is the question whether believers consider it their task to share in the servant spirit of Christ so that they become 'his instruments' and that he can hardly be thought of as separate from them.

It was the experience made during the celebration of the Eucharist the celebration of the Body and Blood of Christ, in which the Early Church reflected on her being the Body of Christ, in which she renewed herself as she allowed the Spirit of Christ to flow through her as a power of renewal and aspired to be what she received (Augustine). In the celebration of the Eucharist the Church becomes the Body of Christ through the Spirit of Christ and the sacramental reality of the body and blood of Christ, a bodily communion with Christ. And she is called to manifest this sacramental essence and meaning of her communion of body and life with Christ in her own bodily form. When Jesus offers himself in the Eucharist as *'body given for others'*, the Church likewise has to become body given for others.

It is the bodily saving presence of Jesus among the people in which he can be touched and experienced through our senses; it is the act of communication through which the Lord wants to come to his people. The Church becomes the body of Christ through the *Corpus Christi* of the Eucharist by way of representing the healing and saving Body of Christ among the people. There is a prayer from the late Middle Ages that has been part of the oral tradition and expresses in a beautiful way this theological intention:

Christ has no hands but our hands to do his work today. He has no feet but our feet to guide others to him. Christ has no lips, only our lips to speak about him. He has no help but our help to call people to his side.

It is our fundamental vocation to build community, that is, to make the concern of Christ our own and to continue his mission by bringing all people to union with God and with each other.[23]

Accordingly, the metaphor of the Body of Christ is unsuitable to justify claims that would imply that the hierarchy is in any way identical with the head of the Body of Christ. Already from the christological point of view, it is not possible either that a human being identifies with God or that a human person claims to be God's representative. On the contrary, according to the faith of the Church, it is God who identifies himself in and through Christ with a human being and his life lived in and through the Spirit of God. And Jesus identifies himself to the point of "mistaken identity" with the "little ones", the exploited and the sinners; and he ultimately suffers their lot. If this is the case, would we not have to accept the theological premise that the risen and glorified Christ does not identify with those who would like to use such identification as a legitimation of their high office? Rather he identifies with those who try to continue the way of the Jesus who walked this earth and sided with those who had no rights and were marginalized?

The "broken mirror" Model

Christian Duquoc, the French Dominican theologian, recently proposed another metaphor, which offers itself rather forcefully as a corrective to the "Body of Christ ecclesiology", especially to those who prefer correct and clear metaphors. He speaks about the Church and its witness character as a "broken mirror".

> The Church is a broken mirror; she reflects only in fragments that for which she is called to bear witness: Jesus Christ. The ecumenical movement was born from the desire to overcome this brokenness. Because the break is still present and manifests itself in the pluralism of the Church — or as Duquoc adds — in a polycentric way.[24]

The pieces of the mirror are a "broken witness". Where the churches of the different denominations are aware of it, they will admit that their witness remains "selective", and that they choose each time what manifests the coherence of her faith and her praxis when she tries to speak of the presence of Christ among his people; they admit that they need to re-store again and again the central position of Christ; and they accept more readily that they do not have any claim to privileges that have been derived from a too direct identification of the Church with the head of the Body of Christ. Such privileges lose their theological and christological founda-tion when it is made clear that the Church cannot be identified with the Kingdom of God. They lose their political foundation because of the lack of unity among the churches which Duquoc can value positively:

> Her division is somehow a means of self-protection: none of the churches can insist that she replaces Christ in the world.... The guidance and leader-ship of the Risen Christ through the mediation of the Holy Spirit cannot be identified with the politics of the churches. It is outside of our realm. The mediation role of the churches is biased and partial at the same time.[25]

The Risen Christ cannot be claimed by anyone. He does not allow the visible churches to simply identify with him. He repeatedly points to the lived witness of the incarnate Logos, the Way of Jesus Christ, which is reflected in various ways in the New Testament and finds a 'polyphonic' and hard to harmonize echo in the witness of the hagiographists. The New Testament itself is a 'mirror' in many small mirrors which cannot form a unified and closed picture of the "historical Jesus", but makes him a chal-lenge for the visible churches who cannot monopolize him.

Vatican II tried to balance this tendency to identify the Body of Christ with one Church, the Catholic Church, and we can see this in the "*subsistit*" formula (*Lumen Gentium* 8). Similarly the pastoral constitution "*Gaudium et Spes*" confirms this when it speaks about the Church in today's world and further develops the understanding of the Church as sacramental real-ity of God's salvific action towards and in the world, as it is expressed in "Lumen Gentium". The Council tried to balance the rather one-sided meta-phor of the "Body of Christ" with that of the "People of God" metaphor. However the tension between the two metaphors was not resolved in the Council's ecclesiology. It seems that these two metaphors, together with others, remain separately side by side.[26]

Yet the metaphor beautifully expresses the divine dimension of the Church without which the Church would remain a purely human institu-tion. It is not we who create the Church, it is not we who haven chosen to be the Church but the choice is God's and Christ's. Despite of all the criticism of the Church, she does remain God's chosen community in which he will always be present and continue his mission on earth no matter how unfaithful and distorted she might represent his Spirit and proclaim his mission.

3. THE CHURCH AS TEMPLE OF THE HOLY SPIRIT

The image of the Church as Temple of the Holy Spirit expresses the constitutive relationship between Church and Holy Spirit. As the Faith and Order Commission sees it:

> Reference to the constitutive relation between Church and Holy Spirit runs through the whole New Testament. Nevertheless there is no explicit image for the relation. The imagery that comes particularly close to the figurative description of this relation entailed in the New Testament, and renders it in a particularly appropriate way, is the imagery of "temple" and "house". This is so because the relation of the Spirit to the Church is one of indwelling, of giving life from within.[27]

Theologically this view had been developed far more extensively by the Orthodox Churches, than by the Western Church. The Christian community at its earliest stage considered itself as the fulfilment of the eschatological expectation promised through the prophets and brought about by Christ. The realization and understanding of who they were came to the early community through the outpouring of the Holy Spirit, THE gift of the risen Lord. The experience of the Holy Spirit was so powerful that Christians regarded their new existence as a Creation of the Holy Spirit.

In John this outpouring of the Spirit happened on Easter Sunday when the Risen Lord "breathes over" the community of the disciples. For Luke it is the day of Pentecost when the eschatological Spirit comes down on the disciples in *tongues of fire*. The Spirit who was at work at the beginning of the world, who "hovered over the chaos," to bring forth the world of creation (Gen 1:1), now hovers over the small group of Jesus' disciples (Acts 2:1-4) and brings forth the new creation, the eschatological community. The Church is created by this event. She is the sphere in which Christ makes himself constantly present through the power of his Spirit. To have received the Holy Spirit means to be in contact with the Risen Lord, and to be in contact with him means to be living already in the sphere of the new creation: "Anyone who is in Christ Jesus is a new creation" (2 Cor 5:17).

The community knows that part of the future hope is already realized in its midst. But it knows equally well that another part still remains in the future. It does experience, at least dimly or as a foretaste, the justice, peace and joy of the Kingdom in the power of the Holy Spirit (Rm 14:17). However, it also still experiences itself and the world as permeated by sin.

The experience of those who allow the power of the Risen Christ into their lives has been described in many ways. The Spirit of Jesus the risen one has given them a new way of life: *"We were all as good as slaves (Gal 4:3) but freedom is what we have, for Christ has set us free"* (Gal 5:1). Now they are called to a new life in community where there is no *"difference anymore between men and women; gentile and Jew, rich and poor"* (Gal 3:28). *"We have moved from death to life because we love our brothers and sisters"* (1 Jn 3:14).

The true sign of whether the Church is open to the Spirit of the Risen Lord present in her midst is her willingness to engage in creating that ultimate community where there will be no more division. Here the ultimate goal of God's intentionality with creation will come to completion, union and communion with the Triune God and with each other in the eternal banquet: "I will be their God and they shall be my people for ever and ever" (Rev 21:3). Christ has already drawn his community through the Spirit into this new union with the Father and each other. An absolutely new intimacy is now offered which we cannot verbalize, but to which the Spirit himself gives expression:

> *We do not know how to pray, but the Spirit witnesses with our spirit that we are God's children since he cries in us ABBA, FATHER (Gal 4:6; Rm 8:15).*

The possession of the eschatological Spirit forbids withdrawal from the world. Those who have the "first fruits of the Spirit" did not receive them for their own selfish needs. Like Jesus filled with the power of the Holy Spirit, the Church is to go out, to proclaim and witness to the Kingdom. Her task is to continue Jesus' own mission in the power of the Spirit she has received from him. In the words of Edward Schweizer:

> The new creation of man and woman by the Spirit is not a flight of faith into heaven or an abandonment of this imperfect world. On the contrary, the new creation means beginning to see the world as it is, suffering with it and taking its suffering to heart. The work of the Spirit is to make us aware of our solidarity with the world.[28]

In the light of the Spirit the Church comes to see that creation is one. It is the possession of the Holy Spirit that leads her into solidarity with the whole of creation in its destiny and its hope. This is well expressed by Bonhoeffer:

> The hour when the Church today prays for the coming of God's Kingdom drives it for better or for worse into the company of the earthlings and world-lings, into a contract to be faithful to the earth, to its distress, its hunger, and its dying.[29]

Since the Church came into existence through the outpouring of the Holy Spirit, it would be better to start with this fact and unfold any ecclesiology from the working of the Holy Spirit. Such an approach would lead more easily to the realization that the Church is ultimately grounded in the Trinity itself.

If we look back at the Council after 35 years, the leitmotif for its idea of the Church seems best described with the word *communio* (as we mentioned already earlier) although this might not have been recognized immediately. Kehl defines the self-understanding of the Catholic Church as it emerged in Vatican II as "Sacrament of communion with God". She is the communion of the faithful united by the Holy Spirit, joined to Christ, and called together with the whole of creation into the Kingdom of God the Father. The Church is viewed as sacramentally expressing here and now the mystery of the communion of the Trinity[30] as Walter Kasper says:

> The mystery of the Church consists in the access we have to the Father in the Holy Spirit through Jesus Christ, so that we may share in God's divine nature. This communion of the Church is made possible and sustained through the Trinitarian communion of Father, Son and Holy Spirit. Finally, the Church as communion, as Vatican II said following up what the martyr bishop Cyprian said, is participation in the Trinitarian communio itself. The Church is in the same way the icon of the community of Father, Son and Holy Spirit.[31]

The notion of the Church as a creation of the Holy Spirit has been further developed in the theology after the Council due, particularly, to the charismatic renewal movement. Some theologians, in search of a deeper appreciation of the Holy Spirit in relation to the Church, have advanced this thesis: the Church *is a sacrament of the Holy Spirit.* That would mean: as the "already" of the "not yet," the Church signifies the new creation, the world to come, which is the work of the Holy Spirit.[32]

Her mission is to release the end-time Spirit, who is operative in her as the future of the world, with the intention of leading creation into its final destiny. This aspect brings out the universality of her mission: to lead the world into the NEW creation, to discover where the Spirit is at work in the world, and to be open to the signs of the times. Boff has put very heavy stress on this aspect. By delineating the way in which the Church came into existence after the Easter event, Boff relies on the Pauline view that the Risen Lord is the Spirit who creates the Church and makes Christ constantly present. This view opens us to the fact that the Spirit, and that means ultimately the Risen Lord, is not bound to the Church alone, but moves where he wills.[33]

The Church, perceived as a "creation of the Holy Spirit", opens a new way of conceiving herself as a charismatic community in which every member has a function to fulfill. Each member has received a charism for the up-building of the whole community (Rm 12; Cor. 12). The well-being of the eschatological community depends on the exercise of these gifts. These charisms are given directly to the individual by the Spirit. They do not need an empowering through delegation by the hierarchy. But, in spite of these hopeful beginnings, this view still suffers from the underdeveloped theology of the Holy Spirit with regard to the Church. This is generally true in Catholic theology. Consequently, the Church as a Creation of the Holy Spirit did not become THE image for the Church either. However, we can say that, together with the image of the Church as People of God, the Church as Creation of the Holy Spirit forms the background for the ecclesiology of the emerging Basic Ecclesial Communities.

Conclusion

H. Küng calls these three images — People of God, Body of Christ, and Temple of the Holy Spirit — "the fundamental structure" of the Church.[34] As such they will remain forever a reference point for any accurate and correct understanding of that entity we call the Church. Theologically they express the essence of the Church and her true nature. We cannot dispense with them. They reveal the real mystery of the Church: the Holy Trinity. This Trinitarian and pneumatic view of the Church runs, thanks to the Eastern Churches, through all sixteen documents of the Council. However, the images the Council employed did not really find the echo they were hoped to evoke among the faithful. The main reason for this phenomenon seems to be located in the diverse situations and surroundings in which people must live their faith today. Their faith experience does not correspond with the modes of faith-expressions that the Church offers in these images.[35] This is mostly true because the unreflected, not spoken of interpretation these images received in the past continue to dominate their application in the concrete life of the Church.

The vision of the Church which these images contain is lofty in their language but, if correctly understood and explained from their original meaning, they image a Church perfectly oriented on the Spirit of Christ himself. Ironically, these images led often to the exact opposite of what they wanted to symbolize as a vision for the Church, be it the image of People of God, Body of Christ or Temple of the Holy Spirit. They often led to a triumphalistic and utterly clerical conception of Church in contrast to what they were meant to express, namely service and mutual equality of all, based on the life principle of Jesus summarized in the words of Mark 10:41-45 I did not come to be served but to serve and to lay down my life for the many or John10:10 I came that they may have life and have it in abundance.

The vision that the Council wanted to express through these biblical images for a renewal of the Church remain valid and viable also today. But we have to admit that many scholars attribute the ineffectiveness of these images and the general post-conciliar ecclesiological void to the fact that the official ecclesiologies expressed in these images do not really reflect the concrete shape the Church actually takes. To proclaim beautiful images is one thing, but to study and reflect seriously on how they are concretely lived at the grassroots level is another. For example, the Church proclaims that all are equal before God as members of the Christian communities, but in fact only the male celibates are allowed to participate actively in the governing power of the Church. If some participation in this power is granted to the laity, then it is done through delegation by the hierarchy and not because the laity has a natural right to participate. The basis for authority and for legitimacy of government in the Catholic Church is the sacrament of orders. Authority here is legitimated neither by majority nor by consensus but by Christ who symbolically instituted the sacrament. It is very difficult to see how more participatory ways of governing could be introduced into such an understanding of authority.[36]

Notes

[1] Medard Kehl, *Die Kirche: Eine katholische Ekklesiologie* (Würzburg: Echter Verlag, 1992) pp. 48-49.

[2] Minar, Paul S., *Images of the Church in the New Testament* (Philadelphia: Westminster Press, 1977 Third Printing).

[3] Ishvani-Kendra Reseach Seminar 2000, "A Vision of Mission for the New Millennium", Sedos Bulletin 32 (2000) p. 100.

[4] Lohfink, G., *Jesus and Community*, p. 80. See also: Jürgen Werbick, Kirche, pp 80-83. Werbick follows here Lohfink but sees this view particularly expressed already in the Gospel of Matthew.

[5] Auer-Ratzinger, *The Church,* p. 26.

[6] Auer-Ratzinger, *The Church,* p. 30.

[7] Auer-Ratzinger, *The Church,* p. 70.

[8] Ferguson, Everett, *The Church of Christ: A Biblical Ecclesiology for Today* (Grand Rapids: Eerman's Publication Company, 1996) pp. 77-88.

[9] Oscar Cullmann, *Christ and Time* (Philadelphia: Westminster 1950) pp. 115-116.

[10] Ferguson, E., *The Church of Christ,* p. 82.

[11] Auer-Ratzinger, *The Church,* p. 70.

[12] Duquoc, Christian, *Provisional Churches. An Essay in Ecumenical Ecclesiology* (London: SCM Press, 1986) p. 39.

[13] Werbick, J., *Kirche,* p. 277.

[14] Werbick, J., *Kirche,* pp. 277-281 titled: "Leib Christi: eine hierarchiologische und anti-ökumenische Methapher?" Werbick shows how the Council reformulated the intent of the encyclical and how carefully it softened the anti-ecumenical interpretation of it.

[15] Schweizer, Edward, *The Church as the Body of Christ* (Atlanta: John Knox Press, 1976),

[16] Schweizer, E., *Body of Christ,* p. 55.

[17] Schweizer, E., *Body of Christ*, p. 46.

[18] Schweizer, E., *Body of Christ,* p. 78.

[19] *The Nature and Purpose of the Church,* Faith and Order Paper No 181, 1998, p. 80.

[20] Wehrbik, J., *Kirche,* p. 300.

[21] Boff, L., *Church Charisma and Power,* p. 145.

[22] Venetz, H. J., So fing es mit der Kirche an. *Ein Blick in das Neue Testament,* Zürich 1981, 131.

[23] Wehrbik, J., *Kirche,* p. 299.

[24] Duquoc, C., Jesus Christus, Mittelpunkt des Europa von morgen, in P. Huenermann (Hg.) *Das Neue Europa, Herausforderung fuer Kirche und Theology* (QD 144), Freiburg i. Br. 1993, 100-110, at 105f.

[25] Duquoc, C., Jesus Christus, p. 108.

[26] Wehrbik, J., Kirche, p. 300.

[27] Nature and Purpose of the Church, p. 23.

[28] Schweizer, E., The Holy Spirit (Philadelphia: Fortress Press, 1980) pp. 109-110

[29] Bonhoeffer, D., Gesammelte Schriften, vol. 3 (München: Kaiser Verlag, 1958) p. 274.

[30] Kehl, Die Kirche, pp. 51-52.

[31] Walter Kasper, "The Church As Communio" New Blackfriars 74 (1993) 232-244 at p. 235.

[32] Kasper, W. and Gerhard Sauter, Kirche Ort des Geistes (Freiburg: Herder, 1976) particularly Part One, "Kirche als Sakrament des Geistes" by W. Kasper, pp. 13-55.

[33] Boff, L., Church Charisma and Power, pp. 144-153.

[34] Küng, H., The Church (New York: Sheed and Ward, 1967) pp. 107-260.

[35] Dulles, A Church to Believe In, pp. 1-4.

[36] Duquoc, Christian, Provisional Churches, pp. 17-19; 99-100.

Chapter Three

The Church in the Context of the Kingdom[1]

I. Church in relation to the world

What is the relationship between Kingdom, Church and World? Whenever the Church in her history was closely identified with the Kingdom now present in history, her relationship with the world was portrayed accordingly. The world was the object that the Church had to act upon or influence. She herself was the active subject. Such deliberations always focused on the internal reality of the Church and affirmed her self-sufficiency in relation to the world. The question asked was simply: What can the world do to build up the Church?

Since Vatican II the question has been reversed. Now people ask: What can the Church do to make the world a better place to live in? Theologically this is based on the insight that the Kingdom of God is meant for the world and that the Church must see herself and her mission in the service of the Kingdom. For the Kingdom is not only the future of the Church but also the future of the world as well. In God's plan of salvation we cannot separate the Church from the world as Yves Congar points out:

> In God's unitary design the Church and the world are both ordered to this Kingdom in the end, but by different ways and on different accounts. Church and world have the same end, but only the same ultimate end. That they should have the same end is due to God's unitary plan and the fact that the whole cosmos is united with man in a shared destiny. That they should have only the same ultimate end prevents a confusion that would be bad for the Church, as raising a risk of dissolving her own proper mission in that of history, and bad for the world, as raising the risk of misunderstanding and hindering its own proper development.[2]

The *Pastoral Constitution of the Church in the Modern World* presents this new understanding of the relationship between the Church and the world in this way. After recognizing the world's legitimate autonomy, the Council asserts that the Church must consider herself part of the total human family, sharing the same concerns as the rest of humankind. Articles 3 and 92 state that just as Christ came into the world not to be served but to serve, so the Church, carrying on the mission of Christ, seeks to serve the world by fostering unity among all people.

The advantage of such a view of the Church in her relationship to the world lies in these points:

(1) It helps the Church to turn away from an exaggerated concern about her own internal affairs and to look at the world for which the Kingdom is meant. The important thing for the Church is not to withdraw into herself and reduce herself to a small group that keeps its distance from the world. Rather, she must take part in constructive action and liberation.

(2) Viewed in this way, the Church can give hope to a world stricken by war, injustice, and hatred by pointing constantly to the coming Kingdom as meant for the whole world and as having appeared already in Jesus Christ. She gives meaning to the small services everyone can do for a better world, a world of justice, peace, and unity. For every good work done in this world means building up the Kingdom that is coming.

(3) This view underlines the principle that *diakonia (service)*, which includes the struggle for a new social order, is as essential to and even constitutive of the mission of the Church as are proclamation and sacramental celebration.

The Kingdom demands the transformation of all human reality, and the Church must be an "agent" of this transformation.

II. The Church as not identical with Kingdom of God now

The Council starts off by describing the Church as the mystery of Christ. In her is realized the "eternal plan of the Father, manifested in Jesus Christ, to bring humanity to its eternal glory." Here the Church is seen in connection with the "bringing about of the secret hidden for ages in God" (1 Col 1:16; see Eph 3:3-9; 1 Co 2:6-10). Therefore the Church has to be seen in this broad perspective of God's plan of salvation, which includes all human beings and creation as a whole (see 1 Tm 2:4; Rm 8:22 ff). The most comprehensive symbol for God's plan with creation is the biblical phrase: *Kingdom of God.*

The Kingdom aims at the transformation of the whole of creation into its eternal glory, and the Church must be seen and understood in the context of this divine intentionality. Her essence and mission make sense only in this setting. Her mission is to reveal through the ages the hidden plan of God to lead all humankind towards its final destiny. She must see herself entirely in the service of this divine plan meant for the salvation of all creation.[3]

Nowhere in the Gospels is the group of the disciples around Jesus identified with the Kingdom of God. The text that is often used for such identification is the Parable of the Tares and the Wheat (Mt 13:24-30). But the "field" in this parable is not the Church but the world as the interpretation of the parable clearly states: "The field is the world" (Mt 13:38). The teaching of the parable is about the Kingdom that invades history without a visible interruption of the present structure of this world. Good and evil will exist side by side and only in the future, when the Kingdom will come in fullness, will there be a separation of both.

To be sure, Jesus' mission is addressed primarily to his disciples. To them it belongs, they will celebrate it, and be in it. But this special proximity of the group to the Kingdom does not turn them into a closed society. The Church has no monopoly on the Kingdom of God. Citizenship in the Kingdom never means a privilege but rather an ongoing summons to solidarity with people, particularly with the excluded and discriminated against.[4]

One of the chief temptations for the Church in history is to claim the Kingdom for herself, to take over the management of the Kingdom, and even go so far as to present herself as the realized Kingdom of God vis-a-vis the world. The Kingdom of God is not the Kingdom of the Christians. God has inaugurated the Kingdom in the world and in history. He did so in two stages. First, the Kingdom was initiated through the earthly life of Jesus, his words and works and fully inaugurated through the Paschal Mystery of his death and resurrection. This Kingdom, present in history, must now grow through history to reach its eschatological fullness at the end of time. The Council clearly accepted this distinction between the Kingdom present in history now and the eschatological fullness still to come (see LG 5,9). But the question not clearly answered is whether the Council also made a clear distinction between Kingdom present in history now and the pilgrim Church.

There are, therefore, two questions to be answered. First, did the Council identify the Kingdom of God in history with the pilgrim Church?

or did it consider the Kingdom of God in history a reality that is broader than the Church and extending beyond her boundaries? Secondly, is the Kingdom of God in its final fulfillment identical with the Church in her eschatological fullness? or does it again extend beyond her while it simultaneously embraces her?

Arguments for an identity

A number of theologians still hold that a close analysis of the relevant texts of *Lumen Gentium* (3,5,9,48) would show that in Vatican II the Kingdom of God remains identical with the Church, be it with the historical reality of the Kingdom now or with the eschatological fulfillment where she will find its fulfillment as well.[5]

This view can be found in the Final Document of the International Theological Commission in 1985. Once again the distinction between the pilgrim Church in history and the heavenly Church in her eschatological fullness is made, but the document continues to identify, on the one hand, the Kingdom of God in history with the pilgrim Church; and, on the other hand, the eschatological fullness of the Kingdom with the heavenly Church. Regarding the fullness of the Kingdom to come the document has this to say:

> It is clear that in the Council's teaching there is no difference so far as the eschatological reality is concerned between the final realization of the Church (as *consummata*]) and of the Kingdom (as *consummatum*)[6]

The reasoning for an identification of the Kingdom in history with the pilgrim Church follows from this argument: if the glorious Kingdom to come coincides with the Church in fullness at the end, it is obvious that the Kingdom here on earth in its preliminary state coincides with the pilgrim Church as well. Since Kingdom and Church will be identical in the final state, one must presume that they are also now identical in their preliminary historical state.

Concerning this aspect the documents comments: Belonging to the Kingdom cannot *not* be belonging — at least implicitly — to the Church.[7] This means positively said: the Kingdom in history now is identical with the pilgrim Church.

However, the commission does adopt the theological phrase, "the Church, sacrament of the Kingdom," although the Council did not use this expression. The phrase is seen as valid under the following perspective:

1. In its ecclesiological application, the term "sacrament" is used analogically, as the first paragraph of *Lumen Gentium* stresses: *"Veluti sacramentum..."*.

2. The expression's aim is to relate, on the one hand, the Kingdom, understood in the plenary sense of its final realization, with, on the other hand, the Church in its "wayfaring" aspect.

3. The term sacrament here is understood in its full sense of *iam praesens in mysterio* (cf. LG 3) ("already present in mystery"), where the reality present in the sacrament (the pilgrim Church) is the Kingdom itself.

4. The Church is not a mere sign (*sacramentum tantum*) but a sign in which the reality signified (*res et sacramentum*) is present as the reality of the Kingdom.

5. The notion of the Church cannot be limited to its temporal and earthly aspect alone. Conversely, the notion of the Kingdom includes a present "already" *in mysterio*.[8]

While this language is very precise and does not claim an absolute identification of Kingdom and Church, it seems to imply it.

Arguments against an Identity

There are a number of theologians who, contrary to the commission's view, would see the documents of Vatican II making a clear distinction between the Church and the historical reality of Kingdom of God now. They even regard this distinction as one of the major achievements of Vatican II. The theological basis for doing so is seen in the Council's definition of the Church as a "Sign (*Sacrament*) of the Kingdom" (LG 9). Since God's saving grace can never be bound exclusively to a sacrament, one has to accept that the Kingdom is still broader than the Church. Such a separation is indirectly expressed in article 5 of *Lumen Gentium* and in article 45 of *Gaudium et Spes*. McBrien comments:

> The nature and mission of the Church are always to be understood in relationship and in subordination to the Kingdom of God. This principle is expressed in article 5 of *Lumen Gentium* and again in article 45 of *Gaudium and Spes*. It replaces what was perhaps the most serious pre-Vatican II ecclesiological misunderstanding, namely, that the Church is identical with

the Kingdom of God here on earth. If it is, then it is beyond all need for institutional reform, and its mission is to bring everyone inside lest salvation elude them.[9]

Schnackenburg affirms McBrien's view regarding the ecclesiological misunderstanding that resulted from the identification of the Kingdom now present in history with the Church when he writes:

> Let us ask ourselves here immediately about the relationship between the Church and the Kingdom or the Lordship of Christ. Is the Church the Kingdom of God on the earth, admittedly in a provisional form, until the Kingdom is fulfilled eschatologically? This view, long held within Catholic theology even though with various nuances, but which leads to a dangerous image of the Church, to a triumphalistic understanding of the earthly Church, is definitely to be rejected. True, in the New Testament the Church is seen in strict relation with the Lordship of Christ, for example in Col 1:12f: "God has delivered us from the dominion of darkness and transferred us to the Kingdom of the Son." We are only received into his Kingdom. Christ exercises his Lordship of grace in the Church by means of the Holy Spirit: but the Church remains a community of human beings who are at the same time sinful and weak.[10]

Karl Rahner says something similar:

> The Church is not identified with the Kingdom of God. It is the sacrament of the Kingdom of God in the eschatological phase of sacred history which began with Christ, the phase which brings about the Kingdom of God. As long as history lasts, the Church will not be identical with the Kingdom of God, for the latter is only definitely present when history ends with the coming of Christ and the last judgment. Yet the Kingdom of God is not simply something due to come later, which later will replace the world, its history and the outcome of history. The Kingdom of God itself is coming to be in the history of the world (not only in that of the Church) whenever obedience to God occurs in grace as the acceptance of God's self-communication.... For [of] this Kingdom of God in the world, which of course can never simply be identified with any particular objective secular phenomenon, the Church is a part, because of course the Church itself is in the world and in its members makes world history. Above all, however, the Church is precisely its special fundamental sacrament, i.e., the eschatological and efficacious manifestation (sign) in redemptive history that in the unity, activity, fraternity, etc., of the world, the Kingdom of God at hand. Even here, therefore, as in the various individual sacraments, sign and thing signified can never be separated or identified (cf. LG 9).[11]

Dulles, who seems to favor a distinction between the glorious Kingdom of God and the Church, however admits that:

> If one looks on both the kingdom and the Church as existing proleptically
> within history and definitively at the close of history, it becomes more diffi-
> cult to see how they differ. With regard to the final phase it must be asked
> — is the consummation of the Church something different from the defini-
> tive arrival of the kingdom of God? The Pastoral Constitution on the Church
> in the Modern World makes the point in article 39 that "all the good fruits of
> our nature and enterprise produced on earth in the Spirit of the Lord and in
> accord with his command" will be found again, in a purified and transfig-
> ured form, in the final kingdom. This text seems to imply that the world
> itself, in all its secularity will be transformed in Christ. It then becomes
> very difficult to distinguish between the glorified Church and the transformed
> cosmos. Perhaps one should say that the heavenly Church, as the place
> where Christ rules in the assembly of the saints, will be at the heart of the
> center of the ultimate kingdom. The new heavens and the new earth, while
> they may include more than the transfigured Church, will serve to mediate
> and express the blessed life of the redeemed.[12]

While one can still argue as to whether or not Vatican II really made this
distinction, some theologians hold that this distinction is clearly made only in
Redemptoris Missio (RM) and in the Document *Dialogue and Proclamation*
(DP), a joint statement of the Council for Interreligious Dialogue and the Congregation for the Evangelization of People. Both documents acknowledge
rather than confess that the Kingdom of God is a broader reality than the Church.

> RM and DP appear to be the first two documents of the recent central doctri-
> nal authority to distinguish the pilgrim Church from the reality of the reign
> of God in history; both documents profess that the reign of God is a broader
> reality than the Church which is present and operative beyond her bound-
> aries among the members of other religious traditions."[13]

Biblical foundation for a non-identity

Dupuis sees the foundation for a non-identity of Kingdom and Church
already present in Jesus' own behavior and actions in his public ministry.
Jesus seems not to have identified the Kingdom with the group of disciples
but envisioned the Kingdom as being broader than the group that became
the Church after his resurrection. Jesus saw his mission limited to the
"house of Israel". Yet there are instances in the Gospel where Jesus over-
steps the boundaries of Israel. Jesus made the Kingdom present through
his miracles like healing and exorcism (see Mt 12:25-28; Lk 4:16-22). The

Gospel tells us that he healed those who did not belong to the people of Israel (see Mk 7:24-30; Mt 15:21-28). These miracles signify therefore that the Kingdom is operative and present among the pagans as well. Thus Jesus did not identify the Kingdom with the "movement" created by him destined to become the Church.[14]

In the letters of St. Paul the Kingdom of God is seen present under a new form, that of the Kingship of the Risen Christ in which it is realized. In Colossians 2:10 and Ephesians 1:10 the Kingship of Christ extends not only to the Church but to the entire world: Christ is the head of the world and of the Church; but only the Church is his body (Col 1:18; Eph 1:22; 4:15; 5:23). Church and world should be seen as two concentric circles, whose common center is Christ. The Kingship of Christ as the presence of the Kingdom in history extends to the whole world, visible and invisible.

> Kingdom of Christ is.. a more comprehensive term than "Church". In the Christian's present existence on earth his share in Christ's Kingdom and his claim to the eschatological Kingdom.... find their fulfillment in the Church, the domain in which grace of the heavenly Christ are operative.... But Christ's rule extends beyond the Church.... and one day the Church will have completed her earthly task and will be absorbed in the eschatological Kingdom of Christ or of God.[15]

The theological fruits of such non-identity

The acceptance of a clear distinction of Church and Kingdom has far reaching consequences for theology, particularly for the Church's relationship with the world and the other religious tradition. The symbol Kingdom of God as being broader than the Church provides the horizon for a solution for two theological problems.

First, in the context of the Church in her relationship to the world, it shows how the work for justice and liberation inside and outside the Church is intrinsically linked with the Kingdom present now, since the ultimate goal of the Kingdom of God is the transformation of all reality.

Secondly, in inter-religious dialogue the Kingdom symbol furnishes the theologian with a broader perspective to enter into dialogue with other religious traditions. If the Kingdom is the ultimate goal of God's intentionality with all of humanity, then the question is no longer how these other religious traditions are linked to the Church but rather how the Kingdom of God was and is concretely present in these religions.

Voiced 'reservations' to a 'Kingdom-centered Church'

While accepting the distinction between the Church and the Kingdom in principle, the Church herself has been very eager lately to assure that both are not to be pulled apart, be it in the liberation theology or in the inter-religious dialogue. Having admitted the distinction, both RM and DP are worried that this view easily leads to two pitfalls. The Kingdom-centered approach seems to stress the Kingdom to such a degree as to leave out the Church almost entirely. Additionally, in so doing it forgets to bind the Kingdom to Jesus Christ. These are clearly the worries the Pope voices in his encyclical *Redemptoris Missio:*

> One may not separate the Kingdom from the Church. It is true that the Church is not an end unto herself, since she is ordered towards the Kingdom of God of which she is the seed, sign and instrument. Yet while remaining distinct from Christ and the Kingdom, the Church is indissolubly united with both (18).

The same concern is also echoed in the document *Dialogue and Proclamation:*

> The Kingdom is inseparable from the Church because both are inseparable from the person and work of Jesus himself ... It is therefore not possible to separate the Church from the Kingdom as if the first belonged exclusively to the imperfect reality of history, while the second would be the perfect eschatological fulfillment of the divine plan of salvation (DP 34).

Some theologians, particularly in India, are at the moment afraid that we are heading towards a crypto-identification of Church and Kingdom once again. By stating strongly that the Kingdom is intrinsically bound up with Christ, and that the Church is his chosen instrument for the Kingdom, the whole argument seems to go so far as to say that you cannot promote the Kingdom unless you are promoting the Church. If the Kingdom can be found only in Jesus and if the Church is the continuation of Jesus' presence through the ages, then, so the argument goes, the Kingdom can be found only in the Church. (In such an argumentation one wonders if the Church is not being compared once again with the physical body of Jesus instead of being compared with the body of the Risen Christ.) They see here a subtle return to an ecclesiocentric approach to the Kingdom which makes it impossible to develop a Kingdom-centered understanding of the Church. The danger is that the universality of the Kingdom is continually reduced to the particularity of the Church once again. In the words of F. Wilfred:

Since certain trends in liberation theology and in the theology of religions seemed to highlight the reality of the Kingdom at the expense of the Church and to distance themselves from the Church, the reaction (of the official Church) has taken the form of barring any access to the Kingdom except through the Church. Or to put it in another way, instead of understanding the Church in relation to the mystery of the Kingdom, this trend wants to understand the Kingdom of God in terms of the Church, and indeed turn the Church itself into the Kingdom.[16]

As these theologians view it: if such a trend would gain the upper hand in Catholic theology today, one of the most powerful sources for the renewal of the Church and its theology could be seriously stifled. Only if we maintain the distinction between Church and Kingdom clearly and uncompromisingly, can such a symbol once again become THE religious symbol of our time. It provides us, on the one hand, with a way to relate to this world and its destiny productively and, on the other hand, with a way to enter into a more open and creative dialogue with other religious traditions and ideologies.

Therefore, we have to be on our guard not to allow such an identification once again as subtle as it may be. The Church is not the Kingdom now since the Kingdom makes itself felt outside the Church as well. Her mission is to serve the Kingdom and not to take its place.

The many qualifications made by RM and DP to the statement that Kingdom and Church are not identical are true to the firmly held position of the magisterium that whatever "traces of the Kingdom" may be found outside the Church must be seen and related to the Kingdom that Christ proclaimed and brought. There cannot exist any "Kingdom revelation" in the world that is not related to or independent of Christ. Referring to the reality of the Kingdom outside the Church DP adds the following caution, which once again makes clear the strong stand of the official teaching authority.

> Part of the Church's role consists in recognizing that the inchoative reality of his Kingdom can be found also beyond the confines of the Church, for example in the heart of the followers of other religious traditions, insofar as they live evangelical values and are open to the action of the Spirit. It must be remembered nevertheless that this is indeed an inchoate reality, which needs to find completion through being related to the Kingdom of Christ already present in the Church yet realized fully only in the world to come (DP 35).

For those theologians who hold on to a non-identity there remains the unsolved theological problem: *How to relate a Kingdom outside the Church to the Kingdom that Christ proclaimed and gave to the Church.* Should one assume that there are other revelations of the Kingdom not related to

Christ? While such views are voiced today by a number of theologians,[17] the official Church has so far steadfastly refused to allow any such propositions to be even considered.

The answer to this question of how the Kingdom of God, which Jesus brought irrevocably into this world through his life, death and resurrection, is now also to be found outside the Church is this: God's Kingdom entered this world finally and definitely with the incarnation of Jesus but took on a more comprehensive presence in the resurrection of Jesus, the Christ. In the resurrection the limitations of Jesus' earthly existence are gone. The Kingdom was definitely present in the Jesus who walked this earth but its presence was, so to speak, restricted to the physical body of Jesus. This is to be concluded from the fact that John could speak about the Spirit who "was not yet because Jesus was not yet glorified" (Jn 7:39). But in his death and resurrection the Kingdom he had proclaimed as having arrived with him took on a new dimension: it now embraced the whole of creation. In the risen Christ, matter has been transformed into the state of the New Creation. In his risen body, Christ is the cosmic Christ, the world to come. He, therefore, assumes a new global relationship with reality as a whole: he is present in creation in a new way.

As the future of the present world, Christ relates to creation in a new way. The whole world belongs to him not only on the basis of creation (Col 1:1-15; Jn 1:1-14) but now also on the basis of its transformation in the resurrection of his body into the New Creation. We cannot limit the presence of the New Creation to the Church alone. This all-pervasive presence of the Kingdom of Christ in the world makes itself visible not only in the Church but also in historical movements outside the Church and in the other religious traditions found anywhere in the world. This was expressed by the International Ecumenical Congress of Theology in Sao Paulo (Brazil 1980) in these words:

> The coming Kingdom as God's final design for his creation is experienced in the historical process of human liberation. On the one hand, the Kingdom has a utopian character, for it can never be completely achieved in history; on the other hand, it is foreshadowed and given concrete expression in historical libera-tions. The Kingdom pervades human liberations; it manifests itself in them, but it is not identical with them. Historical liberations, by the very fact that they are historical, are limited, but are open to something greater. The Kingdom transforms them. Therefore, it is the object of our hope and thus we can pray to the Father: "Thy Kingdom come". Historical liberations incarnate the Kingdom to the degree that they humanize life and generate social relationships of greater fraternity, participation and justice.[18]

There are three dangers which we have to be mindful of:

(1) Church and Kingdom are seen to be so closely connected that an identification takes place. The result is then an abstract and idealistic image of the Church cut off from real history and its traumas.

(2) Church and world are identified with the result that the image of the Church is secular and mundane, and a constant conflict with the powers of the world cannot be avoided. This has been called "the 'secularist temptation' when the Kingdom of God is consciously or unconsciously identified with some earthly goal or other, and the goal of the Kingdom of God entrusted to the care of the Church."[19]

(3) A Church totally centered on herself, out of touch with the world and the Kingdom, becomes a self-sufficient, triumphal, and perfect society not recognizing the relative autonomy of the secular sphere.

According to Boff "these dangers are theological 'pathologies' that cry out for treatment; ecclesiological health depends on the right relationship between Kingdom - World - Church, in such a way that the Church is always seen as a concrete and historical sign (of the Kingdom and Salvation), and as its instrument (mediation) in a salvific service to the world."[20]

Conclusion

Whatever doubts there may remain whether Vatican II did make a clear distinction between the Kingdom in history and the Church in further development, the Church's magisterium seems to have clarified the matter in favor of a non-identification. The Encyclical *Redemptoris Missio* as well as the document *Dialogue and Proclamation* acknowledge the working of the Kingdom outside the Church by seeing there the "values of the Kingdom of God" concretely lived.

> It is true that the inchoative reality of the Kingdom can also be found beyond the confines of the Church among people everywhere, to the extent that they live "Gospel values" and are open to the working of the Spirit who breathes when and where he will.(20)

These "values of the Kingdom" are spelled out as "peace, justice freedom, brotherhood etc." They are clearly seen as manifestation of the Kingdom present right there where they occur in whatever religious tradition or secular situation (RM 17).

It is equally significant that these documents not only clearly distinguish Church and Kingdom, recognizing that the one larger reality of the Kingdom cannot be encompassed by and contained within the Church, but the documents also unambiguously subordinate the Church to the Kingdom by affirming that the Church is meant to be a servant of the broader and more important Kingdom' of God.

> It is true that the Church is not an end unto herself, since she is ordered towards the Kingdom of God of which she is the seed, sign and instrument (RM18).

> The Church is effectively and concretely at the service of the Kingdom (RM 20).

> The Church's mission is to foster the *"Kingdom of the Lord and his Christ"* (Rev 11:15) at whose service she is placed (DP 35; see also 59).

With these statements the official Church has passed another milestone. In Vatican II the Christian Church was no longer totally identifiable with the Catholic Church alone. The Church was seen as embracing other Churches as well. Now it is stated that the Kingdom of God is not to be identified with the Christian Church.

III. The Kingdom of God as present in the Church

Although the Kingdom may not be identified with the Church, that does not mean that the Kingdom is not present in her. The word Church may not appear often in Jesus' teaching but the very concept of the messianic community, intrinsically bound up with the Kingdom, implies the same thing as the concept of Church. It is, therefore, correct to say:

> The Kingdom of God and the Church are two key New Testament concepts, both are crucial for the understanding of God's plan for humanity. They are central to the fulfillment of his redemptive purpose. While the Church cannot be identified with the Kingdom, for the latter is a larger and more comprehensive term, the two are nevertheless in such close correlation that they cannot be separated either.[21]

The Kingdom in 'spatial' and 'dynamic' terms

The following observations should clarify what we mean by saying the Church is not the Kingdom, and yet it is a community chosen by God in which the Kingdom is made present in a special way. In the New Testament we find two sets of ideas connected with the Kingdom of God. These might be helpful to understand better the tension that exists between the Kingdom and the Church. They are the following.

First, in the Old as well as in the New Testament, the Kingdom is mostly understood as God's sovereignty or kingly rule. Perceived as a dynamic concept, Kingdom means God's active rule over all reality but particularly at the end of time. It is all-embracing but still provisional, still to come in all its fullness. This strand is the most dominant one and can be found in all the writings of the Bible. It expresses clearly God's intention to save all human beings and the whole of creation.

Secondly, there is also a strand in the message of Jesus that understands and portrays the Kingdom in spatial terms, as a territorial reality. This is expressed in sayings like these: one can enter the Kingdom (Mt 5:20; 7:21; 18:3); and one can be thrown out of it (Mt 8:120). There are keys of the Kingdom (Mt 16:18-19). The Kingdom is compared with a house into which people are invited, etc. This strand of the message of Jesus is largely new but pervasively present in his Kingdom message.

These two strands create a tension that is fundamental in the New Testament.[22] While they help us to better understand the world in relation to the Kingdom, they certainly could help us also to clarify the tension between Church and Kingdom. They indicate that while the Kingdom is a reality that embraces all of creation, God still has bound it in a particular way to a particular group in space and time now. Dulles makes a similar observation; the symbol Kingdom in the New Testament refers to reign and realm;

> The term basileia in the Greek New Testament frequently means kingship (reign) but it sometimes must be translated as kingdom (realm). The two concepts are inseparable. Christ's kingship or lordship implies a community over which he reigns — in other words, a kingdom. Conversely, the concept of the kingdom always implies a king. Several different expressions such as "kingdom of God," "kingdom of heaven," "kingdom of the Son," and "kingdom of Christ" are used almost interchangeably in the New Testament, and the differences of nuance among them need not concern us here.[23]

It is the Kingdom present now that creates the Church and keeps her constantly in existence. The Church is therefore the result of the Spirit, who makes God's final saving intentionality effectively present as the true source of the community called Church.

Although the Kingdom cannot be identified with the Church, that does not mean the Kingdom is not present in her. While acknowledging the difference between the Kingdom and the Church, the Encyclical Redemptoris Missio is very much concerned that the Church should not be seen and treated as separated from the Kingdom.

> One may not separate the Kingdom from the Church. It is true that the Church is not an end unto herself, since she is ordered towards the Kingdom of God of which she is the seed, sign and instrument. Yet while remaining distinct from Christ and the Kingdom, the Church is indissolubly united with both. (18)

The Kingdom makes itself present in the Church in a particular way. We can say that the Church is an "initial realization" or a "proleptic anticipation" of the plan of God for humankind, or in words of Vatican II, "She becomes on earth the initial budding forth of the Kingdom" (*Lumen Gentium* 5).

Secondly, the Church is a *means* or *sacrament* through which God's plan for the world realizes itself in history (LG 8; 48). As G.E. Ladd puts it,

> The Kingdom creates the Church, works through the Church, and is proclaimed in the world by the Church. There can be no Kingdom without the Church — those who have acknowledged God's rule and there can be no Church without the Kingdom; but they remain two distinguishable concepts: the Rule of God and the fellowship of men.[24]

We should never separate the Kingdom from the Church, since after all, she is God's chosen instrument for his Kingdom here on earth.

Difficulties voiced with this view

This view of the Kingdom (as present in the Church in a pre-eminent way) and of the Church (as an anticipation of the final destiny of humankind) creates a series of difficulties and problems that need to be addressed:

(1). How can the absolute and final reconciliation of the whole of history "already" — although initially — be realized in a particular phenomenon of history?

(2). How can the already realized reconciliation of history be mediated through the Church in the face of human freedom and in view of a constantly open future of history?

(3). In what sense does the Church, as a social entity of salvation, occupy a middle position concerning the question of individual fulfillment and the final universal fulfillment of humanity's social destiny in the universal resurrection of the dead?

Only the Kingdom in its ultimate fullness will be the final reconciliation of the two seemingly dialectically opposed dimensions of human personality: the *individual* (every human being is unique and unrepeatable) and the *social* (communitarian and belonging to the species). Only the coming Kingdom can and will solve this apparent dichotomy between the individual and the social since it will fully reveal the image, according to which we are created: the *Triune God* whose very essence is *One in Three*.

The apparent conflict between both exists only in this present condition of humankind. Only in a sinful and untransformed world does the constant conflict between the rights of individuals and the "structures of society" arise. Both will never really be reconciled as long as the Kingdom has not come in its fullness. This conflict keeps arising to the extent that modern society is becoming increasingly complex and in need of more "sophisticated structuring." The instinctive aversion of many people to all institutionalization will not make it easier for the Church to present herself as a model of human society.

One more difficulty is the growing awareness that the Church herself, as a reality in history, easily falls prey to class-consciousness and yet pretends to be neutral, i.e., not to be affected by such prejudices, though, in reality, she always serves some class interests. There is a refusal to submit to ideological critique, which alone can unmask such class biases.[25]

In the light of such difficulties it is all the more important for the Church to present herself as an "honest institution"[26] or as "God's counter society"[27] to witness to the whole of society what she is really destined for. Her essence and mission are to offer herself as a *"test-case,"*[28] showing that the rights of individual persons and a society of justice, peace and joy are reconcilable and liveable in the present world with the understanding, of course, that they are only a sign of what is to come. A perfect society is not possible in this world. But the Church can offer, in an "initial and anticipatory way," the fulfillment of humanity's social destiny since the Kingdom of God has already broken into this world and indicates the direction towards which all history has to move and to be transformed.

It is therefore the Church's duty to display in an evil age of self-seeking, pride, and animosity, the life and fellowship of the Kingdom of God and of the age to come. This display is an essential element in the witness of the Church to the Kingdom of God.[29]

Conclusion

We know that God's Kingdom is present. Even if the hoped-for future drags on and seems not to come, the choice of living from it is not wrong. The Kingdom releases energies that affect the course of history deeply and in often unintended ways. To live from the future means to have a vision of a world and to stop trying to succeed and to establish our security in the present socio-economic order.[30] It is this vision which created the Church; it is this vision from which the Church lives; it is this vision which is the mission of the Church. Looking at the all-too-human face of the Church, we can easily identify with Pedro Casaldáliga's dream:

I dream of a Church wearing only the gospel and sandals;
I believe in the Church despite the Church,
sometimes, in any case I believe in the Kingdom,
journeying in the Church.

The Kingdom unites.
The Church divides
when it does not coincide with the Kingdom.

Notes

[1] The content of this chapter I have present in almost identical terms already in *The Kingdom of God* (Maryknoll, New York: Orbis 1995) "Kingdom and the Church", pp. 248-272 and in *Throw Fire* (Manila: Logos Publication 1998) pp. "The Community of disciples in the Service of the Kingdom", pp. 287-314.

[2] Yves Congar, *Lay People in the Church* (London: Bloomsbury Publishing Co. Ltd., 1957) p. 88.

[3] Pannenberg, W., *Theology and the Kingdom of God* (Philadelphia: Westminster Press, 1977) pp. 72-75.

[4] Lochman, Jan Milic, "Church and World in the Light of the Kingdom of God", *Church - Kingdom - World. The Church as Mystery and Prophetic Sign,* Faith and Order Paper no. 130, Gennadios Limouris (ed.) (Geneva: World Council of Churches, 1986) p. 6.

[5] Dupuis, J., "Evangelization and Kingdom Values: The Church and the 'Others'" *Indian Missiological Review* 14 (1992) pp. 4-21.

[6] International Theological Commission: Text and Document 1969-85, edited by M. Sharky (San Francisco: Ignatius Press, 1989) pp. 300-304, at p. 302.

[7] Theological Commission, p. 303.

8   Theological   Commission, pp. 303-304.

9   McBrien, R., *Catholicism*, p. 686.

10 Schnackenburg, R., "Signoria e regno di Dio nell'annuncio di Gesu e della Chiesa delle Origini", Communio 86 (1986) pp. 41-42.

11 Rahner, Karl, "World and Church", *Sacramentum Mundi* Vol. 1, K. Rahner et al. (eds) p. 348.

12 Dulles, "The Church and the Kingdom," pp. 17-18.

13 Dupuis, J., "A Theological Commentary: Dialogue and Proclamation," in Burrows, William R., *Redemption and Dialogue*, Reading *Redemptoris Missio and Dialogue and Proclamation* (New York: Orbis Book, 1994) p. 40.

14 Dupuis, J., "Evangelization and Kingdom Values", p. 10.

15 Schnackenburg, Rudolf, *God's Rule and Kingdom* (New York: Herder and Herder, 1968) p. 301.

16 Felix Wilfred, "Once again.. Church and Kingdom," *Vidyajyoti* 57 (1993), pp. 6-24 at p. 10.

17 Knitter, Paul, *No other Name? A Critical Survey of Christian Attitudes Towards the World Religions* (Maryknoll, New York: Orbis Book, 1974).

18 *Challenge of Basic Christian Communities, Papers from the International-Ecumenical Congress of Theology*, February 20-March 2, 1980, Sao Paulo, Brasil, Ed. Sergio Torres and John Eagleson (Maryknoll, New York: Orbis 1981) Chapter 19: Final Document, No 33, pp. 236-237.

19 Lochman, Jan Milic, "Church and World", pp. 59.

20 Boff, L., *Church, Charisma Power,* pp. 1-2.

21 Kuzmi_, "*Church and Kingdom*", p. 49.

22 Lochman, J. M., "Church and World in the Light of the Kingdom of God", pp. 61-63.

23 Dulles, A., "The Church and the Kingdom" in *A Church for all People,* ed. Eugene LaVerdiere (Collegeville, Minnesota: The Liturgical Press, 1993) p. 14.

24 Ladd, G. E., *The Present of the Future. A revised and Updated Version of Jesus and the Kingdom* (Grand Rapids, Michigan: Eerdmans Pub. Co., 1974) p. 277.

25 Boff, L., *Church Charisma and Power,* pp. 108-110.

26 Pannenberg, W., "The Kingdom of God and the Church" in T*heology and the Kingdom of God* (Philadelphia: Westminster Press, Fifth printing, 1977) pp. 82-84.

27 Lohfink, G., *Jesus and Community*, pp. 122-132, "The Church as Contrast-society."

28 Mcbrien, Richard, *Catholicism*, p. 716.

29 Ladd, George Eldon, *The Presence of the Future*, p. 269.

30 Cobb John B., *Sustainability, Economics Ecology & Justice* (New York: Orbis Books, 1992) pp. 13-14.

Part 2

Models of the Church

Chapter Four

Emergence of a World-Church

I. A Theological Interpretation of Vatican II

Introduction

Jesus' vision of the Kingdom has been transmitted to us through the faith community into which we were born: the Roman Catholic Church. Over many centuries this community grasped and framed the message of Jesus according to the culture which received it. The Catholic faith tradition was formulated over the centuries by saints and great theologians who shared a common culture that rested on Greek and Roman foundations as well as on the diverse cultures of people who had joined these empires and had made their own contributions. The theology which gradually arose became the official teaching of the Church. Culture and Gospel became almost identical as the following often-heard phrase might indicate: "Europe is the faith and the faith is Europe." We exported this theology to the Third World in good faith and we established Churches IN many countries. But are they Churches OF these countries?

The philosophical and theological synthesis that was achieved over the centuries is undoubtedly one of the most impressive ever created. But what we realize today is that this grandiose synthesis of theology is built on a particular culture with its values and customs. The message of the Gospel might be so well presented and interpreted through the values and customs of one culture that the people of this culture cannot now perceive that the same message could be expressed equally or even better in any other culture with different value systems and customs. If we accept that the Christian message can be expressed differently in diverse cultures, then we have to accept at the same time that the Bible will read differently in these cultures. But have we really taken inculturation seriously?

There's no doubt that the future of the Christian faith lies with the emerging Churches of the developing world. A few simple statistics support this statement. The Catholic Church is growing by around 15-20 million members a year. This number includes 3 million adult baptisms; 90% of these new members are in the Third World. Today 70% of all Catholics live in the Third World; 50% of these are found in Latin America. These Christians demand the right to express themselves in their own non-Western cultures.

If the future of Christianity belongs to these countries, we will have to expect that they will express their faith experience in a different way and develop a theology accordingly. There will be a back-flow of theology from the Third World to the First World. How should we evaluate this? Something is happening that hardly anyone could have imagined fifty years ago.

The emergence of a World Church in Vatican II

I would like to review a theory which K. Rahner presented fifteen years after the Council in an article entitled: "Towards a Fundamental Theological Interpretation of Vat. II."[1] If Rahner's thesis is true — and I basically agree with it — we can at least see what is coming and what will shape theology in the near and distant future.

Vatican II was THE EVENT of the century for the history of the Catholic Church. Whatever future Synods may have to add or to comment upon, there is no way back. One might well have different opinions but the Council provided official guidelines outlining the directions in which the Church will have to move.

Rahner's thesis: Formally and for the first time the Council was a Council of the World-Church as such.

> The Council for the first time in a formal way was a Council of the world-Church as such. We need only compare it with Vatican I to see its uniqueness in the formal juridical sense. It is true that there were representatives of the episcopal sees in Asia or Africa present at Vatican I. But these were missionary bishops of European or American origin. At that time there was not yet a native episcopate anywhere in the Church. But one appeared in Vatican II. Perhaps this was far from proportionate to the representation from European episcopates. But it was there. These bishops did not come simply as individuals, *"ad limina"* to give an account of their dioceses and to take home missionary alms; Vatican II really was the first assembly of the world-episcopate, not acting as an advisory body to the Pope, but with him and under him as itself the supreme teaching and decision making authority

in the Church. There really was a World-council with a World-episcopate such as had not hitherto existed and with its own autonomy. The actual significance of the non-European part of this total episcopate may have been comparatively slight; the consequences of this conciliar event for the post-conciliar life of the Church may still be very limited, as the Roman synods of bishops have shown since then; none of this alters the essential fact that the council made manifest and brought into activity a Church which was no longer the European Church with its American areas of dissemination and its exports to Asia and Africa.[2]

This thesis sounds innocent but, if true, it has enormous consequences and potential. For Rahner there are — theologically speaking — three great epochs in Church history, of which the third has only just begun and made itself observable officially at Vatican II.

What are these three epochs?

First the period of Jewish Christianity

The disciples of Jesus did not move away from Israel after Easter. They saw themselves wholly as Jews and not yet as a "group alongside others." They continued to take part in the temple cult:

Day after day they met as a group in the Temple" (Ac 2:46).

They kept the Old Testament Law and its tradition (Temple cult, Law and circumcision). To be a disciple of Jesus meant to be a Jew first; only then could a non-Jew enter the circle of Jesus' disciples. The apostles remained in Jerusalem and did not take up mission work to the Gentiles.[3] Peter is reprimanded for baptizing on his own initiative an uncircumcised pagan:

You were a guest in the house of uncircumcised Gentiles, and you even ate with them! (Ac 11:3)

In short: circumcision (sign of the Covenant), keeping of the Law and attendance at the cultic services were regarded as normative for anyone who joined the new movement. However, although remaining in the Jewish tradition, the community had its own rules and celebrations from the very beginning:

(1) BAPTISM as an initiation rite of the new fellowship;

(2) COMMUNAL PRAYER SERVICES in private houses which were directed to Jesus the Lord and not to Yahweh; (Ac 2:46)

(3) The BREAKING OF BREAD as their interpretation of the Passover and the Exodus;

(4) Their OWN LEADERS, Peter and the other apostles;

(5) The FELLOWSHIP OF LOVE which was linked with the breaking of bread that bound them together as brethren who put their possessions at each others' disposal (Ac 4:32-35).

What led ultimately to a separation from "Israel of Old" was the 'YES' or 'NO' to Christ. The disciples did not want this separation; it was forced on them.[4]

Jesus' own ministry was geared to 'gathering together Israel of Old' and he understood his mission in the setting of Israel.[5] Jesus did not take up any gentile mission himself. Granted that Jesus foresaw the coming of a gentile Church after his death (Mt.8:11); yet there was obviously no word from him about how his message should be carried to the Gentiles. Only new situations, new circumstances, imposed on the disciples, made them gradually see that the message was for the pagans as well. And this is not by becoming Jews first but by entering directly into the new community.

We have a beautiful illustration of how difficult it was for Peter and what kind of conversion it demanded for him to accept that God had chosen the Gentiles as well as the Jews without any distinction whatsoever:

About noon the following day as they were on their journey and approaching the city, Peter went up on the roof to pray. He became hungry and wanted something to eat, and while the meal was being prepared, he fell into a trance. He saw heaven opened and something like a large sheet being let down to earth by its four corners. It contained all kinds of four-footed animals, as well as reptiles of the earth and birds of the air. Then a voice told him, "Get up, Peter. Kill and eat." "Surely not, Lord!" Peter replied. "I have never eaten anything impure or unclean." The voice spoke to him a second time, "Do not call anything impure that God has made clean." This happened three times, and immediately the sheet was taken back to heaven (Ac 10:9-16).

However, we have to qualify carefully the distinction between Jewish and gentile Christians. R. Brown distinguishes four types of Jewish/Gentile Christianity.

Type one consists of Jewish Christians and their gentile converts who kept the Law, circumcision and cult and regarded these as necessary for receiving the fullness of the salvation brought by Christ.

Type two consists of those Jewish Christians and their gentile converts who observed only some Jewish purity laws without insisting on circumcision as salvific for gentile Christians. Peter and James seem to have been of this kind.

Type three consists of Jewish Christians and their gentile converts who did not insist on circumcision or demand the observance of Jewish purity laws in regard to food. However, they did not ask for a break with the Jewish feasts and temple nor impel Jewish Christians to abandon circumcision and the Law.

Type four consists of Jewish Christians and their gentile converts who did not insist on circumcision and Jewish food laws and did not ascribe any significance to the Jerusalem temple.[6] Rahner seems to address himself only to the two most opposed types: one and four.

The second period of the Church: the Gentile Christian community freed from Judaic Law

The question was: did the Gentiles, who wanted to join the Christian community, have to become Jews first through circumcision and the keeping of the Law? or could they become members of the community through baptism administered without requiring the observance of the Law and the practice of circumcision?

The problem was felt quite early and some *'ad hoc'* solutions were arrived at, since Jesus had not left them clear instructions on what to do. This can be seen in the way Peter justified to the assembly of the Jerusalem Church his baptizing Cornelius and his household without first making them Jews. Peter reported to the assembly (Ac 10:15-18):

> *"When I began to speak, the Holy Spirit came down on them just as on us at the beginning... Who was I, then, to try to stop God!"* When they heard this *they stopped their criticism and praised God.*

But it was Paul who thought out and formulated theologically what took shape in the history of the primitive Church.. The first Apostolic Council in Jerusalem settled the issue: To become a Christian does not require circumcision and keeping of the Law. The theological reasoning was purely Christological. But the resolution was based on the inspiration of the Holy Spirit and not on the word of the Lord:

> *The Holy Spirit and we have agreed not to put any burden on you (Ac 15: 28).*

One has to concede that something like a mission to the Gentiles would have been possible in the setting of Jewish Christianity, and the solution of Paul and the Council in Jerusalem was theologically not so self-evident as it looks to us today. The Paschal Meal, circumcision, and most of the Law could have been retained just to indicate the connection with the Old Testament.

It is regrettable that Jewish Christianity vanished from the scene. There are many scholars who argue that it was Jewish Christianity that "wrote" our Gospels and that this "formidable minority" had an enormous influence on the Church. In terms of ecumenism, it would be excellent if we still had a Jewish Christianity which could really carry on the dialogue between Jews and Christians once again on a common basis. Some even think it would be easy to recreate such a Christianity for the good of the whole Church.[7] But the fact is that the first Apostolic Council in Jerusalem, with its decision concerning law and circumcision, introduced a radically new period in Church history:

> A Christianity that was not the export of Jewish Christianity to the Diaspora but instead a Christianity which, for all its relationship to the historical Jesus, still grew on the soil of paganism.[8]

What happened here is a transition of Christianity from one historical and theological situation to an essentially new one. Rahner sees this transition extending into the Greek-Roman era as well as into the medieval and modern European era. He regards the Roman-Hellenistic Mediterranean culture and its transmission to the Germanic peoples as one unity.

However, Rahner is not so much concerned with the historical character of such a transition but rather with its theological 'significance.' The abolition of circumcision can certainly not be derived from Jesus' own explicit preaching nor from the preaching about the salvific meaning of his death and resurrection. But Paul regarded this principle as belonging to the Gospel. This principle represents a break with salvation-history which Paul could not undertake on his own. The fact is that we rarely realize what such a break meant: the Church became a gentile Church. (In our own times this break should be worked out in dialogue with the Synagogue of today in order to discover what is still valid from the Old Testament and what is not.)

The third epoch: the transition of the Western Church to a World Church

From this, Rahner proposes the thesis that today we are experiencing a break such as occurred only ONCE before, that is, in the transition from Jewish to Gentile Christianity. He then determines the meaning of Vatican II in the sense that, at the Council the Church, even if only initially and unclearly, proclaimed the transition from the Western Church to a World Church. For Rahner

> the difference between the historical situation of Jewish Christianity and the situation into which Paul transplanted Christianity as a radically new creation is not greater than the differences between Western cultures and the contemporary cultures of all Asia and Africa into which Christianity must inculturate itself if it is now to be, as it has begun to be, a genuinely world Church.[9]

The problem is the following: either the Church sees and recognizes the essential differences of other cultures for which she should become a World Church, and with a boldness draw the necessary consequences from this recognition, or she remains a Western Church and so, in the final analysis, betrays the true meaning of Vat. II.

Here it is useful to recall the distinction made by many scholars today: the Church has to move from being, for example, the local Church IN India to being the local Church OF India. The big question, however, is: does the present Church still have the creative power and authority that she had in the period of her first becoming the apostolic Church? For the decision taken was an irreversible basic decision which affects her very essence. And the authority to do this came to her over and above that which came to her directly from Jesus or now from the Risen Lord. More precisely, Rahner asks: Can the Church legitimately perceive possibilities of which she never made use during her second major epoch because those possibilities would have been meaningless in that epoch and consequently illegitimate?

Vatican II regarded itself as the active subject of the highest plenary power in the Church. The direction which this council gave lacks conceptual clarity but it can only justly be compared with the transition from Jewish to Gentile Christianity. There are many statements in the Council Documents which indicate this break clearly. A few may suffice here:

(1) For the first time and formally the Council was a World Church Council: a gathering of the world episcopate. In comparison Vatican I had no native-born bishop present from the Third World.

(2) The leap to a World Church becomes clear by looking at the decrees of the Council:

> The shift from Latin (as the language of a small and particular cultural region) to the vernacular.

> We can safely say that without the Council Latin would still be the liturgical language throughout the world. We need not be prophets to say that this change can never be reversed.[10]

> *"Gaudium and Spes"* acknowledges the broader perspectives from which theology will have to be done. The great change which came with Vatican II consists in the shift from a classical culture to a more dynamic or evolutionary understanding of culture.

> And so the Council substitutes a dynamic and more evolutionary concept of nature for a static one, and the result is an immense series of new problems calling for a new endeavor of analysis and synthesis. (G S 5)

This means moving away from the official interpretation of the Gospel message in terms of the great "classical culture of the West" to an interpretation which respects the categories, values and attitudes proper to other cultures.

(3) Concerning doctrinal matters:

The Council did two things which are of fundamental significance for a world-wide missionary effort:

> For the first time in the doctrinal history of the Church it initiated a positive evaluation of the great religions of the world.

> Secondly, through the documents on the *Mission of the Church* and on the *Church in the modern world,* it proclaimed a universal and effective salvific will of God which is limited only by the evil decisions of the human conscience and nothing else. This opens the way to accepting the view that other religions are revelatory and salvific, a view which was not previously recognized. "Dialogue" becomes the main word when the Church's mission is explored and discussed.

A basic objection against Rahner's thesis is that he seems to regard the break from the Gentile Church to the World Church as just as important as the break from Jewish Christianity to Gentile Christianity. The first break, so the objection goes, was not just a break from a CON-text it was a break in the TEXT.

Paul particularly realized the newness of the Gospel and the impossibility of reconciling it with the Jewish tradition. For him the break seems to have been necessary in order to create a new TEXT. Others would say that Paul does not present a new TEXT he only gives the correct interpretation of the TEXT; namely, that the Old Testament found its correct interpretation in Jesus Christ. The Temple, circumcision, the Law and the tradition which the Jewish Christian kept and the Council in Jerusalem approved should be regarded as CON-text which had to be changed once the TEXT was moved into a new culture and environment. It seems that Jewish Christianity and the Gentile Church lived on for some time side by side and only historical circumstances brought it to an end.

Conclusion

Rahner's thesis that Vatican II was the great event in which the Church for the first time came to the reality of being world-Church[11] calls for a new understanding of the relationship between the Church and cultures. Now that the Church is a World-Church, it must incorporate a world perspective into its *"modus operandi"*. It cannot be exclusively married to the Roman or European way of life. In Rahner's view, now that the Roman Catholic Church is a World-Church, it is time to act like a World-Church. Each culture has contributions it can and must offer the Church. Conversely, the Church must accept and incorporate these gifts into herself.

In his book *Charisma and Power*, Boff underscored how the Church assimilated secular organizational structures from the Roman Empire and from feudal society. It would be very difficult to defend the theological position that all these structures are in themselves *"ius divinum"* and constitute the very nature of the Church. As history shows, the Church has always been influenced by the society in which it has lived. Now that the Church is no longer strictly a European creation, it ought to incorporate the variety and diversity brought to it by the cultures and societies of its world-wide membership. Josef Ratzinger defines this tension in a very impressive manner.

> After decades of concentration on 'Roman', which followed the (First) Vatican Council, (theological inquiry) the Church has again directed more attention to the other side of the scale, to 'Catholic'.[12]

It is far easier to focus on the "Roman" aspect of the Church than on the "Catholic" aspect. "Roman" implies unity in and allegiance to the Church of Rome. "Catholic" implies the diversity of the Church throughout the world.

It seems to me that the struggles over authority which are occurring in the Church today are partly the price the Church is paying for being "Catholic". Certainly before Vatican II, the Church prided itself on being "Roman", the "same thing always and everywhere". With the advent of Vatican II and the World-Church, we come to realize once again what being "Catholic" really means. Universality includes an ambiguity which is at times not easy to live with. If the Church is at the same time "Roman" and "Catholic", then there is no way to avoid this struggle. With the advent of Vatican II the Church set herself on an irreversible course which will be marked by the attempt to balance "Roman" and "Catholic" in the Church. As Rahner succinctly says:

> The Church at the Council surrendered a good deal of power that it formerly assumed. At this point a frontier has been crossed behind which it will never again be possible to return, even to a slight degree.[13]

Rahner argues that the emphasis in the past has been placed too heavily on the "Roman" side of the scale to the detriment of the "Catholic" side. One can sense his frustration as he writes:

> Have not the Roman Congregations always had the mentality of a centralized bureaucracy, claiming to know what is best everywhere in the world for the service of the Kingdom of God and the salvation of souls and do not their decisions appear to be shockingly naive, based as they are on the assumption that the Roman or Italian mentality is the obvious standard of judgement?[14]

II. Megatrends affecting the Church Today

There are two simultaneously evolving realities the Church must reckon with: first, the ever more felt importance of the local cultures concerning the Church's mission; secondly, the almost opposite, the emergence of a global culture that affects almost all cultures. This shows itself in particular trends which are all pervasively present everywhere. These trends have to be evaluated critically but they cannot be ignored.

From now on the CON-text into which the Gospel has to be translated will be global. The world with its different cultures and perceptions of reality will become the arena in which God's Kingdom has to be discovered as already present and has to be articulated in the words of these cultures. Looking at the new situation we have to realize that "profound transformations are taking place at the moment which characterize today's world especially in the southern hemisphere."[15] No one can attempt to do any serious theological reflections on the Church and her mission in the world today and the near future without taking these facts into account. Different names have been given to these "profound transformations" and different aspects have been stressed depending on what part of the world and out of what kind of situation one sees and evaluates these trends. European theologians will come up with a different list as will the Asians or Latin Americans but the differences are not that great. Since they affect all cultures and people in the whole world they are rightly called by some authors "megatrends." Some of the most important of these for our topic concerning the future of the Church and her mission in the world seem to be the following:[16]

Resurgence of Cultural Traditions

Among all peoples of the world there is a resurgence of a sense of their cultural identity. This phenomenon is present in every continent and is manifested in a return to the roots of culture, to the original and living traditions, customs, understandings, values, and relationships — a return not for its own sake, but for the sake of rediscovering identity, in order to cope with the modern world in ways that differ from one culture to another.

Inculturation is a process by which the Gospel enters into a culture, takes from the culture all that is already gospelled, and is enriched by it. In addition to this, the Gospel challenges the culture in those aspect that are un-gospelled and the culture challenges the Gospel in those aspects which are merely Western and thus both are purified and universalized. So the dynamics between culture and Gospel are such that each is enriched and challenged by the other. There is a call and a response. There is a rejection of elements of the culture which are contrary to the Gospel as well as a critique of and removal from the Church of those elements which are not the genuine Gospel but rather westernized interpretation.

Globalization: the trend towards socio-economic and political globalization

While not a radically new concept, globalization has adopted a particularly important relevance in our days. Most of us accept the idea that humanity is rapidly becoming a global society. But this trend has to be treated in a critical fashion. Globalization is a double-edged sword, both a blessing and a curse - but it is here to stay. There are those who extol the virtues of globalization and who say, it is about tearing down borders, eliminating world poverty, uniting divided peoples and securing world peace. But there is the seamy underside: the aim of globalization is often seen only in economic terms. As such, it tries to impose a single vision of how national economies should function and be structured, it is a modern neo-colonial process by which global economic powers are securing their hold over the so-called developing world but not less over the developed countries.

Positively we have to appreciate the universal outlook globalization provides. Universalism means not only opening our windows to the outside but also keeping them wide open so that the mutuality between our Church and other churches, religions, all sorts of movements for the good of God's Kingdom, is not stopped but continues with unrelenting determination.

Revival of Religious Experiences

People are longing for personal religious experience: a hunger for the divine, a search for the absolute. Religious revival happens in all religions in the world, including Asia and Africa alike.

The Churches, the synagogues, the temples, all the structural religions of today, will have an influence on the lives of the people insofar as they provide opportunity for genuine religious experiences. They will be judged unimportant if they become obstacles to this experience.

Basic Ecclesial Communities: the need for personal encounter of God within small faith communities

With the support and encouragement of a small group, people find their way to God, and God finds a way to people. People long to experience God, to relate to God, to share their own faith with others in freedom and spontaneity, in an atmosphere of confidence and trust.

The basic unit of the Church, the parish, seems to fall short in many parts of the Church. What is called for is the small faith community, which is today's response to the individual's quest for God and to personal meaningful involvement for the transformation of humanity.

Problems in Ministerial structures:

People's needs for God are not met anymore in present structures of the ministry: priest, male, celibate, ordained. A whole range of new ministries is required.

There are 400 000 priests. 68% care for 40% of Christians in Europe and USA and 32% minister on behalf of the 60% of the rest of Catholics. There are not enough to take care of the sacramental needs, never mind mentioning other pastoral needs. The Church needs to develop different ministries and new styles of ministry.

The Western Church in Crisis

The Western Church as an institution is in deep crisis. It is in crisis because it is Western, because it has modified the universality of her nature and defined herself in terms that may have been relevant to Westerners in the past but are irrelevant to them at the present, and even irrelevant to non-Westerners. The ultimate reason for this crisis is that the Church has become identified with an antiquated form of Western culture and expresses the mysteries of God, of Jesus, of community and ministry in these terms; consequently" the Church today appears irrelevant to its own Western members and totally alien to non-Westerners.

Many trends towards a global church have been developed not in the West but in the mission churches: liturgical renewal, ecumenism, interfaith dialogue, movements of inculturation, being true to one's own identity, new understanding of ministry.

The Poor as the New Evangelizers: the centrality of the poor and oppressed in the plan of God for humanity

The poor are again at the center of our understanding of God's plan for humanity. Once more, God has chosen them to evangelize the world, to help the world to come to a new understanding of the gospel, of the real value of life, of the true value of community and of the joy of sharing.

New Presence and Significance of Women

The new awareness of the presence of women in the life of the church and society. Theology, spirituality and ministry take on new dimensions where women enter the field. This will start a new era of evangelization and mission. What is asked for is: equality, partnership, co-responsibility and co-ministry.

New frontiers for Mission

The rapid increase in the number of people who have not been exposed to the Christ event. Christians will decrease from one-third in 1970 to one fifth in the year 2020. A whole new approach to mission outside and beyond the parameters of the Church is a must.

Co-partnership with the earth

The earth is the first sacrament of God's love for its inhabitants; it is the womb which gives life and nurtures it constantly, as the partner in the journey of humanity towards the Kingdom. The earth can no longer be considered as an object to be controlled and dominated, or as a means to be used and misused as one pleases. The earth is part of humanity, and humans are part of the earth: they have a common destiny. To abuse the earth is to commit suicide, to misuse the earth is to threaten life, to respect the earth and to treasure it as one of God's greatest gifts is to assure life. We need to develop a renewed theology of the earth and to promote ecology in all its aspects

Conclusion

As a consequence of this new openness, an enormous number of books have been written; seminars, and meetings on inculturation and contextualization have taken place and are constantly taking place. As a consequence two pastoral priorities seem to be emerging in the Church today: Contextualization and Solidarity with the Poor. Contextualization or inculturation follows theologically from Rahner's thesis quite easily. Inculturation has a particular urgency in Asia with its great cultural and religious traditions. In Africa also the Church is faced with the task of inculturating itself into the different African traditions. The second pastoral priority today is the Church's solidarity with the poor, an option which many regard as belonging to inculturation. We have to expect different views in theology stemming from the different situations in which the Gospel is read and lived.[17]

Chapter Five

The use of models in Theology to describe the Church today

Since Vatican II different concepts and descriptions of the Church have emerged. Some are the result of the Council's own deliberations, others emerged out of the experience of very concrete situations in which the Church finds herself today. These new circumstances have given rise to various understandings of the Church's essence and mission. Theologians have analysed these different approaches and views and tried to synthesize them in order to come to grips with at least the main thrusts. A. Dulles, Models of the Church, outlines five descriptions of the Church as most prevalent in the post-conciliar Church. Jerome P. Theisen presents nine models.[18] R.P. McBrien, *Catholicism*, sees three dominant models or ways of perceiving the Church.

I. What is a model?

For the last 50 years the concept of theological model has been used by theologians. Although this way of scientific investigation is primarily a tool employed by the empirical sciences, its use in theology has become accepted. Why such an empirical approach like "model" can be applied to theological topics at all is indicative of what has happened to theology over the last 50 years. In the words of B. Lonergan:

> Theology has become largely an empirical science, in the sense that Scripture and Tradition are not premises but data. The steps from data to interpretation are long, arduous, and at best, probable. An empirical science accumulates information, develops understanding, masters more of its material and, out of this, new insights and more comprehensive views will emerge.[19]

Model thinking in theology can prevent us from making concepts and symbols into idols. It helps us realize that the infinite can never be captured in the finite structures of language. It opens an almost infinite possibility to theological development and, therefore, goes beyond any purely conceptual definition or symbolic representation.

Since Avery Dulles published his book on *Models of the Church* in 1974, many other scholars have followed him in approaching theological topics with the hermeneutical tool of model. Today we find books like *Models of Christology, Models in Moral Theology, Models of Original Sin, Models of Inculturation*, etc. Howard A. Snyder has followed this line by investigating the biblical phrase Kingdom of God under the theological concept of model.

What is a model? A model is a conceptual and symbolic representation or system by which we try to grasp and express reality or part of reality.[20] A model is to some degree an intentional abstraction from reality in order to clarify issues. It is a relatively simple, artificially constructed case, which is found useful and illuminating for dealing with realities that are more complex and differentiated.[21] Or in the words of Luzbetak:

> Models are simplified rough drafts, rough but effectively able to call up appropriate mental images. They are analogues around which inquiry can be usefully organized. Models have a great potential for expanding human knowledge. Their utility lies in the fact that they proceed pedagogically from the known to the unknown, not only summing up but, so to speak, dramatizing the implications of the particular analogy.[22]

Dulles distinguishes between explanatory and exploratory model: EX-PLANATORY model serves to synthesize what we already know or, at least, are inclined to believe. EXPLORATORY model can lead to new theological insights. This kind of model is new, at least for theology, since it works more with hypothesis, which in turn depends on the data available.[23]

Luzbetak sees a good model as having the following characteristics:

> Good models will always be (1) *useful*, (2) *open*, (3) *fitting*, and (4) *stimulating*. By *useful* we mean that good models are well suited for organizing a body of knowledge. They explain a large quantity of data and allow few exceptions. Good models are useful also in the sense that they not only serve informational purposes but also help solve practical problems. By *open* we mean that good models recognize their limitations. Models are presented only as approximations of truth, only as tentative statements of reality, as hypotheses, and as invitations and challenges to further refinement and clarifications. By *fitting* we mean that good models are logical, consistent, and neat. That is, they are simple, clear, aesthetic, and balanced. By *stimulating* we mean that good models have a capacity to arouse the imagination and thus to contribute to further and deeper understanding.[24]

Models do not have to be exclusive. Various models balance or supplement each other. A chosen model has normally one or two secondary aspects and rejects only the polar opposite of the primary model. According to Lambino when we choose a model, we should regard the following points as important:

1. *Inadequacy* of models: Each model comprehends only a different area of reality; it does not exhaust it. Reality is always greater and richer than any model that tries to grasp it.

2. *Relativity* of models: Each model focuses on one aspect of reality. No single model can claim to be exhaustive or exclusive in the sense that it grasps and expresses the whole of reality completely. There is no model to end all models.

3. Models as *responsive to needs*: Each age of history and historical community tends to develop a model that best responds to its felt needs. In that sense we can say: "A model is accepted/acceptable if it accounts for a large number of biblical and traditional data and accords with what history and experience tell us about the Christian Life."

4. *Historicity* of models: When the historical situation changes i.e. if there is a shift in the human person's understanding of self, the need for new models arises.

5. *Time-limits* of model: In time every model reaches the limits of insight. New models will emerge.[25]

Hans Küng has described the way new models or paradigms in theology may come into existence by using parallels from natural science and existing theology. He mentions five links in the chain of reasoning, which could be summarized in his five provisional theses.

1. As in natural science so in theology, there is a "normal science", the established position with its classic authors, text books, and teachers that is characterized by

   – a cumulative growth of knowledge;
   – a solving of remaining problems;
   – resistance to everything that might lead to the alteration or replacement of the established model of understanding or paradigm.

2. As in natural science so in theology, the awareness of a growing crisis is generally the point of departure for a crucial change in certain previously valid assumptions. This leads to breakthroughs in new interpretative models or paradigms. Where the available rules and methods fail, they lead the search for new ones.

3. As in natural science so also in theology, an old model of understanding or paradigm is replaced when a new one is ready.

4. As in natural science so also in theology, both scientific and non-scientific factors play a role in deciding whether a new paradigm will be adopted or rejected. Thus the transition to a new model cannot be forced rationally but may be described as a conversion.

5. As in natural science so also in theology, it is hard to predict, amid the great arguments of the day, whether a new model will be absorbed by the old one, or the old one replaced or archived. If it is accepted, the innovation solidifies into tradition.[26]

The positive result of such a process is that we gain new insights and ever more comprehensive views to the degree that the data increases. Exegesis has been proceeding that way for a long time. What we have gained today is more and more data. Out of this data the theologian can construct a working hypothesis that he will have to substantiate with the data available to him. Today this procedure is at the root of doing theology on the basis of models. All theologians will agree that theology is not just an empirical science, for one must take into consideration the fact that it has an abiding norm in the past, a norm given to us once and for all in the revelation of Israel's history and ultimately in Jesus Christ.

There is no way back. The ultimate reason for this shift is the insight that the old dogmatic theology, with all its splendor and glory, misconceived history with its 'classicist mode.' It thought not in terms of evolution and development but of universality and permanence.[27] The Second Vatican Council recognized this shift in the often quoted sentence:

And so mankind substitutes a dynamic and more evolutionary concept of nature for a static one, and the result is an immense series of new problems calling for a new endeavor of analysis and synthesis. (G S 5)

What is new is the understanding that history itself becomes a means of revelation as well. As Lonergan put it: "There is a dimension in man which strives for meaning which makes culture possible. In bringing out

this meaning in culture man makes himself the creator of his own history."
The different cultures must be taken more seriously if the Gospel should
really be able to reveal its universal significance for all nations and people.
In his massive work on Church and Culture, Louis Luzbetak puts it this
way when he writes about the Church's mission in the future:

> The Church needs anthropology if it is to be able to evaluate and be in a
> position to offer to nations around the globe a two-thousand-year-old tradi-
> tion, much of which is both spiritually and culturally precious, while much
> might best be described as mere trappings of history. The Church needs
> anthropology because it must be able to speak today as it did on that first
> Pentecost (Acts 2:1-12), in a way that all peoples of the world might under-
> stand. The Church ought to be able to speak in respective native tongues
> about the marvels God has accomplished - whether the people be Parthians,
> Medes, or Elamites; whether they be from Mesopotamia, Judea, Cappadocia,
> Pontus, or the province of Asia; from Phrygia, Pamphylia, Egypt, or Libya;
> whether they be Romans, Cretans, or Arabs. The Church must understand
> *all* peoples and be understood *by all*, despite deep cultural differences. It
> would be unfortunate indeed if the Church were to overlook the fact that it
> has today at its disposal, as never before, a vast treasury of human knowl-
> edge in the social sciences, not the least important of which is the Science of
> Human Beings called *Anthropology*.
>
> But even local churches *qua local* addressing their own people, with whom
> they share the same culture, need a *culturally oriented* approach to mission
> and therefore should avail themselves of the Science of Culture. As we
> have emphasized over and over again, there is no more effective or more
> genuine way of being Christian-that is to say, of being,"of the mind of Christ"
> (1 Cor 2:1 6)-than in terms of culture. The local church is not fully and
> effectively proclaiming the Kingdom unless the Gospel is preached in the
> cultural "language" of the community concerned: in other words, unless the
> proclamation of the Word, the participation in worship and manifestation of
> God's presence, and the specific forms of communication, fellowship, ser-
> vice and organization are all as closely as possible tailored to the culture
> and social situation of the time and place. What every local church needs is
> a truly local theology, local in understanding and local in practice.[28]

If it is true that all human beings are *cultural* beings then Jesus must
be *culturally* relevant if he is really to be understood and appreciated. And
so it is with the Church: it must be culturally relevant if she is to be understood and appreciated. This is a most obvious fact unfortunately only too
often overlooked.

II. Different Models of Church

Introduction

After Vatican II the Church's interest gradually shifted towards the developing countries whose voices were rather tolerated than seriously listened to during the Council. Suddenly there emerged formidable theologians from continents like Latin America, Asia and Africa who had not been present during the council. The first fruit of their effort to do theology from their situational and cultural background was the emergence of Liberation Theology. This was the first really non European systematic approach to theology that brought movement into an otherwise very stable and fixed way of doing theology. The reaction of traditional theologians and the Church's own teaching office ranged from outright condemnation to a gradual acknowledgment as the years went by. The questions raised by these theologians could not be ignored since traditional theology could not provide answers anymore with its way of doing theology.

In the wake of these insights and developments after the Council, different understandings and views emerged concerning the Church. Theologians like K. Rahner, A. Dulles, Johannes Metz, and Hans Küng realized that the emerging "Global Church" or "World Church" would have to give way to different conceptions of Church built on different cultural and sociological situations. W. Bühlmann, L. Boff, A. Bellagamba, and most of the Latin American Liberation Theologians envisioned a Church that would be able to respond to the changing situations in the world and in turn could help the traditional Church in the West open herself to new situations which are emerging there as well.

The Bible presents us with 95 images, applied mostly to the Covenant people, which are applicable to the Church as well. Dulles remarks that, when image is employed reflectively and critically to deepen one's theoretical understanding of reality, it becomes what is called a model. In our exposition of the Church we will follow the five models that A. Dulles regards as the most important ones for the Church at the moment. The Lumko Pastoral Institute in South Africa has presented five models of its own in an attempt to renew the Church through small communities. Their approach starts with the changes that occurred after the Council in the actual structuring of the Church on the parish level. They want to present a vision for the Church of tomorrow that is viable and, in their view, the only one feasible if the Church is to survive.

Theologians have analyzed these different approaches and views and tried to synthesize them in order to come to grips with at least the main ones. A. Dulles, Models of the Church, sees five descriptions of the Church in the post-conciliar Church.[29] We will follow his models as a guide in our presentation.

1. The Church as "community of disciples"

Eight years (1982) after his publication of the *Models of the Church*, Dulles came out with another major book on the Church titled, *A Church To Believe In: Discipleship and Dynamics of Freedom*. In chapter one of this book Dulles proposes a new conception of the Church in the light of which the five models he had presented earlier should be seen, re-evaluated and judged. He calls this new conception of the Church *Community of disciples*.[30] Behind this image we find an expression of the newly discovered realization that the basic vocation of any Christian is first and foremost to follow the Lord as he walked over this earth (*Perfectae Caritatis* 2). The emphasis here is on following the Lord rather than following the Church, on being constantly on the road rather than having already reached the goal. Church must be seen as the community of those who have made it their life profession to follow the Lord and as such build a community that is called Church. Dulles regards the following elements as basic for such an image of Church as Community of Disciples.

The group around Jesus: Community of Disciples

Although this conception of Church is not common in Catholic ecclesiology, it has a good biblical foundation, particularly the book of Acts, where the primitive Church is often called the "community of the disciples". This conception links the Church to Jesus himself in the sense that the earthly Jesus founded the *"community of disciples,"* men and women whom the Father had called and given to him in order that he should lead them to a radical commitment to him and the Kingdom he preached. They became the group that was to emerge after Easter as the Church.

The Church based on the Community of Disciples

What all the Gospels are concerned with is fellowship with the Lord. They could be called "Manuals of Fellowship". It is difficult to decide to what degree we can say that the earthly Jesus founded a Church. But we can say with certainty that Jesus deliberately formed and trained a band of disciples to whom he gave a share in his teaching and healing ministry. Therefore, we can say: Jesus did found a *"community of disciples"*. The Church which emerged after Easter should be understood and seen in continuity with that *community of disciples* which Jesus himself had created in his life time. This community is the place where authentic discipleship to Jesus himself and to his Kingdom message becomes possible. In order to know what it means to be a disciple of Jesus, we have to look at these men and women whom Jesus chose and called to follow him and to learn from them what the Lord asked of them. This vision of a Church as "community of disciples" seems to tune in with what many regard as their own experience of Church today.

Like the first disciples, the present day Christian has first to hear a personal call from the Lord and to respond to it in a free and self-conscious manner. This call must be heard as coming from the Lord of the Church and not simply from the Church so that Christ himself is seen as the focal point of the Christian life. Dulles puts the stress on the personal experience of a call to become a Christian over against just being a Christian because one was born into a Christian Church.

Discipleship a constant becoming

According to the New Testament one is never a disciple but is always on the road to becoming one. Discipleship is a precarious thing, something one can easily betray or deny. To remain in the company of Jesus requires a fresh grace from the Lord every day. The emphasis here is that being a disciple means to be on the road towards discipleship. It means to be constantly learning strange words and deciphering puzzling experiences. It means "to go behind the master" and let him determine the way, to let oneself be corrected every day. It is here that the community becomes quite important, because it is in the community that one finds support and discerns with others which way the Lord leads. Once again, it is not just a matter of receiving instruction only; rather, it is a question of learning and of actively participating in ministry and mission. This affirms what we said earlier about the identity instilling power of the image of discipleship.[31]

This view follows closely the insight of the Latin American theologians for whom concrete fellowship with the Lord is the first step before any theory about the Kingdom and the Church can be brought forth. Only in the praxis of following Christ do we glimpse the mental categories that will enable us to understand the real nature of the Church and formulate it in a meaningful way.[32]

Disciples in community

In the experience of our dependence on each other we come to realize that without community there would be no Scripture, no sacraments nor any other means of access to Jesus himself. What counts is the experience of the individual disciple who again needs the *community of disciples* for making and discerning this personal experience. It is a matter of staying in contact with the community which goes back to the first disciples of Jesus and which was founded by them in order to know what authentic fellowship is all about.

This view is most explicitly presented in the gospel of Matthew. For him the Sermon on the Mount is the New Rule and the New Law for the disciples. This *"Magna Carta"* of Christian behavior is to be understood as the new way of life for those who want to follow the master. But Matthew makes it clear that the Sermon on the Mount presupposes the existence of a community of those already committed to the Lord and in which the demands of the Sermon are practiced and lived. It presupposes a Christian community, we could even say the Church. Without such a community we cannot live discipleship.

The Beatitudes show very clearly that the Gospel is to be proclaimed and lived in a community where the living out of the same Beatitudes is made possible through the community that provides the necessary support for the individual. The individual alone cannot live these virtues except as a member of a Christian community and the Beatitudes assume that there are people in the community who have made them their rule of life. All the hard sayings in the Sermon on the Mount are meant to remind us that we cannot live without the support and trust of others. For Matthew we can only be and remain disciples of Jesus by joining the community of disciples. Only the community can provide the atmosphere, the concern, the mutual love and the experience of Christ risen and alive that will enable the disciple to live true discipleship. Outside community we cannot live discipleship.

Another feature of Jesus' ministry that Matthew emphasizes strongly and which expresses his idea of discipleship is Jesus' custom to sit at table with his followers who represent all kinds of people and always include the outcasts of society. Some authors even think that the Kingdom of God movement can best be summarized as a "table community movement." The authors base the validity of this phrase on the undeniable fact that one of Jesus' basic behaviors was his frequent sharing of meals with the poor, the hungry, and the outcasts who made up the majority of his followers. What marks the community of Jesus' disciples is therefore the continuous practice of "sitting at table" and remembering that Jesus will remain with them in this celebration until the day he will come again to fulfill it (Mt 26:29). But it is also the community which decides who can become a member and under what conditions an individual can remain a member of the community of the disciples (Mt 18:15-18; 22:11-13).[33]

Disciple and ministry

Dulles thinks that, in a Church described as *community of disciples,* we will have to view ministry differently. Competence and authority should only be invested in mature and faithful disciples. A leader selected and commissioned on this basis of proven discipleship may have a wide range of responsibilities, but authoritarianism of any kind needs to be outlawed in a *community of disciples.* However, this is possible only if the governing power in the Church is no longer based solely on sacramental power. The ecclesiology of Vatican II seems to make such a distinction between Sacrament of Orders and governing power theoretically possible. But as long as the liturgy, the place of the sacred, remains the only model for Church organization, it will be difficult to see how the model *Community of Disciples* would be allowed to develop at the grass-roots level, by giving the laity a share in the government of the Church, not on the basis of hierarchical delegation but on the basis of their own vocation.[34]

By seeing ministry as discipleship we can avoid making sharp distinctions between the disciples and would introduce into the Church once again true equality among all. Discipleship is the common denominator which unites all, because all are followers and learners in relation to Jesus Christ.

2. The Church as Institution

Cardinal Robert Bellarmine +1621 proposed a definition of the Church, mentioned earlier, which became classical in Catholic tradition.

The one and true Church is the assembly of human persons bound together by the profession of the same Christian faith and the communion of the same sacraments, under the rule of legitimate pastors and in particular of the vicar of Christ on earth, the Roman Pontiff.[35]

Pius XII took up this definition in his encyclical *Mystici Corporis.* However, far from being a real definition, it is actually a list of requirements necessary for belonging to the Catholic Church. It puts the stress on the exterior features, i.e., on the visible form of the Church while the internal dimensions of membership are left aside. Clear and decisive as it may be for apologetic reasons, it is too external and minimalistic: external profession of faith, communion in the sacraments and subordination to proper authority. These three criteria are determined by the central government, the Roman Pontiff. They exclude from the Church all those who do not correspond to these visible criteria of which the central government is the author. Only Roman Catholics are true members of the Church; others belong to her only by desire. As a consequence, the Church of Christ "exists" only in the Roman Catholic Church. In such a model the power and functions of the Church are divided into three: teaching, sanctifying, and governing. This leads to the distinctions between

- The Church teaching and the Church taught
- The Church sanctifying and the Church sanctified
- The Church governing and the Church governed

The result of such distinctions is that the Church is identified with the governing body or the hierarchy. While the teaching and sanctifying functions of the hierarchy are seen as mediating the doctrine and grace of Christ, the governing function is perceived as being handled by the hierarchy themselves.[36] This in turn leads to a strong hierarchical conception of authority. The Church is conceived as a society in which the fullness of power is concentrated in the hands of the hierarchy and handed down through sacramental ordination. There is hardly any room for active participation of the laity in the governing power of the Church based on the reality propounded by Vatican II that all the members of the Christian community are first and foremost all equal and called to active participation in the life of the church. In the words of Vat. I:

But the Church of Christ is not a community of equals in which all the faithful have the same rights. It is a society of unequals, not only because among the faithful some are clerics and some are laymen, but particularly because there is in the Church the power from God whereby to some it is given to sanctify, teach and govern, and to others not.

A definition of the Church, which in contrast stresses the interior invisible and christo-centric aspect of the Church was given by K. A. Möhler (also mentioned earlier) during Vatican I:

> The Church is the Son of God perpetually appearing in human form among men, always renewing himself, eternally regenerating his enduring incarnation; for the Christian faithful are called in Holy Scriptures the Body of Christ.[37]

Putting both definitions, that of Bellarmine and Möhler, side by side brings into focus two basic elements: the VISIBLE, social form and the INVISIBLE, transcending reality of the Church. The first definition envisions the Church as a perfect society in human history while the second puts a strong emphasis on the christo-centric aspect of the Church to the extent that it has been called "christo-centric mysticism." Both, however, lead easily to a conception of Church as being a "divine institution" beyond and above all human ambiguities and corrections.

However, the definition given by Bellarmine has remained the one that determined to a large degree the concept of the Church still today. This model sees the Church primarily as a hierarchically structured, visible society which mediates salvation to its individual members through preaching and teaching of the Word and the administration of the sacraments. This was the dominant model in Roman Catholicism before the Council, and it inspired the first draft of the Council's Dogmatic Constitution of the Church. The Council fathers rejected such an approach to the mystery of the Church as being too juridical and too rigid.

The strength of this model

1. It enjoys *strong endorsement* in so many Church documents in the past and Vatican II did maintain this aspect as well. The document *Lumen Gentium* remains ambiguous since it adopted the hierarchical view without a serious attempt to reconcile the new and the old view.

2. It provides a strong sense of *corporate identity*, each person knows his/her place and role in the Church.

3. It is attentive to *historical continuity* connecting the present Church with the Church of the past. It provides a feeling of security against any present theological uncertainty and theological fad.

The weaknesses of this model

1. It is based not so much on Scripture as on a particular "world view" with a definite understanding of the universe, of the human person and culture which is composed of a set of meanings and values informing a common way of life. This view is a perfect expression of the classical world view. It consists of a "dominant mentality" which enshrines a certain tradition, it implies certain presuppositions or assumptions, it regards certain concepts as fundamental.

The presuppositions and assumptions are the following: Christ founded the Church as a visible society and equipped her from the beginning with institutional means adequate for every occasion. The hierarchy, having the fullness of the apostolic authority, is in charge of the official doctrine, worship and discipline of the Church.

> God created the hierarchy and thus provided more than sufficiently for the needs of the Church until the end of the world. (A. Möhler)

The Church bases therefore its authority not on the community but on the Sacrament of Orders. In democracy authority rests with the people and is delegated by the people and is legitimate only to the degree that people give credit to it. In the Church authority derives its legitimation not from the people but from God or Christ. Democratic procedures for determining governing power in the Church are, therefore, just not possible. The ultimate reason given is the understanding that salvation comes to us from elsewhere and cannot be drawn from the grass-roots. To say that all are equal does not affect the social organization of the Church but is seen only as a spiritual reality. What might be rightly assumed in the secular world — that social and political equality is a basic human right — cannot be applied to the Church in its organization. It might seem paradoxical for the Church to defend the equality of social and political rights of men and women in the secular world and not to admit those same rights in the organization of the Church.

Another paradox heard so often today is the claim of the Church to be a historical anticipation of the Kingdom of God in space and time now. The symbol Kingdom itself stands for a community of brothers and sisters where there are no rulers nor ruled, where all are equal and one in Christ (Gal 3:27-28). How does the Church concretely witness to this Kingdom of equals in its external structures? The Catholic Church finds itself in a constant dilemma: on the one hand she defends social and political equality, on the other hand she withholds this to her own members in the exercise of authority in the Christian Community itself. She firmly holds to the principle of authority based on the Sacrament of Orders which is claimed to be the only one to do justice to revelation as it was proclaimed in Jesus Christ.[38]

  2. There are only a few passages in Scripture that support this view. It seems that Catholic ecclesiology knew only Matthew 16:17-19 "You are Peter and on this rock I will build my Church."

In Matthew 16:19 Jesus tells Peter that what he binds or loses on earth will be held as bound or loosed by God. But this statement is repeated in almost exactly the same words in 18:18 and applied to all the disciples or even to the Church in general. As has been observed:

It is only if we were to fail to read on after 16:18-20 that we might make the mistake of thinking that only Peter and his successors were permitted to make decisive pronouncements.[39]

With the exception of the pastoral letters, the New Testament described the assembled community and not individual officials in the community as being ultimately responsible for making decisions in matters of doctrine and morals. Accordingly, the Christian community played a much more active role in any decision making process in the early Churches than we usually assume.[40]

  3. The hierarchical and societal aspect is disproportionately over-stressed at the expense of the communitarian. The role of the *ordained* is exaggerated at the expense of the missionary responsibility of the entire Church.

The institutional structures are those which are regularly established, publicly recognized, stable, respectable, and uniform. Dulles singles out four categories of institutional structures in the Church: (1) Doctrines and doctrinal formulations which are normative for all the members such as creeds, dogmas, and canonical writings (Scriptures, Conciliar pronouncements). (2) Forms of public worship, such as sacraments and other approved rituals. (3) Structures of government i.e. offices with the powers and duties attached to them.(4) Laws and customs regulating the behavior of members.[41]

  4. The scope of the Church is limited to the Roman Catholic Church, the ecclesial reality of other Churches is not recognized.

5. The mission of the Church is limited to the preaching of the Word and the administration of the sacraments, at the expense of the Church's broader social and political responsibility.

6. It is a real obstacle to creative and fruitful theology. Other essential ministries in the Church, like the prophetic and teaching ministry are entirely subjected to the magisterium. The charismatic ministries in the Church are either ignored or are presumed to have been legitimately taken over by the ministry of office.

These are the main objections voiced against the institutional model as it has existed in practice and theory in the church since the Council of Trent. As all short summaries are easily one-sided exaggerations, the hierarchical model has often been made responsible for all ills in the Church. How did the Council react to this model and how did it change?

The Council and the hierarchical model

The revolutionary vision of the Church that emerged during the Council put a stop to a Church image that portrayed the Church in almost exclusive terms of hierarchy. However, many theologians still think that, in spite of all the corrections the Council made, the effective institutional and legal structures of the Church seem to render this new vision of the Church largely ineffective at the grass-root level. The old perception of the Church still seems to be the image that is prevailing in many circles of the Church up to the present. One does not have to be so pessimistic but the reform introduced by the Council still has a long way to go.

The first question to be asked when correcting the hierarchical model will certainly be: How democratic or participatory can the Church really be? Our time with its passion for equality and participation will use this as the litmus test whether the Church has a future or not. Her understanding of world order in hierarchical terms is alien for many people today. But can she really be defined and understood as *total equality* of all even in her very structure of authority and governing power?

B. Ashley in his book on *Justice in the Church* introduces a distinction that might help us concerning the question of equality and inequality. He writes:

> We must distinguish *functional* from *personal* equality and inequality. Functional inequality requires an order or hierarchy of functions if these functions are to be coordinated in a unified action.[42]

How we understand hierarchy is what's important. As Ashley points out: there are two conceptions of hierarchy one linear and one nonlinear. The linear one conceives the universe as a linear order of entities emanating from the Divine One in which each entity totally contains all its inferiors and is totally contained by its superiors. The Christian Neo-Platonist Pseudo-Dionysius applied this linear conception to the celestial hierarchy of angelic spirits and to the ecclesiastical hierarchy of Church offices. In such an ecclesiology the laity are totally dependent on their priests for all graces, the priests totally dependent on the bishops, the bishops on the pope, the pope on Christ and Christ on God.[43]

Such a linear concept of hierarchy is not the way ecclesiological office has necessarily to be conceived although in practice it might have been done so. This conception seems to be in the mind of those who today reject radically any hierarchical model as unacceptable to the modern mind and who want to see it replaced by the principle of participation. Ashley quotes here Sandra Schneiders who writes:

> It is not that those in authority are exercising authority badly or that those who should be obeying lack faith, humility, or some other virtue (although both are sometimes true). It is that principle of hierarchy which is the nerve of both secular and religious obedience as they have been traditionally understood, is being radically questioned and the principle of participation is supplanting it in more and more sectors of life.

Ashley thinks Schneiders is seeing authority in the linear way in her harsh judgement on authority and her demand for abolishing the principle of hierarchy all together.[44]

But there is an other view of authority developed by St. Thomas. This second model of hierarchy does not accept the linear conception of the order of being. Any entity in the chain of being is generically subordinated to its superior but not totally so, since it also has unique specific or individual characteristics not contained in any of the superiors except in the creator. It likewise contains its inferiors only generically and not totally, so that they are in some respects superior to it. This view certainly does justice to a Christian anthropology which sees every human being as absolutely unique in so far as it expresses something of God's very being that is not expressed in any other co-creature. The identity of a human person rests ultimately in his or her unique relationship with a personal God.[45]

This concept of hierarchy applied to an ecclesiology constitutes its members as functionally unequal yet because each member functions to make a unique contribution to the common good, all members equally have a right to participate in the common good. Thus the *principle of hierarchy and the principle of participation* need not stand in opposition, but can complement each other in an ecclesiology based on a nonlinear model. In such an ecclesiology, while the laity receives the broad range of graces through the Church's official hierarchy, this general subordination of the laity to the hierarchy does not render the laity more distant from God since each Christian has unique graces directly from God, mediated only through Christ, his Divine Son, by Christ's Holy Spirit.[46]

> The Christian view of justice does not confuse the personal equality due to all members of the church and of society because they are created in God's image with the necessarily hierarchical inequality of gifts, offices and kinds of status required for a community to achieve the common good of its members and to permit the maximum participation by all. Yet the inequality of function and status must always be in the service of personal equality, and must never override that more fundamental equality. The Christian in whatever functional status must imitate Christ who came not to be served but to serve.[47]

But as long as all governing power remains practically, if not theoretically linked to the Sacrament of Orders, the Church will have great difficulty in coping with the charismatic element of the People of God which in theory is not denied. The uniqueness of every person is precisely revealed in his or her having received a charism or charisms given to build up the Christian community (1Cor 12). Therefore, the charismatic structure, in contrast to the hierarchical office, contains the functional inadequacy of every person. Admittedly charisms were of great importance for the infant Church. But these charisms are not considered as belonging to the essence of the Church, because the Church is not primarily a merely charismatic movement but a hierarchical institution, founded on the apostles and their authority. But if we take Ashley's nonlinear model of hierarchy into consideration, the charisms are then to be understood as unique contributions made by the members of the Church and are, as such, not contained in the office. And yet they belong to the essence of the Church. Only if one sees hierarchy in the linear model can there be no unique contribution to be made through the charisms of the laity.

Paul's conception of the Church as a "charismatic entity" entails a community that is kept alive constantly through the charisms which the

Holy Spirit gives to each member of the community for the well-being of the community and demands the full exercise of these unique contributions of the individual if the Church will remain what she really is supposed to be: the anticipation of the Kingdom community in which everyone will contribute to the happiness and full identity of very person.

Realizing the danger of neglecting the charismatic element in a highly structured Church, Pius XII tried to show that the structures of the Church contain both elements: hierarchic and charismatic and that they could never be separated from each other. Their mutual relationship is constantly explained in terms of service and harmony and that there cannot be any conflict between the two. The historical reality of the Church, however, has shown that these moral values will not do away with concrete conflicts and that it is too easy to put the blame on the factor of sin. In fact, the hierarchical remained so highly stressed that the connection between it and the charismatic element is neither seen nor reflected upon most of the time.[48] The ultimate reason seems to be once again the linear model of how to perceive an hierarchical order.

Conscious of this danger Vatican II tried to balance such a one-sided, exaggerated hierarchical picture of the Church by re-evaluating the charismatic elements". The Council clearly stated that the Church is not only built by institutional structures but also by the infinite variety of gifts that each person "has the right and duty to use... for the building of the Church" (LG 4; 12).[49]

By seeing the Church as built on office and charisms the Council grounded a set of rights and duties for all Christians, it includes the right to "receive in abundance the help of the spiritual goods of the Church, the right and at times the duty of the laity to express their views on Church matters, and the right to initiate activities in the service of the Church". In addition it affirms the ability of the laity to engage in more immediate forms of cooperation in the apostolate of the hierarchy and to be appointed to some ecclesiastical office (LG 33, 35).

The relationship between office and charism is here conceived in such a way that the Council regarded the Church as being

> a spiritual organism in which, from the early days, there have been permanent ministries and charismatic ministries, all regarded as gifts of the Spirit.[50]

A strong addition to this view — held by almost all churches — is made by the "catholic" Churches. They point out that institutional ministries have always been associated with the apostolic authority. The Twelve exercised a particular role within the early communities. Now, as Christ chose and sent these Twelve, Christ continues through the Holy Spirit to choose and call persons into the ordained ministry.

The concrete question is how these charismatic ministries can function effectively besides the institutional ones without being rendered ineffective by the latter. Can we perceive of an institutional model that would give room for the other ministries to function well? Many think that this is possible if the hierarchical model recognizes the proper importance and relative independence of these charismatic ministries from the office ministry in the Church. In terms of Ashley's non linear model of hierarchy that would mean to acknowledge that the charisms are the unique contribution of the individual who in exercising his/her charism is *functionally unequal* with the hierarchy as the hierarchy is unequal to the laity in exercising its function for the well-being of the whole. This would require that government in the Church would not be based entirely on the sacramental dimension but on the charismatic element as well. What are these other ministries? We will deal here with only two, which are of great importance in the Church as a whole: the prophetic ministry and the ministry of teaching.

Paul presents us in 1Corinthians 12:28 and in Ephesians 4:11 with a list of ministries in the Church which he lists according to their importance by stating: first, second, third.

> *And God has appointed in the church first apostles, second prophets, third teachers, then workers of miracles, then healers, helpers, administrators, speakers in various kinds of tongues (1 Cor 12:28).*

> *And his gifts were that some should be apostles, some prophets, some evangelists, some pastors and teachers (Eph 4:11).*

Implied in this listing is that these ministries are supposed to be permanently present in the Church. To the question of who succeeded the apostles in their ministry the answer seem to be easy: the hierarchical ministries. The problem arises however with the other ministries. Are the prophets to be a permanent ministry visible and tangible in the Church like that of the hierarchy? What about the ministry of the teachers? Do these ministries have their own function or have they just been taken over by the hierarchy who regard themselves as those who are called to discharge the ministry of the prophets and the teachers as well?

CHART: THE CHURCH IS BUILT ON: I COR 12:28; Eph 4:11

Apostles	Prophets	Teachers
SUCCESSORS: - bishops	SUCCESSORS: - individual Prophets - institutional groups	SUCCESSORS: -Theologians
STATUS: ecclesiast. Office	STATUS: charismatic ministry	STATUS: charismatic ministry
FUNCTION: - sound doctrine: Apostolic Tradition - ordered Liturgy - administration of the Sacraments. - order and tradition - to assure unity of conviction in matters of faith and morals	FUNCTION: - To discern God's will for the Church of today; to read the signs of the time. - to present "NEW MODELS" of following Christ in new social, political and economic situations. - to play a "CORRECTIVE ROLE" in the Church's constant tendency for too much accommodation	FUNCTION: - responsible for passing on the TRADITION of the Kerygma and the Word of Jesus: CONTINUITY - To INTERPRET the tradition by providing "NEW MODELS" of interpretation.
DANGER: - to absorb the charismatic ministries into the ecclesial office - to become stagnated in traditional forms and ways and to end up in mere BUREAUCRACY	DANGER: - unwilling to let itself be "proven" and "tested" by the ecclesiastical office - to forget that this ministry is meant to serve the well-being of the whole Church and not to dictate.	DANGER: - to become only the mouthpiece of the hierarchy - to pretend to be the offical teaching office of the Church.

The Ministry of Prophets: succession of prophets in the Church

The Christian understanding of prophetism has its roots in the Old Testament. Here prophetism arose as a charismatic criticism of the institution. Whenever established Israel forgot the Covenant with its demands for justice and aligned itself too conveniently with the surrounding societies, the prophets appeared on the scene in order to protest. The classical prophets are among the most remarkable people who ever lived. They were 'verbal mediators' between the two worlds of the primordial tradition. Their special characteristic was the passionate and critical involvement in the historical life of their people in their own time. They radically criticized their own culture in the name of God and called for an alternative consciousness contrary to the dominant consciousness of their culture.[51]

As a rule, the institutional representatives could not accept this critique. Since they could not ignore it they always tried to domesticate it, i.e., control it and integrate it into the institution. But there were always prophets who would not allow themselves to be domesticated. Prophetism was always like a thorn in the flesh of the institution.

In Israel it was expected that in the end time the prophetic spirit would be poured out on all; the whole messianic community would be prophetic (Joel 3). The perennial tension between institution and prophetic charism would finally cease. The early Church was convinced that this was happening now in their midst (Ac 2). If all were prophets, was there any need for a special prophetic ministry?

Ephesians 2:20 insists that the Church is built on the "foundation of apostles and prophets," while in 1 Corinthians we read that "God has appointed in the Church first apostles, second prophets, third teachers" (1 Cor 12:28). All three words — apostles, prophets, teachers — refer to persons having clearly defined roles and recognized ministries in the community.

Therefore we must distinguish between the recognized ministry of the prophet and the occasional gift of prophecy, as well as the general belief that in the New Testament everyone has received the prophetic spirit (Ac 2:17; 1 Jn 2:20; Jer 31:31-34 Ezk 36:24-28).

The question is: if this ministry belongs to the "foundation of the Church", who has taken over these functions of the prophets and the teachers? Is there a succession of the prophets in the Church? That the bishops are the successors of the apostles has long been an accepted thesis, but what about the prophets and teachers?

In the Catholic understanding of priesthood the three different ministries: prophet, teacher and priest, seem to have once again been made into one. In the Old Testament the priest had three functions in the beginning. He was to proclaim God's will to people (Urim and Thumim); to teach as part of the levitical priesthood (Dt 33:10) and to sacrifice and offer cultic offerings. However, the first function was taken over by the prophets, the second by the scribes. Sacrifice was the principle function left for the priest at the end of the Old Testament period.[52]

The New Testament started from a different perspective of priesthood than the Old Testament. Its understanding of priesthood emerged over a long period and the different steps it took before it reached its present concept are difficult to delineate. The accumulation of a whole range of functions is historically explainable but hardly justifiable theologically. It is important that we come to see that these functions do not all belong by nature to the successors of the apostles but that some are meant to be exercised by different people in the Church and are to be regarded as their charisms.

Paul and Luke regard "prophets" as important members of the Christian community. Paul lists them second after apostles (1Cor 12:28) and they belong to the foundation of the Church (Eph 2:20); to them the mystery of the calling of the Gentiles has been revealed (Eph 3:5); and they belong to the gifts of Christ to his Church (Eph 4:11). Luke portrays the same view. There are five men whom he calls "prophets and leaders" (Ac 13:1-2) of the community at Antioch; Judas and Silas are named prophets (Ac 15:32) and are leading men among the brethren (Ac 15:22).

Accordingly, we must assume that, at a very early stage, charismatic, impulsive prophecy became institutionalized and prophets were then seen as the holders of a spiritual office. This office had its own standing in the community between or on a par with apostles and teachers. (1Cor 12:28; Eph 4:11); next to apostles (Lk 11:49; Eph 2:20; 3:5; Did. 11:3); next to teachers (Ac 13:1; Did. 15:1) next to saints and apostles (Rev 18:20).

What are the proper functions of the prophets?

We have to distinguish three groups concerning the possession of the prophetic spirit:

1. The eschatological community was convinced that each one had received the great gift of the end time, the prophetic spirit (Ac 2:27; 1 Jn 2:20, 27).

But as for you, the anointing you received from him remains in you,
and you do not need anyone to teach you; since the anointing he gave
you teaches you everything, and since it is true, not false, remain in
him just as it has taught you (Jn 2:27).

2. There was "congregational prophecy", which describes the prophesying that was done by members of the early Christian communities who were not given the title "prophets" and who did not have the leading role in the community that those called prophets had.[53]

3. The ministry of the prophets which became institutionalized and had its own standing in the community.

We are concerned with the last group and its function. The letter to the Ephesians sees the "prophetic role" as mediation of revelation, receiving insights into mysteries and communicating them to the Church. The prophet's role in Acts is a more practical one: giving direction to the Church.[54]

More generally their role was to encourage, edify, console, call to penance. They differ from the apostles in that they do not speak as official witnesses of the Risen Christ. In contrast to the teachers they are not concerned with general points of doctrine, but urging the course to be taken in the present concrete situation.[55] James Dunn, in *Jesus and the Spirit,* sees the function of the prophets in line with the Old Testament prophets: they express warnings, admonish, give occasional premonitions and insights into the future and are the mouthpiece of the Holy Spirit in giving guidance for the Church's mission. Another very important function of the prophets in the early Church was that they helped to interpret the prophecies of the Old Testament, and the sayings of Jesus in the light of what happened (death, resurrection and outpouring of the Spirit), and in relation to their own changing situation. Furthermore, it seems that the prophets delivered prophecies, not merely in the name of Jesus, but as the very word of Jesus, and in doing so they influenced the tradition of the kerygma of Jesus.[56]

Further development

In the first two centuries it was taken for granted that the ministry of prophecy was a permanent endowment of the Church (Did. 11-13). In all of the controversies of the second and third centuries with the Montanists, the Fathers were adamant that the prophetic charism should not be suppressed in the Church.

The prophetic gift must, according to the teaching of the apostles, be maintained in the whole Church until the final advent (Miltiades).

Some go so far in their zealous battle against false prophets that they reject the grace of true prophecy in the Church (Irenaeus).

From the third century on, prophecy belonged to the past and became the "Christian underground." St. Thomas no longer knew what to do with prophecy as it was understood in the early Church. The growth of clericalism in the Church meant that prophecy faded into the background. The fruitful tension between apostolic succession and prophetic succession had to give way to an increasing sacerdotal, hierarchical Church. During Vatican II Cardinal Ottaviani summed it up well when he declared that the early Church did indeed have prophets and other charisms, but that with the death of the last apostles not only revelation but also the reality of these charisms ceased.

But prophecy never died in the Church. The great saints like Bernard of Clairvaux, Francis of Assisi and Catherine of Siena show that the prophetic role remained alive and in lively tension with the institutional Church. Yet the Church became less and less receptive to prophetic criticism. The history of the Reformation might have been different if the Church had been open to the prophetic Spirit of the time. The whole history of Western Christianity after the Reformation is dominated by the struggle between the prophetism of the Reformation Churches and the sacerdotalism of the Catholic tradition. Prophecy as disclosure of God's plans and purposes in history was almost totally disregarded, and as Knox put it: "More than all other Christian Churches, the Catholic Church became institutional."

For the Catholic Church there could be no friction between prophets and magisterium. Prophecy was nothing more than the discharge of what they called the "prophetic office" of the Church which was identified with the magisterium. In short, the ministry of office had taken over the ministry of the prophets.

Prophets in the Church today

Though Vatican II speaks fourteen times about charisms and recognizes their importance, nowhere does it state how they are related to the institutional element of the Church. In the documents of the Council one can hardly find anything that would come near to what the New Testament meant by this ministry.

The crucial point, however, is that the Church admits that God manifests his presence and purpose in events of the present age. Only through the assistance of all can the Church "hear, distinguish and interpret the many voices of our age and judge them in the light of the divine word" (GS 44; see also 33).

The question hotly debated during the Council was whether or not the charismatic element in the Church is distinct from the institutional. *Lumen Gentium* seems to imply a real distinction between the institutional and the charismatic, and the superiority of the latter over the former (LG 4, 7, 8, 12).

> He (Holy Spirt) furnishes and directs the Church with various gifts, both hierarchical and charismatic...

> He (Holy Spirit) distributes special graces among the faithful of every rank. By these gifts He makes them fit and ready to undertake the various tasks or offices advantageous for the renewal and up building of the Church...(LG 4; 12).

But the Council left the question open. Today most theologians are saying that the institutional and the charismatic are irreducible and distinct aspects of the Church in its pilgrim condition. This means that the magisterium as such cannot appropriate this ministry and claim it as its own. In the non linear model of hierarchy this is obvious. Both are linked to service and are subordinated to the life of the Christian community as a whole. The ministry of prophecy belongs to the charismatic ministries and it must be exercised. The Church needs this ministry, i.e., men and women capable of discerning God's hand in the history of our times.

Since prophets cannot appoint themselves as prophets but need to be recognized as such by others, prophetic movements stand in need of approval by the Church at large. But office holders are always tempted to suppress the prophetic element, for it is a disturbing element. By upsetting people's settled views and challenging their complacency it continually threatens the unity and stability of the institutional Church. Yet,

> a Church in which the prophets have to keep silent declines and becomes a spiritless organization, and its pastors would become mere bureaucrats... In such a Church people would be suffocated by the fumes of a decaying sacerdotalism... History has shown that when prophets are not given their say within the Church they rise up to condemn it from outside.[57]

Prophets are essential not only for the Church but for humankind as a whole as well. Only the prophet engages in imagining different possibilities. He never asks whether his vision can be implemented. First, there has to be a vision before it can be implemented. Modern cultures are normally competent enough to implement everything but it seems impossible for them to imagine anything. The prophet's task is to keep alive the ministry of imagination, to keep on proposing alternative solutions and futures never thought of. They have to propose new visions to enthuse and to energize people since it is the 'Not Yet', the promised and that which is about to begin that can energize us and not that what we already possess.[58]

Religious Orders as "Institutional Prophetic Ministry"

Is there a constant bearer of the prophetic ministry in the Church? or is this ministry totally sporadic, based on an ad hoc inspiration of the Holy Spirit without any permanence? There are individual prophets, but can there also be an institutional prophetic ministry? A number of theologians see religious life as a kind of "institutional prophetic ministry".[59] Not all theologians share this view. They accept that we do find prophetic orders and schools in Scriptures as well as in the history of other religions. But they insist that such institutions have rarely proved successful in the long run. All they could do was to provide a discipline and an environment conducive to prophetic sensitivity.[60] Dulles does accept a *succesio prophetarum* but he defines it differently:

> Because prophecy is not ordinarily transmitted by continuous succession or by induction into office, prophets do not 'succeed' their predecessors in an unbroken line as pastor commonly do. Yet when the prophetic charism is bestowed, the recipient can become not simply a successor of the prophets but a prophet in the succession. Thus a *successio prophetarum* exists, even though it be *discontinuous and unpredictable*.[61]

Thomas Merton held that prophetic witness was integral to monastic life. For him the religious called out of the world to live a life radically different from humanity at large was well positioned to see the present from God's point of view and to discern the signs of the time more critically.[62] The Congress on Religious Life (1993) had this to say:

> In the Church religious life forms a liminal group. That is, an alternative group, separated by its life style and ministry from the normal structures of society. It forms a liminal group by its life style of community celibacy, the option for the poor and permanent discernment in search of the will of God

the Father. To live this way in all its radicality is to be in society in a manner distinct and somewhat distant from it. As Religious this is our prophecy. It is our way of being symbol of the Kingdom. [63]

With Jesus a new reality has entered this world: the Kingdom of God. This is such a concrete and challenging reality that people are repeatedly drawn into its spell. In the end such people can do nothing else but dedicate themselves totally and unconditionally to this Kingdom. In the words of the Congress:

> Religious place themselves in the service of the Kingdom. This they do with the intention of being transparent signs, living parables, messianic anticipations of the full realization of the Kingdom. They attempt to represent existentially the poor, obedient, chaste and compassionate Christ in the World.[64]

Since "radicalism" has not provided a completely adequate manner of distinguishing religious life from ordinary Christian life, there are a number of other possibilities which try to do this. Among these are the following:

Rahner favors a view which has been called "transcendalism". Religious life is seen as a way to realize the eschatological and transcendental dimensions of the Christian life.

Schillebeeckx and Gutierrez regard religious life as a particular "anthropological" form of Christian existence. Religious life offers authentic values. Some people turn towards these values which normally are not chosen by the majority. This way of life is found in all great religions of the world. It is important to recognize today that religious life is not only a Christian phenomenon.

It has always been the role of religious persons to communicate their experience with the "Holy". The role they played made them distinct witnesses of precise human values like simplicity and austerity. They give witness to the centrality of relationship and encounter with the "Holy", to compassion and non-violence, to self-control and inner harmony with the cosmos and people living together. This way of life offers an alternative scale of values, as a critical contrast to the "status quo" and will become a model of inspiration for society.

The Latin American theologians have forwarded the thesis that religious life is a way to realize "prophetic solidarity" with the people of God, especially the poor. They see religious life as a "prophetic exaggeration" of the fundamental call of every Christian to follow the Lord in concrete situations today. In the words of Michael Amaladoss:

> In the Church religious are a "prophetic pole", not only counter-cultural, but creatively prospective. Their prophecy is not only directed to the world, but also to the Church community. By radically living and /or promoting through their apostolic action some of the values of the Reign of God they are reminders of and invitations to a possible new world for all the People of God. They are also the cutting edge of the Church's mission to the world, in so far as they symbolize in a specially visible way the radicalism of the Kingdom of God which is being proclaimed.[65]

Or in the expressive language of Joan Chittister:

> It is not the loss of institutions that religious must fear; it is the loss of the fire/heat of the charism itself. It is the potential loss of prophetic presence that strikes at the root of religious life today. Religious life is to remind the world of what it can be, of what it must be, of what it most wants to be: deep down, at its best, at its most human core. Religious life lives at the edge of society to critique it, at the bottom of society to comfort it, at the epicenter of society to challenge it. Religious life is a reminder of the will of God for the world.[66]

It was J. B. Metz, who in recent time has developed this view most strongly.[67] For him, part of a formal definition of the essential nature of religious orders is the fact that they are charismatic signs, resulting from the activity of the Spirit; in other words, they are charismatic institutions and movements.

The founders of religious orders like St. Francis, Dominic, Teresa of Avila, Ignatius etc. were often prophets, and their prophetic message remains present in the communities they founded. In the sense that the communities carry on the charismatic inspiration of the founders, we can speak of an "institutionalization" of a prophetic ministry without denying that individual prophets can arise at any time, without creating a community in which they "incarnate" their prophetic spirit. The danger for these charismatic movements is that they easily become domesticated. In the words of N. Lohfink:

> Canonization, recognition of religious orders, even the development of canon law regarding religious orders, well-intentioned as they are, can have the effect of domesticating charism. Another way the Church, more than general society, tries to tame charism is to suppress and eliminate prophetism.[68]

The origin of religious orders: "a prophetic protest"[69]

We know that religious orders as we understand them today came into existence in the fourth century. But that does not mean that there were no antecedents to them. In the early Church we find people who wanted to follow the Lord in a more radical way by renouncing possessions and marriage in order to be closer in fellowship with him. They lived in their respective Christian communities, and there gave their witness that ultimately there can be no difference between being a disciple and being a Christian. Actually they were following the general call of the Christian but felt the Lord inviting them to a different way of being his disciples, the way he himself had lived so radically.

The early Christian communities lived in a society which did not share their values; and, therefore, they became automatically what Lohfink calls "counter society," witnessing to a different set of values and way of being human.

This situation changed dramatically when the Church became the state religion and people entered in droves. The Church ceased to be a counter society. By conforming herself to society many felt that the Christian faith was compromised. At that moment the prophetic charism rose anew within the Church and began to protest. Many scholars see here a remarkable resemblance to the beginnings of the prophetic movement in the ninth century B.C. when established Israel had forgotten to live in Covenant love with her God and in justice and peace with each other.

John Cassian comments that the first religious went apart "to practice those things which they had learned to have been ordered by the apostles throughout the body of the Church in general" (Collationes XVIII, ch. 5). According to him, monks formed communities to see that these ideals be not just talked about but lived. Religious life came into existence as a protest movement against a Church that had conformed too much to society at large. Religious life was seen as following the model of the prophets in the Old Testament.

Many individual Christians at that time moved out into the desert and soon created new communities, which in turn took over the former mission of the Church to be "counter society." These communities patterned themselves on the community model of the early Church as described by Luke in Acts where everything was held in common by people of simple hearts who called themselves brothers and sisters.

Later other communities took their orientation from the group that had "followed Jesus when he walked this earth"; in short, the disciples of Jesus. The best examples are the communities founded by Sts. Francis, Dominic and Ignatius. Vatican II seems to have this pattern more in mind in its description of religious life

No matter which pattern we consider, that of "counter society" or radical discipleship, both witness to the fact that there is always seems to be a need within the Church for healing and a reminder of our basic call. In short, religious orders have a therapeutic task to fulfill for the Church. There seems to be a link between the Church's task to be a "contrast society" and the existence in the Church's history of monasteries and religious orders. Religious communities arose whenever the Church forgot and betrayed her social mission.

> It is not wrong to say that when the Church began to get sick, God ordained monks, nun and cloisters as its therapy. When the Church forgot that it was to be a contrast society, a contrast society was created in its midst.[70]

The three basic functions of religious life in and for the Church

Metz sees the functional definition of religious life with regards to the life of both the Church and society under two aspects: Religious orders and communities have an "INNOVATIVE FUNCTION" and a "CORRECTIVE ROLE" in the life of the Church. Both functions are prophetic.

(1.) The "innovative function" of religious life

What does it mean to say that religious life has to fulfil an "innovative function" for the Church? The first mission or function of religious life consists in providing a clear reminder of the intimate link between being a Christian and following Christ. The general demand to follow Christ is too abstract. Its concrete meaning and content have to be demonstrated by means of very concrete models in every age and situation. The Church as a whole and society at large need patterns, models and visible forms which clearly and unmistakably reveal what the Gospel demands of following Jesus means today. (In the past this was always seen as provided by the Saints.)

Who can provide these new patterns or models? Metz sees that the role of religious is to offer "productive models" for the Church as a whole. These models should illustrate how fellowship with Christ is to be lived in the new social, economic, intellectual and cultural situation of today. Following Christ is not just a subsequent application of the Church's Christology to our life. Who Christ is can never be known unless we embark on the way of following him. Following Christ can never be a purely spiritual endeavor. It has to be lived and demonstrated in the concrete circumstances of our time.

To provide "productive models" means to show what being a disciple of Jesus is all about and to show what Jesus would do in the setting of our time. Their basic function should be to help the Church move out of entrenched positions, to read the signs of the time and to show where the Church's mission should move to now.

(2.) The "corrective role" or the "shock therapy" of religious life

The constant danger of the Church as a large-scale institution is accommodation and questionable compromise, the ever-present tendency of making the Gospel liveable in a consumer society and, thereby, watering down its radicalism to the point that it does not hurt any more. It is over and against a too nicely balanced view of things and too much compromise with the standards of the time that religious life is seen as having to play a "corrective role."

> A prophet is someone called and sent to recall to people God's saving interventions in the past, to challenge them to conversion from their disloyalty to God in the present and to urge them to build up a new humanity that is God's promise to people. It is a call to active hope based on experience and memory. It is a call to be a counter-culture not merely being critical and negative but proposing alternative ways of being and living community. The horizon of the prophetic mission of the Church is the Reign of God, a community and fellowship, justice and love.[71]

We can call it a "prophetic role" because religious life is not situated in the hierarchical office of the Church but in its prophetical ministry. As such, it possesses a particular sensitivity to the signs of the time. After all, the prophets' task has always been to proclaim to the people of God the will of God for today. Their function is, therefore, at times, to upset the so-called balanced view and thus move the Church out of stagnated perspectives and positions to fresh viewpoints and situations, towards the frontiers, into new circumstances and challenges. This task is not a self-appointed ministry but a call to fulfill a function in and for the whole Church. In this sense, Lohfink seems to be correct in calling religious orders "God's therapy for the Church."

Why should this be their task?

It is because religious congregations are the heirs of great founders like Sts. Francis, Dominic, Teresa etc. These men and women upset the Church of their times by demonstrating the uncompromising nature of the Gospel and by moving the Church, as a large scale institution, into new situations and circumstances. This they had to do on the basis of their prophetic charism. One of the greatest (and perhaps the most deadly) temptations of religious life is to move too far into the middle ground where everything is nicely balanced and moderate and to forget to be a prophetic challenge in and for the Church. To use Brueggemann's image, they are in danger of losing their imagining powers and of becoming unable to envision new alternatives for the Church that could help her out of the "only thinkable" solution born out of the present factual world. While many religious do excellent work in numerous institutions; very often we have to admit that they fulfill a role which society has assigned to them. They have been nicely integrated into society and are regarded as useful and appreciated for what they do as long as they stay where they are and do what they are "supposed to do": care for the old, serve in hospitals, run some boarding schools, etc. By no means are they to meddle in any way with issues of society.

But we should not forget that the prophetic ministry needs the "office ministry" as well. From here it gets its approval and is discerned as being a movement in the Church brought about by the Spirit for the benefit of the whole Church. The whole Church must recognize the relative independence of this ministry and listen to its voice and message. Both are meant for the well being of the Church although their functions are different.

(3.) The Witness of "community living"

There is a considerable number of spiritual writers who say that the priority of religious life today is the WITNESS TO COMMUNITY LIFE. Their life in community must be a clear sign that our Christian faith can create communities in which peace, justice, love and true brotherhood/sisterhood are not just empty words, but lived realities. As communities within the Church, they serve as the visible and tangible anticipation of the final community which God intends for the whole of creation. The reconciling power of the Holy Spirit creates a community which, already here on earth, reveals that unity and harmony among men and women, which is to find its fullness at the end of time. Because of all the brokenness of human life and the impossibility of ever creating any perfect community, the sign that God's Kingdom has broken into the world has to be demonstrated in our time.

This making the Kingdom at least initially present in our world is the task of the whole Church but, once again, religious communities should offer themselves as concrete test cases showing that the Kingdom has indeed already appeared in this world. In a time when people hunger after signs of God's Kingdom as present, the question is: Who can give this witness to real community if not the religious communities themselves? Who else can provide a more visible and tangible demonstration of the power of Christ's reconciling love in the Church as a whole if not religious communities which claim to have made it their mission rather than 'task' to follow the Lord more freely and to imitate him more exactly? Once again the function of religious communities is seen as being a "counter society" or a "contrast society" for our time.[72]

Conclusion: Prophetic criticism applied

The most genuine form of prophecy in the Church comes in the form of communities which as such serve a prophetic function over against the entire Church. Prophetic communities can actually exercise two functions: On the one hand, they can provide prophetic criticism within the Church itself which questions accommodation to the world; on the other hand, they provide prophetic criticism over against the total society, which is the specific mission of the whole Church.

Prophets are called but no one can make himself a prophet. If others proclaim us as prophets then we can accept this and should feel good about it, but not if we make ourselves into prophets. The prophet lives in a given context to which he offers an alternative through his word, action and life. Since he challenges ways of life he has to reckon with opposition. He is an outsider and will have enemies. A prophet without enemies is no prophet. His vocation is first a charism, not an office.

Several questions may be posed at this juncture: Are religious today really offering this prophetic critique to the Church and to society as a whole? Have religious orders betrayed their calling so that God must devise other means to take up this task in the Church? Is God's history of salvation moving in a different direction? These are difficult questions to answer. The drop in religious vocations raises such questions. We should not forget, however, that if we religious have failed there is always the way of conversion.

Many however find in the emergence of small communities and community movements in the Church of today a hopeful sign that here God is furnishing his Church with a new prophetic charism. Their very existence is a prophetic criticism within the Church and they offer the much needed "counter society" to society at large. In our world today the traditional forms of religious life might not suffice anymore to serve as God's therapy for his Church. God might call alongside the religious order other forms of community, including all of the faithful, in carrying on his therapy for the Church. These communities may in turn well serve as a pattern after which religious orders may have to renew themselves if they do not wish God to bypass them in his desire to reach all human beings and to make his prophetic critique heard.

Corresponding to the reasons why there is a particularly urgent call for a prophetic ministry of religious orders, the following points could be offered by religious orders themselves as prophetic criticism within the Church.

As we noted earlier, the constant danger for the Church as a large scale institution is accommodation and questionable compromise, the ever-present tendency of making the Gospel liveable in a consumer society by watering down its radicalism to the point that it does not hurt anymore. Over against a too nicely balanced view of things and too much compromise with the standards of the time, religious life is seen as having to play a "corrective role." For these same reasons N. Lohfink sees religious orders as 'God's therapy for his Church."

To call their mission a "prophetic role" is justified because religious life is not situated in the hierarchical office of the Church but in its prophetic ministry. As such, it possesses a particular sensitivity to the signs of the time. After all, the prophets' task has always been to proclaim the will of God for today to the people of God. Its function is therefore at times, to upset the so-called balanced view and so move the Church out of stagnated positions into new situations, to the frontiers, into new circumstances and challenges of our time. Or in the words of Walter Brueggemann:

> The task of prophetic ministry is to nurture, nourish, and to evoke a consciousness and perception alternative to the consciousness and perception of the dominant culture around us... The alternative consciousness to be

nurtured, on the one hand, serves to criticize in dismantling the dominant consciousness. To that extent, it attempts to do what the liberal tendency has done, engage in a rejection and delegitimatizing of the present ordering of things. On the other hand, that alternative consciousness to be nurtured serves to energize persons and communities by its promise of another time and situation towards which the community of faith may move. To that extent it attempts to do what the conservative tendency has done, to live in fervent anticipation of the newness that God has promised and will surely give.[73]

The prophetic task is a way of evoking, forming, and reforming an alternative community. The two key words are critical and energizing, two qualities which a prophetic ministry must hold together.

Corresponding to the reasons why there is a particularly urgent call for a prophetic ministry of religious orders, H. Arens[74] thinks that the following stances could be taken by religious orders themselves as forms of prophetic criticism within the Church:

(1). The crisis in the Church herself

Over against a too hierarchically structured Church, religious orders are to be more consensus-oriented, more fraternal, less hierarchically organized. The model of leadership within religious orders could be a challenge within the Church for better cooperation and collegiality. Offices in religious orders are normally held for a limited period, which allows for more flexibility, and protects against stagnation and immobility.

Religious congregations today are trying to get away from clericalism by placing the emphasis more on the common vocation. Consequently, there is a greater esteem for the lay person.

(2.) The rift between Church and society

Religious orders as prophetic communities seem to offer to marginalized groups an alternative model wherein they feel more at home. Communities, in which the faith is lived more holistically by taking into consideration all aspects of human life, are extremely attractive. The option for the poor and marginalized is obviously a clear sign that a community will not have its role dictated by society, but only by the Gospel.

(3.) Consumerism and materialism

The evangelical counsels, which promise a freedom from the concerns of this world, should enable the religious to let go, to be available, to be transferred, to change, and to die.

It is the eschatological dimension of this way of life that relativizes all earthly values and could serve as a strong critique of a society that puts all of the stress on having and consuming. These communities could offer a counter society in which truly human, i.e., Christian values are lived and promoted.

Who are the Successors of the Teachers?

1 Corinthian 12:28 as well as Galatians 6:6 imply that in Corinth there was a recognized group of teachers. They had a double function: First, of "passing on the tradition" which they themselves had received from the founding apostles, in particular, the tradition of kerygma and Jesus' words (Rm 16:17; 1Cor 4:17; 11:2; Col 1:28; 2:7; 2 Thes 2:15; 3:6); and secondly, "of interpreting the tradition" and thus, its development. New situations demanded such fresh interpretations. Concerning their authority within the community we can say:

1. The teaching function had more the character of "office" than any of the other regular ministries. They were a more trained group who had the ability to retain, understand and teach the tradition of the Kerygma.

2. In comparison to the apostles, the teachers would only teach, while the apostles could demand and give orders.

3. As the teacher moved beyond the simple passing on of tradition to its interpretation, he moved into the charismatic ministry, not unlike the prophet.

With regard to the prophetic ministry we could say:

the teaching function provided an indispensable complement to prophecy; the normative role of the Gospel and of Jesus' words provided an invaluable control on charismatic excess. Prophecy without teaching degenerates into fanaticism; teaching without prophecy solidifies into law.[75]

It is obvious that the successors of the teachers are the theologians and the exegetes. Although like the charism of prophecy, the charism of theology can never be adequately institutionalized, their ministry is to be a constitutive element in the Church as well. The magisterium has often described their ministry in too narrow terms as this definition shows:

> The noblest office of the Theologian is to show how a doctrine defined by the Church is contained in the source of revelation (Pius XII).

This task might fall under the first function of the teacher, but it ignores the second function of interpreting the tradition anew. The Church has increasingly acknowledged of late that theology has a task independent from that of the magisterium. As Pope John Paul II puts it:

> The Church wants independent theological research, which is distinct from the ecclesiastical magisterium, but knows itself responsible for the common service to the faith and the people of God. It will, however, not be possible to exclude all tension and conflicts between both (Pope's speech in Fulda, Germany).

The Pope sees this tension rooted in the limits of our mental capacity and the pilgrim state of the Church.

Dulles sees the tasks of theologians "to reflect synthetically and critically on the Christian message, bringing out its meaning and coherence." Concerning the critical task of the theologians he observes:

> Yet the critical observations of theology are often no more enthusiastically welcomed than the denunciations of the prophets. Theologians, too, are at times suspected of disloyalty to the institutions.[76]

Conclusion:

The institutional model of the Church, when maintained, will only be accepted when the charismatic ministries are taken seriously once again. If the ministry of prophets, the ministry of teachers, and in a similar way the other charisms, are allowed to fulfill their functions, are given relative independence in the Church, and can operate freely in the service of the whole Church, the Catholic Church will once again become a renewed Church. These ministries are created and willed by the Spirit for the benefit of the whole. Tensions and conflicts may at times be unavoidable, but this belongs to the eschatological community that lives in the "condition of this world". There will never be perfect harmony and peace, and the one who at all cost wants peace between these different functions can only have the peace of a cemetery where no life is left.

There is a number of theologians who regard the "charismatic element" in the Church as the essence of the Church, and "office" only as a necessary regulative of the "charismatic". Rahner sees the main task of the office holders as "nurturing and discerning the charisms" in the Church by referring to 1 Thessalonians 5:19-20, "Do not stifle inspiration (other translations: quench the Spirit; suppress the Spirit; smother the Spirit; treat the gift of prophecy with contempt), but test everything and then keep what is good."

The official Church has made statements concerning the relationship between hierarchical and charismatic which are ambiguous. The charismatic elements are highly praised and set over against the institutional or hierarchical, yet those who preside in the Church have received the competence to judge the authenticity of charismatic gifts (LG 12). On the other hand, we are told that the society furnished with hierarchical agencies is an instrument of the "spiritual community ... enriched with heavenly things, even as the humanity of Christ was an instrument of his divine nature" (LG 8). This seems to imply that the Council accepted a superiority of the charismatic over the hierarchical. Yet as we observed earlier, as long the Church ties the exercise of governing power in the Christian community exclusively to the Sacrament of Orders, it hardly seems possible that the other ministries will be allowed to function really independently.

Can the Catholic Church reform herself in this way? Many doubt this others say she can, presupposing that she is willing to analyze which system of government would be most suited for a particular new cultural and social situation.[77]

One could answer this question affirmatively if the Church acknowledged seriously that these three authoritative ministries are essential for her life. In the words of Dulles:

> For successful interaction, it is important that none of the three functions usurp the specialization of the others or seek to reduce the others to innocuous servitude. For theology or prophecy to perform its distinctive task it must retain a certain measure of autonomy and critical distance from the official leadership, while at the same time accepting the latter's supervision.[78]

Each of these three vocations contains built in hazards.

The apostolic leadership, left to its own, tends to encourage passive conformity and blind conservatism. It suppresses troublesome questions and challenges and avoids any new provocative issues. Many Church leaders still hold (in practice at least) to the view that they themselves have all these other charisms and that there is no real need for further charismatic ministries. They will only complicate matters.

The prophetic leaders can easily be caught up in their own insights. They can fall victims to the illusion which take their own fantasies for the directives of the Holy Spirit. They forget that only a false prophet can proclaim himself a prophet.

Teachers can easily get caught up in their own world of speculations and proclaim their insights as THE magisterium.

At the present moment there is a felt tendency to reaffirm the role of the hierarchy. This is understandable in the wake of excessive criticism of all authority in the Church. Such an attitude of endemic suspicion can become destructive for the Catholic faith. The Church cannot do without an authorative ministry if she wants to remain faithful to her origin of apostolic tradition. In the words of Dulles:

> The Scriptures, the tradition the creeds and the dogmas must be trusted, and so must ecclesiastical authorities who vouch for them. Dissent from authority cannot and should not be totally ruled out, but should be the exception rather than the rule. The presumption should be that the Catholic accept the official teaching of the Church. Dissent, where it cannot be prevented, should be expressed in modest and discreet ways that do not undermine the very principle of authority. For the Church is by its very essence a community of faith and witness. The pastoral office exists in order to authenticate sound doctrine and to assure unity of conviction in matters of faith and morals.[79]

3. The Church as Communion[80]

This model perceives the Church primarily as *koinonia* or community. The word koinonia appears 19 times in the New Testament; 13 of these are found in the Pauline writings. Community puts the stress on "interpersonal relationship", be it to the triune God or to the members themselves, rather than on describing the Church in terms of "institution of salvation" or as a perfect society. It aims at personal growth through interpersonal relationship.[81] The ecclesiology of communion has been hailed as one of the achievements of Vatican II. It has gained more and more attention in the post conciliar Theology. Walter Kasper describes his approach to ecclesiology with these words:

> For the Church there is only one way into the future: the way pointed out by the Council, the full implementation of the council and its communion ecclesiology. This is the way which God's Spirit has shown us.[82]

The Synod of Bishops in 1985 affirmed that "the ecclesiology of communion is the central and fundamental idea of the council's documents."[83] And the Congregation for the Doctrine of Faith observed in 1992 that "the concept of communion can certainly be a key for the renewal of Catholic ecclesiology."[84] The congregation links to this approach the biblical images which the Council had used such as the church as the body of Christ, the people of God, the temple of the Holy Spirit and the sacrament of salvation and unity.

> The communal model views the Church as the Body of Christ, as the People of God, as a fellowship in Christ deeply committed to the well-being of its members. Theologically, the strength of this model lies in its deep Scriptural roots; anthropologically, its strength lies in a deeply ingrained human trait, the human need and subconscious craving for fellowship in almost everything we do as humans. The favorite model of Vatican II, as the Extraordinary Synod of Bishops of 1985 emphasized, was precisely this communal model, the Church as a People of God. The Church exist because human beings need each other: they need community.[85]

The primary meaning of communion in the Council's documents refers to the intimate relationship the faithful have with the triune God. The Christian community is regarded as the anticipation of God's ultimate plan with humanity and the whole of creation into union and communion with the triune God. The Church is seen as an icon of the Trinity. This is also called the vertical dimension of the primary meaning of *koinonia*. The secondary meaning of communion is its horizontal dimension. It refers to the relationship among the believers based on the prior communion with God. As Jon Sobrino sees it, "Communion expresses the ideal of the church and an eternal aspiration of humanity; the communion of brothers and sisters is at the heart of Scripture and tradition." In the ecumenical dialogue we can say the communion model is the one that is most congenial to both Orthodox and to Protestants. In the words of the Faith and Order Commission:

The notion of koinonia has become fundamental for revitalizing a common understanding of the nature of the Church and its visible unity... The term is being reclaimed today in the ecumenical movement as a key to understanding the nature and purpose of the Church. Due to its riches of meaning, it is also a convenient notion for assessing the degree of communion in various forms already achieved among Christians within the ecumenical movement.[86]

Although this description of Church is not new, St Augustine and St. Thomas referred to it frequently when dealing with the Church; the idea was mostly taken up and further developed by the Protestant Churches after the Reformation often in contrast to the Catholic view with its heavy stress on institution. The whole theological controversy of charism against office, of "charismatic" against "legal", was often a question of how to perceive the Church. Stronger emphasis on the charismatic dimension of the Church over against a too hierarchically conceived Church image led to a communion ecclesiology.

Among Catholic theologians, Y. Congar and J. Hamer in particular developed this model prior to the Council and laid the foundation for the councils renewed view of the Church as communion. The Church is seen here as a fellowship of persons — men and women in union with God and one another in Christ. Or, as Y. Congar puts it: "Church is the totality of means by which this fellowship is produced and maintained — it is a community of salvation and not so much an institution of salvation."

In choosing as the fundamental structure of the Church the biblical images: People of God, Body of Christ, and Temple of the Holy Spirit, the communion ecclesiology of the Council emerged almost as a logical consequence. Particularly by taking the image "People of God" as the central metaphor for the Church, the Vatican Council gave Catholic Christians a new root metaphor for themselves. What happens here is a change from a self-understanding as an "institution" to that of being the People of God. This shift in metaphor has significant consequences in how the Church sees herself and understands her very essence and mission.[87] The Church is first the People of God. That means an entity that exists prior to all structuring and prior also to the call of individual members. With this conception of Church the Council did away with any pyramidal system and restored the fundamental equality of all members in the Christian community. All are equal: "There is no longer Jew nor Greek, nor male nor female but all are one in Jesus Christ." (Gal 3:28) The differentiation which emerges in the structuring of this people is secondary and cannot touch the primary rights. That at least is the ideal of the Church conceived by the Council. How effectively institutional and legal structures do justice to this ideal has yet to be proven at the grassroots level.

Strength of this model

It has a very good biblical basis.

Among scriptural images of the Church, some referring to the Trinitarian dimension of the Church, became particularly prominent. Among these, the images of the "people of God" and the "body of Christ", accompanied by the imagery of "temple" or "house" of the Spirit, are particularly important. We must note, however, that none of these images is exclusive; all of them implicitly or explicitly include the other Trinitarian dimensions as well.[88] These three images have been chosen because of their central importance in the New Testament and because of their significance for the Trinitarian dimensions of the Church. The Council saw the fundamental structure of the Church most adequately expressed in them. Each of them aims at community and presupposes it.

Yet there are other images of the Church in the New Testament, most of them christological, like vine, flock, wedding party, and bride. They all serve to highlight certain aspects of the Church's being and life: the vine-image stresses its total dependence on Christ, the flock-image stresses its trust and obedience, the party-image stresses the eschatological reality of the Church, the bride-image stresses the intimate though subordinate relation of the Church to Christ. At the same time these images have their limits: the vine-image does not take into account the interpersonal relationship between Christ and the Church; the flock-image does not take into account the freedom of the believers; the party-image does not take into account the not-yet fulfilled dimension of the Church's life in via; the bride-image presupposes the subordinate status of women in ancient times.[89]

Vatican I had already intended to deal with two topics concerning the Church: The internal and the external form of the Church. The first preparatory documents were based on A. Möhler's view of the Church: "The Church as Christ's Mystical Body" and the "Church as a true, perfect, spiritual and supernatural community". Neither of the two documents were taken up during the Council. Concerning the external structures of the Church only the questions of primacy and infallibility (which had not even been on the agenda of the Council) were treated and became the *"pars prima"* in ecclesiology.

This view determined all treatises on the Church up to Vatican II. In his famous Encyclical Mystici Corporis Christi (1943) Pius XII wanted to complete what the Council had left unfinished. The concept *"Corpus Christi Mysticum"* is here regarded as the most comprehensive and precise description of the Church. The statement that the *Mystical Body* is identical with the Roman Catholic Church is critical. It almost sounds like a paradox: Pope Pius's intention was to soften the one-sided or exaggerated rather than too heavy stress on external structures; yet by identifying the Church with the physical body of Christ, he made the hierarchical structure even stronger. In spite of every critique of this encyclical most of the impulses for a new ecclesiology before the Second Vatican Council derived from this encyclical.

The Second Vatican Council took up the image once again. By dropping the word "mystical" and changing the phrase the Church "exists in" to "subsists in" the Roman Catholic Church, it removed from the Body of Christ image the triumphalism that was easily associated with it. By employing the third image, Church as the Temple of the Holy Spirit, the council brought in the charismatic aspect of the Church to counterbalance the hierarchical. The Church according to this image is seen as an organism that is held together by the different functions of the members and organs which compose it. Each person or member of the community has received a charism which he or she is asked to exercise for the well-being of the whole. What keeps the community alive and healthy is the exercise of the charisms of the individual members. The Holy Spirit, as the creator of the Church and as the sustainer of the Christian community, is powerfully expressed in this way. The Eastern Churches were always particularly strong on this aspect. Their view of the Church is first and foremost Trinitarian.[90]

This image of Church is based on good tradition.

Augustine and Thomas by far preferred the image "community" to describe the Church. Augustine used the phrase "Body of Christ" to stress the invisible community which embraces not only the members here on earth, but the heavenly beings as well. He was the first to talk about the "Church since Abel". Thomas used the community aspect of the Church to emphasize in particular the divine aspect or the vertical dimension of community.

This view corresponds to the present experience

Almost all modern renewal movements in the Church which emerged in the Church after Vatican II put strong emphasis on the Church as community. They experience the Church in this way. The Charismatic renewal movement, Better World Movement, Neo-Catechumenate, etc., and in particular the Basic Christian Communities of the Third World Church, all adopted this model, very often unconsciously. Church is seen as a community that guarantees not only the spiritual but also the human growth of the members. This model brings out very forcefully the Church's abiding responsibility to be a sign of Christ's presence or of the Kingdom of God present in the "already" form, by being a community in which justice, peace and mutual love are realized and lived.

Weakness of this model

While granting the richness of the ecclesiology of communion, we should not overlook its inborn weaknesses. Luzbetak describes them in these words:

> The basic danger of this model is the fact that the image may led people to become too introspective and not concerned enough about the world outside the Church-community. To get lost in the joy and blessing of Christian fellowship means to forget the Kingdom for which the Church exists; it is also to forget the Church is mission. Furthermore using the images of Body of Christ and People of God we can become too mystical and possibly get lost in cliches and platitudes. One more danger with this model is that the communal character becomes so dominant that the institutional dimension of the Church can be made to appear unimportant.[91]

Wherever this model is chosen consciously to offset a too hierarchically conceived church the dangers are the following:

1. The relationship between the visible and spiritual dimension easily gets blurred. The Church, seen purely in terms of "charismatic entity" easily leads to regarding the charism of office as useful but not absolutely necessary. The community can fulfill all its needs without a priest.

2. The community model does not always clearly identify those elements which make such a community different from other communities.

3. A clear sense of identity is often missing in the sense that everyone can participate, irrespective of his or her affiliation (the best example are the charismatic groups). The three elements, which make a Catholic a member of his Church, are often neglected. Orthodoxy is downplayed.

4. It tends to concentrate on the values of the individual's growth both at the expense of the social and political responsibility of the whole Church and at the expense of the community's abiding commitment to the renewal and institutional reform of the Church herself.

5. It easily looks at itself as "exclusive community", tending towards an inwardness that keeps others out. Members of such communities often feel at home only among themselves and regard others as intruders. There is the danger of looking at themselves as the perfect community which becomes the measure for judging the rest of the world.

In spite of its weaknesses this model seems to have become one of the most dominant and growing perceptions of the Church at the moment. A Church which takes community as its basic model will have to rethink its understanding of ecclesiastical office. The growing awareness of charismatic ministries as constitutive of the Church alongside ecclesiastical office will demand a new look at the functions which ecclesiastical office has to exercise in such a Church. What is the role of an office holder in a Church that understands itself first of all as a "charismatic entity" in which everyone has a role to play? A few points could be outlined here:

First, the office holder has to make sure that the whole "apostolic tradition entrusted to him" will be proclaimed and lived in these communities. The precise purpose of the charism of office is to ensure that the "apostolic tradition" is being preached faithfully, not just partially.

Secondly, he should be a man who has the "gift of discernment" i.e. the gift of being able to discover the many charisms in the congregation and letting them become active for the well-being of the whole community. His function, then, is to discover charisms and to co-ordinate them for the good of the Church. He should be a man with "ability to dialogue", who can sense the Spirit operative in the community rather than constantly acting as if he alone had the Spirit. For him St. Paul wrote: "Do not stifle the Spirit, but discern everything and then keep what is good" (1 Thes 5:19-20) . But the question has to be asked: are future priests trained in this way? Is their suitability for this ministry judged by whether they have such abilities or not? Under what criteria are seminarians ordained and accepted to the priesthood for a church in which a communion ecclesiology is valued as the one most advocated by Vatican II?

Pope John Paul II in his Post-Synodal Apostolic Exhortation: PASTORES DABO VOBIS (1992) speaks explicitly about the necessary ability of cooperation for any candidate for the priesthood:

> The ordained ministry has a radical "communitarian from" and can only be carried out as "a collective work"(17)... Of special importance is the capacity to relate to others. This is truly fundamental for a person who is called to be responsible to community and to be a "man of communion" (43)... Awareness of the Church as "Communion" will prepare the candidate for the priesthood to carry out his pastoral work with a community spirit, in heartfelt cooperation with the different members of the Church: priests and Bishops, diocesan and religious priest, priest and lay people. Such a cooperation presupposes a knowledge and appreciation of the different gifs and charisms of the diverse vocations and responsibility which the Spirit offers and entrusts to the members of Christ's Body... It is particularly important to prepare future priests for cooperation with the laity (59).

Thirdly, on the basis of his own charism he has an obligation to prevent any community from closing in on itself. He has to present to them the universal aspect of the Church. He, himself, as a member of the collegially structured charism of office, shares in the Church's universal pastoral ministry although he is put in charge of a local community which demands of him a local pastoral ministry.

These three points do not define the ministry of office in the Church conceived in the model of community, but they indicate which direction a rethinking of the priestly role in such a Church must take. It seems that the renewal of the Church through the basic Christian communities in the Third World Church will stimulate a thorough, vigorous and even radical rethinking of the priestly ministry and its role in the Church.[92] Dulles has made similar demands in his church model *Community of disciples* where he discusses the shape of a future ministry in such communities.[93]

Conclusion

The model of Church as communion contains many positive aspects particularly for our age and time. Just to list a few:

First, the idea of communion is based on the human experience found in any culture of our globe. The need for sharing and intimacy is inborn in every human being. Theologically, the strength of this model lies in its deep Scriptural roots; anthropologically, its strength lies in a deeply ingrained human trait, the human need and subconscious craving for fellowship in almost everything we do as humans.

Secondly, the communion model can bring together a whole range of theological issues. It can be used to: relate the institutional and the spiritual dimensions of the Church; deal with pluralism and unity; bring out the relationship of the universal Church to the local Churches; attend to the issue of primacy and episcopacy as well as the issue of evangelization and salvation. Yet the danger is that, since it can cover so many issues, it ends up with little meaning or no point of reference.

Thirdly, since it contains a vertical and a horizontal dimension it can bring out the spiritual dimension of the individual as well as that of the community in its relationship with God on the one hand and with our fellow human beings on the other hand. It can help to realize that the *vertical-transcendent* and the *horizontal-communal* dimension of communion are of equal value and that any emphasis of one over the other will only result in a flawed vision of the Church.

Fourthly, the model is suited very well in the ecumenical dialogue since it is congenial to both Orthodox and to Protestants alike.[94]

In view of the fact that the Church must see itself and its mission in the service of the Kingdom of God the communion idea reveals most clearly what the Kingdom is all about and what the Church's mission consists of: the Church is an anticipation in space and time of that great vision, spoken of by the prophet Isaiah and by Jesus himself, of the heavenly banquet where all human beings will be united into one community of brothers and sisters in union with God and the whole of creation. It is the fulfillment of the age old dream of all humanity for union with God and fellow human beings in justice, peace and joy. The Church's mission is to demonstrate this vision at least partially and to work for its coming about in all sectors of human life. The very phrase Kingdom of God means communion including all three aspects of the new transformed world: union with the triune God, union with all creatures and union with the whole cosmos.

The Faith and Order Commission described the Church from this aspect as follows:

It is God's design to gather all creation under the Lordship of Christ (Eph 2:10), and to bring humanity and all creation into communion. As a reflection of the communion in the Triune God, the Church is called by God to be the instrument in fulfilling this goal. The Church is called to manifest God's mercifulness to humanity, and to restore humanity's natural purpose — to praise and glorify God together with all the heavenly host. As such it is not an end in itself, but a gift given to the world in order that all may believe (John 17:21).[95]

4. The Church as Sacrament

The notion of the Church as SACRAMENT was hailed by ecclesiologists as THE achievement of the Council as far as a theological definition of the Church goes:

> The statement of the Second Vatican Council with regard to the total sacramentality of the Church is probably the most important pronouncement it made concerning the Church... All the Council's other statements about the Church are affected by this insight. The key to the new understanding of the Church reached by the Council is the teaching of the christocentric character of the Church.[96]

This model of the Church tries to come to grips with the divine and human elements of the Church. It is the most theological view presented. Most moderate theologians accept this model as basic and most adequate since it expresses the essence of the Church in traditional theological terminology. H. de Lubac, K. Rahner, O. Semmelroth, E. Schillebeeckx, and Y. Congar all contributed to this model before and during the Council. For the first time Vatican II used this description of the Church in an official document of the Church:

> The Church is a kind of Sacrament of intimate union with God and of the unity of all humankind, that is, she is a sign and instrument of such union and unity. (L G 9 and 48)

After Vatican II the image of the Church as sacrament gained momentum even in Protestant Churches which preferred the terminology "instrument and sign" rather than sacrament.[97] The Faith and Order Commission expressed it accordingly:

> The Church is the sign and instrument of God's design for the whole world. Being that part of humanity which already participates in the love and communion of God the Church is a prophetic sign which points beyond itself to the purpose of all creation, the fulfilment of the kingdom of God. ... at the

same time the Church is the instrument through which God wants to bring about what is signified by it: the salvation of the whole world, the renewal of the human community by the divine Word and the Holy Spirit, the communion of humanity with God and within itself.[98]

What does it mean to say the Church is a sacrament?

As Christ is the Sacrament of God, so the Church is seen as the Sacrament of Christ. She makes him present and tangible in this world until he comes again. Here the Church signifies and effects the unity of humankind, one with the other and all with God in Jesus Christ, in virtue of being "sign and instrument" that really contains the grace it confers.

Following K. Rahner's argument, we can say: God created the world in order to lead it into his own glory. All history must be seen and understood as manifesting and realizing the salvific plan that is the self-communication of God to all humankind. But history as such remains an ambiguous sign of this self-communication the 'yes' and the 'no' each person gives to God who communicates himself. Only in the history of Jesus is the realization of the self-communication of God to all humankind achieved in an unambiguous way.

Christ the sacrament of God

Jesus is the sacrament of God in history. In him who God is and what he has in store for all of his creation becomes sacramentally visible. Jesus' life is marked by two essential aspects: IDENTIFICATION and REPRESENTATION. He became one with us by identifying himself with us and he is 'God with us' (Phil 2). Christ is the historically real and actual presence of the eschatologically victorious mercy of God (Rahner). He is God made visible and present to us with the aim of communicating himself once and for all to us. God has bound himself to this person.

> From the moment the Logos assumes this human nature redemption cannot be canceled anymore, the grace of God no longer comes steeply down from on high, from God absolutely transcending the world and in a manner that is without history, purely episodic. The Logos is permanently in the world in tangible historical form, established in the flesh of Christ as part of the World, of humanity and of its very history.[99]

Now it is possible to point to a visible, historically manifest fact, located in time and space and say: here is a concrete sign that effects what it points to: God's self-communication to humankind. Having assumed our nature (identification): Jesus, who is God's union and communion with us and one of us as well, represents us to God: he is our union and communion with God. He said YES for us once and for all to God's self-communication which has now become irreversible. God cannot withdraw from the world again. Therefore we say: CHRIST IS THE SACRAMENT OF GOD. That means, he is an efficacious sign of our union with God and God's communion with us. He signifies this union and he brings forth this union. A sacrament is a sign of something really present.

According to Trent a sacrament is the "visible form of an invisible grace". Theologians would say a sacrament is an "efficacious sign, it produces or intensifies that of which it is a sign". The reality signified achieves an existential depth; it emerges into solid, tangible existence. All spiritual realities are accessible to us only through signs because of the incarnational structure of the human spirit. A sacrament as a sign of a spiritual reality contains the grace it signifies, and confers the grace it contains. Jesus, God in human form (sacrament), signifies union with God and brings forth this union. This union of humankind with God is accomplished through the life, death and resurrection of Christ. The transformation of the "earthy Jesus" by the Father through the power of the Holy Spirit (Rm 8:11; Eph 1:18-20) is the great break through into the "New Creation", the final act in the bringing about of this union of humankind with God.

This new creation is the final accomplishment of God's salvific plan with humankind. The Risen Lord, in his identification with us, is already for us the final fulfillment of our future destiny. Anyone who comes in contact now with the Risen Lord, is drawn into his sphere of life, is "already a new creation" (2 Cor 5:17). The question now is: How can this redemption accomplished in Jesus Christ become effectively present in time and space for every human being since Christ is not physically present in the world in the way he was when he walked this earth? Or, how can we come in contact with him in a manner that is certain and reaches into this our world? Who represents him, "the historically real and actual presence of the saving love of God?" It is here that we have to locate the Church.

The Church the sacrament of Christ

We presuppose the principle that God touches men and women through other human beings and through tangible historical events. Salvation is mediated through concrete historical-social realities. Hence it is easy to see that the Church becomes the sign of Christ present now in the world. She becomes his hands, his mouth his body through which he communicates his words and saving actions to the world.[100]

> The Church is for us the sacrament of Christ, she represents him, in the full and ancient meaning of the term, she really makes him present. She not only carries on his work but she is his very continuation, in a sense far more real than that in which it can be said that any human institution is its founder's continuation.[101]

Or in the words of Adam Möhler:

> The Church is the Son of God perpetually appearing in human form among men always renewing himself, eternally regenerating, his enduring incarnation, for the faithful are called in the Holy Scripture the Body of Christ.

The Church in this view is conceived in terms of the mission of the Son in the Holy Spirit. The idea to perceive the Church as sacrament takes on its full meaning within a trinitarian perspective in which God's plan is revealed. The Kingdom of God content-wise means God's final revelation of who he is and the final fulfillment of every person's social destiny in union with the triune God. In the words of Vatican II:

> Lifted up from the earth, Christ draws all men to himself (Jn 12:32) risen from the dead, he has sent his life-giving Spirit upon the disciples, through the Spirit he has established his body, which is the Church as the universal sacrament of salvation, sitting at the right hand of the Father he is at work in the world without ceasing to bring men to the Church, to join them more closely to himself through her. (*Lumen Gentium* 48; *Ad Gentes* 2-5: *Gaudium et Spes* 45)

K. Rahner defines the Church from this perspective as the

> continuance, the contemporary presence of that real, eschatologically triumphant and irrevocably established presence in the world, in Christ, of God's salvific will.[102]

The mission of the Church is seen here as placing the world in the presence of the mystery of Christ in the Spirit. All her structures are completely subordinated to the mystery of Christ. In short, her mission is to bring people in contact with Christ and through him with the Kingdom. She is a sacrament, i.e., a sign that brings forth what it signifies: First, she is a sign of God's presence in the world, her mission is to bring people into contact with God and his Kingdom.

Secondly, she is an anticipation of what is to come, she effectively mediates the salvation that is already present in her. In the words of the Council: "She is a kind of Sacrament of intimate union with God and of the unity of all humankind; that is, she is a sign and instrument of such union and unity."(LG 9; 48)

Church universal Sacrament of Salvation

The Church is described as being by its very essence the *universal sacrament of salvation*. The description, which holds a prominent place in the *Dogmatic Constitution on the Church* (LG 48), is quoted both in the *Degree on the Church's Missionary Activity* (AG 1) and in the *Pastoral Constitution on the Church in the Modern World* (GS 45).

By Sacrament the Council means a symbolic reality established by Christ, a sign that contains and confers the grace it signifies. The Church, therefore, is not a mere cognitive sign, making known something that already exists, but an efficacious sign that brings about the redemption to which it points. Since the Church is seen as a universal sacrament, that means as *"an instrument for the redemption of all"* (LG 9), we must assume that the salvation of all human beings does in some way depend on the Church. The Church is involved in the salvation of all who are saved (LG 16). Whatever kind of faiths and beliefs people may confess we must assume that the grace which saves them is in a *mysterious way* linked to the Church. In the words of the Council, through this grace they are *ordered* to the Church. That means the saving grace they receive outside the Church gives the recipient a positive inclination towards the Church so that all who live by God's grace are in a certain sense affiliated with the Church.[103]

The question that arises is whether the Church saves simply by being the reality towards which people are oriented or whether she acts to bring about the salvation of such persons. The perception of the Church as "a universal instrument" of salvation (LG1) suggests that the Church is actively at work in the salvific process but does not explain by what activities the Church accomplishes this result.

Referring to the Constitution on the Liturgy many theologians see that it is through prayers and the eucharistic celebration that the Church unceasingly intercedes with the Lord for the salvation of the entire world (SC 83).[104]

The problem that arises when we state that the Church is a *universal sacrament of salvation* is that it easily leads to an exclusive understanding of salvation as being totally *ecclesiocentric*. To avoid this danger, we constantly need to be reminded that God's saving grace can not be restricted to the sacrament alone. There is grace outside the sacrament and therefore salvation outside of the Church. Whatever interpretation is given to this definition, we may not interpret it so narrowly that we restrict all saving activity to that mediated through the Church alone. The theological solution that is generally offered today is that it is through the Holy Spirit that the grace of salvation, linked to the incarnation, death and resurrection of Christ, will reach all people in ways not known to us.[105] In the words of *Redemptoris Missio:*

> The Spirit manifests himself in a special way in the Church and in her members. Nevertheless, his presence and activity are universal, limited neither by space nor time (RM 28) .... Thus the Spirit blows where he wills (Jn 3:8), who was already at work in the world before Christ was glorified and [it is he] who 'filled the world... and holds all things together (and) knows what is said' (Wis 1:7).. He leads us to broaden our vision in order to ponder his activity in every time and place (RM 29).

We already touched on this subject in the chapter on the Church and the Kingdom and return to the subject in the Chapter on the Church's mission today.

Weaknesses of this model

First, there are very few passages in Scripture that support this model at all (Eph 5:32). Secondly, for some this model encloses the Church within boundaries that remain introverted and cultic (sacramentalism). Others believe that by allotting to the world such a high degree of sacramentality (God's self-communication through history and matter), the Church gets so immersed that it loses its own identity since sacramentality is granted to all reality. Thirdly, while this model explains (theoretically in words) the mystery of the Church very beautifully, it does not offer concrete criteria by which to evaluate, judge and discern the divine and the merely human in the Church. Where, for example, is the divine in a Church so human and so often defeated? Fourthly, because the language explicating the Church as sacrament is so technical and sophisticated, it is very difficult to preach about such a model. It remains basically a Catholic model only, although the World Council of Churches in Uppsala in response to Vatican II called the Church "a sign of the coming unity of humankind."

Conclusion

The Council wanted to be a pastoral Council according to the intention of Pope John XXIII. This meant that all topics taken up by the Council were to help the ordinary faithful see their faith in relation to the concrete situation in which they lived. The profound theological meaning and importance of the image of the Church as Sacrament remains a model highly appreciated by theologians but hardly understood by the ordinary faithful. Yet, as Luzbetak points out, the important dimension of the Church as universal Sacrament is ritual because religion is never divorced from ritual. Applying this to the Church's missionary task, he concludes:

> What is important to remember is that, just as in the case of community building each culture has its own way of respecting an individual, bearing each others burden, listening, forgiving, caring, sharing, serving, and spending oneself for each other, so it is in the case of ritual: *each culture has its own set of ritual symbols and meanings that should be used as much as possible to make the local church even more recognizable as God's Universal Sacrament.*[106]

5. The Church as Herald

The Church as Herald is a characteristically Protestant conception of the Church. This type of theology was highly developed by Karl Barth, who relies heavily on Paul and Luther. For him the fault of Catholic ecclesiology is that it concentrated too heavily on its own being with the result that it becomes triumphalistic. The correct attitude for the Church must be to point away from itself, like John the Baptist, by pointing to Christ. The Church is essentially a herald of the Lordship of Christ and a herald of the future Kingdom.

According to K. Barth, the Church is the living community of the living Christ. God calls the Church into being by his grace and gives her life by means of his Word and His Spirit, with a view to his Kingdom. The Church is not a permanent fact or an institution: she is an event constituted by the power of the Word of God in Scripture. There is no authority in the Church except the Word of God, which is to be let free to call into question the Church herself. It is God's Word that creates and renews the Church and that urges her on to her mission: the constant proclamation of the salvific event, Jesus Christ, and of the advent of the Kingdom of God. Besides Karl Barth, R. Bultmann also promoted this view of the Church very strongly. The Church is so much an event that she can have no solid socio-logical or institutional dimension. All historical forms that the Church has to take are always provisional and even paradoxical. The Word alone re-mains central and the only true reference point. There are three catch-words concerning the Church to which Bultmann constantly refers: wor-ship, eschatological, and vocation. The Church is first of all a community of worship where the Word is proclaimed. Secondly, she is an eschatological community which means that God makes himself present in the accep-tance of Jesus by the believers. Thirdly, the worshiping community becomes a community with a prophetic vocation, a kerygma that calls for a decision.

The mission of the Church is to proclaim that which she has heard, believed, and been commissioned to proclaim. The emphasis is on "faith and proclamation" over interpersonal relations and mystical communion, which the community model stresses highly. This model is also called "kerygmatic", for it looks upon the Church as a herald — one who receives an official message with the commission to pass it on. The biblical picture for this model is: The herald of a king who comes to proclaim a royal decree in a public square. This model is not strongly present in the docu-ments of Vatican II as a whole except in the passages found in the Decree on Ecumenism and the Constitution on Revelation. Catholic theology has accepted the all importance of the Word of God and regards the magisterium under the Word and not above it. However the hierarchy in particular has the responsibility of watching over the proclamation and interpretation of the Word. In and for the community the magisterium is to be seen as repre-senting Christ's power and authority with regard to the fidelity to and con-tinuity of his message. Among Catholic theologians H. Küng has pre-sented a similar view: for him the Church is the Congregation that has been summoned ('ecclesisa' = being called out) by a herald. This gives to the Church an "event character" rather than seeing it as an unchanging entity "Ecclesia" like "Congregation" means both the actual process of congregating and the congregated community by itself. The theology of the Word of God has become very central in the ecclesiological outlook of the Basic Ecclesial communities. The Word here has become the immediate point of reference and the source of inspiration. It is the primary catalyst of the community since the Word, unlike the sacraments, is always within its reach.

The Word of God is here experienced in its direct relationship with life since it is read, reflected and meditated upon by the faithful almost daily. It is the foundation of the faith and the spirituality of the BECs. In the measure the BECs grow and develop in the Church this model will become more and more important and in need of being developed in the Catholic Church.

Strength of the model

First, it has a good and sound biblical foundation in the prophetic tradition of the Old Testament and in the theology of St. Paul. Secondly, it gives a clear sense of identity and mission to the Church: a congregation that heralds the good news of Jesus Christ and is not afraid of being opposed by contrary views. Thirdly, its spirituality focuses on God's sovereignty and man's infinite distance from him, which leads to virtues like humility, readiness for repentance and reform. Fourthly, it has given and can give rise to a very fruitful "Theology of the Word." In comparison with the sacramental model, the Word here "has a unique capacity to express not only what is present but what is absent, not only what is but also what is not, and hence to protest against what is actually given and to condemn it." (Dulles)

Weaknesses of the model

The Word of God appears NOT to have become flesh but simply word. From a Catholic point of view, the incarnational aspect is not seen and appreciated. Secondly, the "event character" is at times stressed so much that any "continuity" in time and space is questionable. The "permanence of Christ's real presence as we see it in the sacramental model seems to be lost. This aspect is strongly stressed by the Council in the Constitution on the Liturgy and in the Constitution on Divine Revelation. Thirdly, the Catholic understanding of the Church as a "stable community in history", in which Christ continues to make himself present and available, leads to a different view of authority in the Church. Fourthly, the model focuses too exclusively on witness to the neglect of action. It has a very pessimistic outlook on the Kingdom's power to change this world. Nor is much said about the Christian's obligation to create a new social order. The stress is too strongly placed on the Kingdom as totally the work of God, entirely and exclusively produced at God's initiative. We humans can only patiently await its coming. The socio-political dimension of the Gospel as a call to change this world is not taken seriously or even denied. Lastly, the model easily gives rise to biblical fundamentalism, one of the greatest threats to the Gospel message today.

6. The Church as Servant

In all of the models up to now the Church is seen as the active subject, and the world as the object that the Church acts upon or influences. The question formerly asked was: What can the world do to build up the Church? Now the question is: what can the Church do to make the world a better place to live in? This view is based on the theological insight that the Kingdom of God is meant for the world and that the Church must see itself and its mission in the service of the Kingdom. The pastoral Constitution of the Church in the Modern World presents a completely new understanding of the relationship between the Church and the world. After recognizing the world's legitimate autonomy the Council asserts that the Church must consider itself as part of the total human family and sharing the same concerns as the rest of all humankind.

Articles 3 and 92 of the Constitution of the Church in the Modern World point out that just as Christ came into the world not to be served but to serve, so the Church, carrying on the mission of Christ, seeks to serve the world by fostering unity among all people. The disposition of the whole Church is one of universal service to humanity as such, which is seen as one big family. Service becomes the central inspiration of ecclesiology. What is most important here is the 'Theological Method' used in this type of theology. Dulles calls it "secular-dialogic" because the world is considered to be a properly theological source in order to discern the signs of the times. The "concrete situation" is taken as the starting point for theology and only after an analysis of the situation is any theological reflection done. The method is "dialogic", because it seeks to operate on the frontier between the contemporary world and the Christian tradition. The model perceives the Church primarily but not exclusively as an "agent of social change" in the name of the Kingdom, which is coming among humankind - a kingdom of justice, peace and joy as well as of holiness and grace.

Strength of this model

First, it helps the Church to turn away from being overly concerned about its own internal affairs and look at the world for which the Kingdom is meant. Secondly, the Church as understood in this model can give hope to a world stricken by war, injustice and hatred by pointing constantly to the coming Kingdom as having appeared already in Jesus Christ. It can give meaning to the small services all can do for a better world of justice, peace and unity. Thirdly, this model underlines the principle that "diakonia", which includes the struggle for a new social order, is as essential to, and even constitutive of, the mission of the Church as are proclamation and sacramental celebration. The Kingdom demands the transformation of all human reality and the Church must be an "agent" of this transformation. Snyder sees three significant strengths in this model:

First, its optimism provides motivational power for social change. Generally this model is a conscious critique of other worldly viewpoints that see the Kingdom either as irrelevant in present society or, worse, as encouraging passivity and discouraging Christian action on behalf of the public good.

Secondly, it sees positive values in human culture. In its insistence that the Kingdom is present and social, not just individual, this model stresses the good in human nature, in human cultural achievements and often in the physical environment. Rather than merely being a "kingdom of darkness" or a negative drag on the higher, nobler realm of non-material spirit, the world in this view is a place of beauty and value within which Christians add their efforts to perfect society and heal its diseases.

Thirdly, this model stresses human action and responsibility. God has made us responsible creatures, capable actors in the world's drama. Not to accept this role is to fail to seek first God's Kingdom and its justice. Sin is not just acts of personal immorality; it is a failure to accept God-given responsibility for this world.

Weaknesses of this model

First, only general biblical indications will support this model, since direct biblical references cannot be found. There are only references in a broader sense. The main argument is drawn from creation. Secondly the separation of Kingdom and Church, although done by Vatican II, can easily lead to the assumption that the Church is merely one of a number of agencies within history that are building up the future Kingdom. Why should one belong to the Church if one can work more effectively for justice and peace outside of it? What are the elements that make such an "agent of social change" distinct from other agents? We can easily lose sight of the christocentric aspect of the Kingdom, not to mention its ecclesiological dimension.

Thirdly, the stress on "social or structural change" can easily lead away from that necessary constant stress on personal conversion which the Bible demands. The cultic or celebrative aspect of the Kingdom now is often rated secondary and not absolutely necessary.

Conclusion

We have been following the 5 models (or 6 if we include that of Community of Disciples as one as well) which Dulles presents in his book. Each model has its strengths and its weaknesses. The issue is not a matter of exclusiveness, but is rather a question of one's basic stance in looking at the Church. For example, I can hold that the sacramental model of the Church is the one I favor most, but that does not mean I exclude the positive aspects of the other models. My image of Church will basically be formed from the sacramental model and I will modify this accordingly. My basic model, however, will remain the sacramental one. In the same way I can presume that someone who chooses the servant model as his or her basic model for perceiving the Church does not exclude the aspects which are strongest in the sacramental model. To choose a model means I accept a particular vantage point from which I look at the Church and from which I take the valid observations of the other models into consideration and thus allow my self to adjust my understanding of Church. It follows, therefore, that one has already chosen a model out of which one operates whether he or she knows it or not.

Is it possible to conceive a model that would contain the best of all models? Most probably not. One can use different models to come up with a description of Church but to press the idea of Church into only one model would violate the very mystery of her being. McBrien uses the five models of Dulles for his description of Church, but believes that they can be summarized in just three models: *institution, community, servant.* For him the institutional model contains the Sacrament and the Herald model. McBrien sees these three models as complementary and comprehensive in order to understand the Church and her mission adequately. He defines the Church in the following way:

> "The Church is the whole body, or congregation, of persons who are called by God the Father to acknowledge the Lordship of Jesus the Son in Word and Sacrament, in witness and in service, and, through the power of the Holy Spirit, to collaborate with Jesus' historic mission for the sake of the Kingdom of God".

The mission of the Church he outlines as follows:

The *first task* of the Church is to keep alive the memory of Jesus Christ in Word and Sacrament and to express hope in the world to come, a totally new creative manifestation of the future Kingdom. The Eucharist in particular presents the past and present aspect of the Kingdom and creates hope in its future fulfilment. The *second task* of the Church is to make the future present in its midst. The Kingdom is a present reality and tangible in the "community of disciples" and this reality must be made visible on the community level and not just individually. The *third task* of the Church is to take up responsibility for the humanization of the world in its fullest sense. Because the Kingdom of God is also a Kingdom of justice, peace and communion and the Church exists for the sake of the Kingdom, this Kingdom must be made visible in the form of anticipation of what is to come. Without this we cannot create or maintain a firm belief that the fullness of the new creation is not just a "pie in the sky" but the ultimate fulfilment of God's grand design of creation and salvation.

Although McBrien uses all five models to describe the essence and the mission of the Church it is obvious that he sees the Church from the vantage point of the servant model. For him the Church must basically be understood from the central message of Jesus himself: the Kingdom of God in the service of which she must find her identity and her mission.

The description of the Church as we find it in the "The Faith and Order Commission" seems to contain almost all essential aspects of the different models mentioned above but it emphasizes strongly the social mission of the Church:

> The Church is the community of people called by God who, through the Holy Spirit, are united with Jesus Christ and sent as disciples to bear witness to God's reconciliation, healing and transformation of creation. The Church's relation to Christ entails that faith and community require discipleship in the sense of moral commitment. The integrity of the mission of the Church, therefore, is at stake in witness through proclamation and in concrete action for justice, peace and integrity of creation. The latter will often be undertaken with those outside the community of faith. This is a defining mark of *koinonia* central for our understanding of the church.[107]

Excursion: The meaning of the term "Church" in Vatican II.

The Council did not give us a definition of Church, as a matter of fact, the term Church is used in different ways in the conciliar documents. There are six different descriptions of the Church as G. Baum[108] has shown:

1. Church as "CATHOLIC CHURCH"

The Church is equated with the Catholic Church as defined in the traditional teaching of the Church:

- – the same faith,
- – sevenfold sacramental liturgy,
- – legitimate pastors with the Pope as supreme authority.

The argumentation for the equation of church with the Catholic Church starts with the definition of the Church as the "universal sacrament of salvation" (LG 48). The Church of Christ and the Catholic Church are not two realities but one. The analogy is made between the incarnation and the Church.

> Just as the eternal Son of God assumed only one individual body for the ransom of humanity, so the Spirit of Christ through "the social structure" of the Catholic Church (*socialis compago*) is the organ of salvation for the world. Thus the Church develops a special pneumatic "life of its own in all the forms which are proper to it as a social structure in the Spirit.

The conclusion drawn is therefore: It can be deduced that the ecclesial elements and the means of salvation which are present in the separated churches and communities are present there to the extent of their union with the Catholic Church. Separated churches and communities function as means of salvation because elements of the Catholic Church subsist in them. This means that they draw their efficacy from the fullness of grace and truth found in the Catholic Church.[109]

2. Church as "LOCAL CONGREGATION"

Although the Council adopted a universalistic perspective most of the time when it was talking about the Church, asserted quite strongly that it is only in and out of the particular churches that the one and single catholic Church exists (LG 23). This has been called by some theologians "the most important ecclesiological formula of the council."

> It guarantees, or should guarantee, that the relationship between the whole church and the individual churches is seen as one of reciprocal or mutual inclusion, that individual churches are not considered administrative subdivisions of a pre-existent reality, nor the one church as a subsequent federation of individual churches. The many churches are not churches except in the one Church; the one Church does not exist except in and out of the many

churches. Since the council, these carefully nuanced and mutually condi-
tioning statements have prompted what some called a *Copernican revolu-
tion* in ecclesiology, a renewed interest in the local churches, whose communion is the whole church.

The council's teaching in finely balanced: The church is not *catholic* if it is
not particular, that is, *local*; but the particular or local is not the church
unless it is *catholic* at every level, that is, redemptively integrated.[110]

This has been called one of the great achievements of Vatican II.
Through the celebration of the Word and the Eucharistic meal Christ is
present in the worshiping community and the power of the Holy Spirit
transforms it into his body (LG 26). This idea of "local congregation" or
"Church in action" is of great importance particularly for the Basic Ecclesial
Communities. The Faith and Order Commission expresses it this way:

The Communion of the Church is expressed in the communion between local churches in each of which the fullness of the Church resides. The communion of the Church embraces local churches in each place and all places
at all time. Local churches are held in the communion of the Church by the
one Gospel, the one baptism and the Holy Communion, served by common
ministry. The communion is expressed in service and witness to the world.[111]

3. Church as "COMMUNITY OF THE BAPTIZED"

The Council stated that baptism, properly celebrated, incorporates believers into Christ (Ec 3; 22; LG 14; 15). There exists a Spirit-created
sacramental communion between Catholics and other Christians, even if
one dimension of communion is incomplete. The Council acknowledged
that other Christian Churches are communities in which Christ is present
and that they are instruments of the Spirit in saving and sanctifying people.

There are two basic reasons why the Church cannot just be identified
with the Roman Catholic Church alone. First, the reality of communion
exceeds the boundaries of the Catholic Church. There are baptized non-
Catholics who, by their faith, hope and love live the life of communion
with Christ and the Spirit; and there are Roman Catholics who do not live
in the Spirit.

Secondly, if we consider the elements, spiritual, sacramental and ministerial that constitute and animate the Church, we can discover these elements in various degrees also in other Christian churches and communities
where they can mediate salvation as well.

Correspondingly the Council nuanced the claim that the Roman Catholic Church is the true Church of Christ and asserted that the Church of Christ subsists in (rather than simply is) the Roman Catholic Church. By accepting such elements as justifying grace, incorporation into Christ, communion with the Holy Spirit, Holy Scripture, sacraments, devotion to Mary etc., the Council found the phrase the "true Church subsists" more appropriate since these elements can also be found to some extent in the other churches.

Those who maintain the equation between Church of Christ and Catholic Church argue that those ecclesial elements found in these churches are elements of the Catholic Church which subsists in these non-catholic churches and communities.[112]

4. Church refers to the "PEOPLE OF ISRAEL"

The Council realized that the roots of the Church lie in the past. She is in continuity with the people of the Old Covenant. By tracing back the beginnings of God's calling of humankind to a Covenant people, the Council sees the entire "ABRAHAMIC COMMUNITY" as Church, which is the "Community of the called" beginning with Abraham and stretching through history as a whole This view sees the Jewish people once again as belonging to the Church in a broader sense.[113]

5. The Church "FROM ABEL ON"

The Council saw God's searching for humankind right from the beginning of history. The word "universal Church" refers to the entire family of the human race inasmuch as it is touched and transformed by God's saving grace. G. Baum sees here the Church as the community of all persons extending as far as the human race extends.

However, he maintains that the grace of God, which is operative in the whole of humanity, is dependent on Jesus Christ, the one mediator between God and each human being and hence also related to the Church which is his body. What he means is equal to saying that the whole history and the dynamism of human life are supernatural. To designate the entire family of the human race as Church Universal is equivalent to saying, in scholastic terminology, that the whole of human history is supernatural.

The following question, however, has to be asked: "Is it permissible to extend the concept 'Church' to such an extent that it actually includes everybody?" For Baum the axiom "Outside the Church, no salvation" does not cause any problem since the Church is to be identified with the whole of the human race.

H. Küng, in various writings, has opposed this use of the word Church. As a thesis he holds: As against the extra-ordinary way of salvation, if this is rightly understood, the ordinary way of salvation for non-Christian humanity exists in following their own religious traditions. The concept Church should be applied to the Christian Churches only and not to non-Christian communities because:

1. It is contrary to the evidence of the New Testaments and the tradition based on it.

2. The extension of the notion of Church is not necessary to account for the salvation of non-Christians.

3. The broad notion of the Church renders missionary work unnecessarily difficult, for it presumes that people of good will really belong to the Church.

4. It offends non-believers to be told that they are Christians at least in implicit desire; and they reject such theological speculations.

6. The "HOUSE CHURCH" (Lumen Gentium 11)

The community of father, mother and children is called Church. In recent years in particular the theology of marriage has come to discover the ecclesial dimension of marriage. As Paul VI put it:

> The family is a place where hospitality is experienced, the paschal mystery is fulfilled and evangelization occurs. The Family is Church by its mission and its special aptitude for transmitting the Gospel.

There are four elements that we might mention here which constitute a family as Church:

1. Christ's presence: The sacrament of marriage guarantees Christ's presence in the family, since this sacrament "contains and radiates" the mystery of Christ's union with the Church. Where Christ is, there is the Church.

2. Evangelization: A healthy experience of family life is the best preparation for grasping and accepting God's message of salvation. God's self-disclosure to humankind is most intimately described in the Bible through images that are taken from family-life: spouse, mother, father, bride etc.

3. Prayer: Vatican II encourages the family to become a "sanctuary of the Church by its common prayer." Family prayer, scriptural reading etc. should lead the whole family to a better participation in the Church's liturgy.

4. Experience of love: The family is the place where children experience love in all its aspects: love as fidelity and affection; they come to know its freeing aspect and its power to grow and to open up to others; and finally, they are led to discover God's love as the ultimate source of all human love and freedom.[114]

Notes

[1] Rahner, Karl, "Towards a fundamental theological interpretation of Vatican II" *Theological Studie*s 40 (1979) pp. 716-27.

[2] Rahner, K., "Towards a fundamental theological Interpretation", pp. 718-19.

[3] Brown, R., *Priest and Bishop, Biblical Reflections* (New York: Paulist Press, 1970) pp. 51-52.

[4] Schweizer, E., *Church Order in the New Testament* (London: SCM Press, 1961) p. 41.

[5] Lohfink, G., *Jesus and Community*, pp. 7-29.

[6] Brown, R., *Biblical Exegesis & Church Doctrine* (New York/Mahwah: Paulist Press, 1985), pp. 133-34. See also "Not Jewish Christianity and Gentile Christianity but Types of Jewish/ Gentile Christianity" The Catholic Biblical Quarterly 45 (1983) pp. 74-79.

[7] Rossi de Gasperi, F., "Continuity and Newness in the Faith of the Mother Church of Jerusalem" in, *Bible and Inculturation, Inculturation Working papers on living Faith*, Rome (1983) (17-69) at p. 63.

[8] Rahner, K., "Towards a fundamental theological interpretation", p. 721.

[9] Rahner, K., "Towards a fundamental theological interpretation", p. 723.

[10] Rahner, K., "Concern for the Church," *Theological Investigation* XX. (New York: Crossroad Publ., 1981) Chapter 6 & 7, 77-102, at p. 92.

[11] Rahner, K., "Concerns for the Church", p. 78.

[12] Karl Rahner and Josef Ratzinger, *The Episcopacy and the Primacy* (New York: Herder and Herder 1963) p. 38.

[13] Rahner, K., "Concerns for the Church", p. 94.

[14] Rahner, K., "Concerns for the Church", p. 79.

[15] Pope John Paul II, *Redemptoris Missio*, No. 37.

[16] What follows is a summary from the book by Anthony Bellagamba, Mission & Ministry... in a *Global Church* (Maryknoll, New York: Orbis books 1992) pp. 1-9.

[17] Schreiter, R. J., *Constructing Local Theologies* (New York: Orbis Books, 1985) p. 1.

[18] Jerome, Theisen P., *The Ultimate Church and the Promise of Salvation*, (Collegeville, Minnesota: St John's University Press, 1976).

[19] Lonergan, Bernhard, "Theology in its new Context" W.E. Conn, Ed., *Conversion* (New York: Alba House, 1978), (3-21) at p. 6.

[20] Lambino, Antonio B., "A New Theological Model: Theology of Liberation" *Towards Doing Theology in the Philippine Context* (Manila: Loyola Papers 9, 1977), (pp. 2-25) p. 6.

[21] Snyder, *Model of the Kingdom*, p. 20.

[22] Luzbetak, L. J., *The Church and Culture*, p. 136.

[23] Dulles, Avery, *Models of the Church*, pp. 22-24.

[24] Luzbetak, L. J., *The Church and Culture*, pp. 136-137.

[25] A. B. Lambino, "A New Theological Model", pp. 6-7.

[26] Küng, Hans "Paradigm Change in Theology: A Proposal for Discussion", in: *Paradigm Change in Theology A Symposium for the Future*, Edit by Hans Knng and David Tracy, (Edinburgh: T&T Clark LTD, 1989) pp. 3-31.

[27] Lonergan, B., "Conversion", p. 7.

[28] Luzbetak, L. J., *The Church and Culture,* pp. 374-375.

[29] Dulles, Avery, *Models of the Church* (Expanded Edition) (New York: Doubleday, Image Books, 1987).

[30] Dulles, A., *A Church to Believe In: Discipleship and the Dynamics of Freedom* (New York: Crossroad Publishing Company, 1982) Chapter one: "Imaging the Church for the 1980s", pp. 1-18.

[31] Schoelles, Patricia, "Liberation Theology and Discipleship: The Critical and Reforming Tendencies of Basic Christian Identity", *Louvain Studies* 19, 1994, pp. 46-64.

[32] Sobrino, Jon, *Christology at the Crossroads: A Latin American Approach* (New York: Orbis Books, 1978) p. 60.

[33] Fuellenbach, John, *Throw Fire*, pp. 110-113; Hendrickx, H., *A Key to the Gospel of Matthew* (Manila: Claretian Publications, 1992) pp. 10-13.

[34] Duquoc, C., *Provisional Churches*, p .101.

[35] Schmaus, Michael, Dogmatic 4: *The Church its origin and Structure* (London: Sheet and Ward, 1977) p. 8.

[36] Dulles, A., *Models of the Church*, pp. 34-46.

[37] Moehler, Adam, *Symbolic*, paragraph 36.

[38] Duquoc, Christian, *Provisional Churches An Essay in Ecumenical Ecclesiology* (London: SCM Press LTD, 1986) pp. 6-7; 98-103.

[39] Bas van Iersel, "Who according to the New Testament has the say in the Church" *Concilium* 148 (1981) (11-17) at p. 11.

[40] Bas van Iersel, pp. 15-16.

[41] Dulles, A., *A Church to believe in*, p. 22.

[42] Ashley, Benedict M., *Justice in the Church: Gender and Participation* (Washington. D.C.: Catholic University Press, 1996) pp.10

[43] Ashley, Benedict M., *Justice in the Church*, p. 11.

[44] Ashley, Benedict M., *Justice in the Church*, p. 10

[45] Fuellenbach, J., *Throw Fire*, p. 17.

[46] Ashley, Benedict M., *Justice in the Church*, pp. 11-12.

[47] Ashley, Benedict M., *Justice in the Church*, p. 164.

[48] Dulles, Avery, *A Church to Believe In. Discipleship and the Dynamics of Freedom* (New York: Crossroad Publishing Company, 1982) pp. 24-25.

[49] Enrique Nardoni, "Charism in the Early Church Since Rudolph Sohm: An Ecumenical Challenge" *Theological Studies* 53 (1992) (646-662) p. 655.

[50] "Charism in the Early Church," p. 662.

[51] Borg, M. J., *Jesus, A Vision, Spirit, Culture, and Life of Discipleship* (San Francisco: Harper &Row, 1987).

[52] Brown, Raymond E., *Priest and Bishop, Biblical Reflections* (New York: Paulist Press, 1970) pp. 10-13.

[53] Sullivan, Francis, *Charisms and Charismatic Renewal: A Biblical Theological Study* (Dublin: Gill & Macmillan, 1982) p. 95.

[54] Sullivan, Francis, *Charisms and Charismatic Renewal*, pp. 91- 95.

[55] Dulles, Avery, "The Succession of Prophets in the Church", *Concilium* 4 (April 1968) Vol. 4, pp. 28-32.

[56] Dunn, James DG., *Jesus and the Spirit* (London: SCM Press, 1975) pp. 172-173.

[57] Dulles, A., "The Succession of Prophets in the Church", pp. 31-32.

[58] Brueggemann, W., *The Prophetic Imagination,* pp. 11-14.

[59] Rahner, K., *Spirit in the Church* (London: Burns & Oates,1979) p. 50.

[60] Dulles, A., "Successio Apostolorum", *Concilium* 148 (1981) pp. 61-67 at p. 62.

[61] Dulles, A., "Successio Apostolorum", p. 65.

[62] Merton, Thomas, *Prophets in the Belly of Paradox,* ed. G. Twomey (New York 1978).

[63] Union of Superiors General, *Consecrated Life Today. Charisms in the Church for the World,* (Montreal: St Paul, 1994) p. 214.

[64] *Consecrated Life Today,* p. 201.

[65] *Consecrated Life Today,* p. 133.

[66] *Consecrated Life Today,* p. 133.

[67] Metz, Johannes B., *Followers of Christ The Religious Life and the Church* (London: Paulist Press 1978).

[68] Lohfink, Norbert, "Where are today's prophets?" *Theology Digest* 37 (1990) p. 107.

[69] Fr. J. Moloney, *Disciples and Prophets: A Biblical Model of Religious Life.*(London: Darton, Longman and Todd, 1980) pp. 155-170.

[70] Norbert, Norbert, "Religious Orders: God's Therapy for the Church," *Theology Digest* 33 (1986), pp. 203-212, at page 208.

[71] *Consecrated Life Today,* p. 131.

[72] Lohfink, G., "Religious Orders", pp. 209-212.

[73] Brueggemann, W., *Prophetic Imagination,* p. 13.

[74] Heribert Arens, "Das Prohetische am Ordensleben" *Ordenskorrespondenz* 33 (1992) pp. 8-22.

[75] Dunn, J., *Spirit,* pp. 282-284.

[76] Dulles, A., "Successio Apostolorum", p 63.

[77] Duquoc, C., *Provisional Churches,* p. 99.

[78] Dulles, A., "Successio Apostolorum," p. 64.

[79] Dulles, A., "Ecclesial Futurology: Moving Towards the 1990s" pp. 1-15 at p. 4

[80] Dulles, A., *Models of the Church,* pp. 48-62.

[81] McBrien, Richard, *Catholicism* (London: G. Chapman, 1980) pp. 712-13.

[82] Kasper, Walter, *Theology and Church* (New York: Crossroad, 1989) p. 150.

[83] Extraordinary Synod of Bishops, "The Final Report," II,C, 1 *Origins* 16 (1985) p. 448.

[84] Congregation of the Doctrine of the Faith, "Some Aspect of the Church Understood as Communion," *Origins* 21 (1992) p. 108.

[85] Luzbetak, *Church and Culture*, p. 376.

[86] The Nature and Purpose of the Church, Faith and Order Paper No. 181 (Bialystock, Polan: Ortdruck Orthodox Printing House, 1998) 48.

[87] Lee, B. J. and Cowan, M. A., *Dangerous Memories. House Churches and our American Story* (Kansa City: Sheed & Ward: 1986) pp. 4-9.

[88] *The Nature and Purpose of the Church*, 16.

[89] *The Nature and Purpose of the Church*, 25.

[90] Chenu, M. D., "The New Awareness of the Trinitarian Basis of the Church", *Concilium* 146, (1981) pp. 14-22.

[91] Luzbetak, *Church and Culture*, p. 337.

[92] Boff, Leonardo, *Church Charism & Power. Liberation Theology and the Institutional Church* (London: SCM Press, 1985).

[93] Dulles, A., *Church to believe in*, pp. 17-18.

[94] Granfield, P., "The Concept of the Church as Communion", p. 753.

[95] *The Nature and Purpose of the Church*, 26.

[96] Schmaus, M., *The Church as Sacrament* (London: Sheed & Ward, 1975) p.5. See also Kasper, W., *Theology & Church* (London: SCM Press, 1989) pp. 111-147.

[97] See Grassmann, Günther, "The Church as Sacrament, Sign and Instrument," in *Church Kingdom World* by G. Limouris (editor) (Geneva: World Council, 1986) pp. 1-16.

[98] *Nature and Purpose of the Church*, 43, 45.

[99] Rahner, K., *The Church and the Sacraments* (London: Burns & Oates, 1963) p. 15.

[100] Theisen, J., *The Ultimate Church and the Promise of Salvation* (Collegeville, Minnesota: St. John's University Press, 1976) p. 131.

[101] de Lubac, H., *Catholicism*, p. 29.

[102] Rahner, K., *Church and Sacrament*, p. 18.

[103] Dulles, Avery, "Vatican II and the Church's purpose", *Theology Digest* 32(1985) pp. 344-345.

[104] Sullivan, Francis A., *The Church We Believe In* (New York: Paulist Press, 1988) p. 128.

[105] Stafford, Francis, J., "The Inscrutable Riches of Christ: The Catholic Church's Mission of Salvation" in *A Church for All People. Missionary Issues in a World Church,* Ed. E. La Verdiere (Collegeville: Liturgical Press, 1993) pp. 31-50.

[106] *Church and Culture*, p. 382.

[107] *The Nature and purpose of the Church*, p. 56, No. 112.

[108] Baum, G., "The Meaning of Church" in *The Credibility of the Church Today* (New York: Herder & Herder, 1968).

[109] For a in depth treatment and a critical evaluation of this aspect see J. Francis Staffort, "The Inscrutable Riches of Christ: The Catholic Church's Mission and Salvation" in *A Church For All People,* pp. 35-44.

[110] Komonchak, J., "Ecclesiology of Vatican II," p. 765

[111] *Nature and Purpose of the Church*, 66.

[112] Stafford, Francis, J., "The Inscrutable Riches of Christ: The Catholic Church's Mission and Salvation" pp. 38-39.

[113] Lohfink, G., *Does God need a Church*, pp. 51-106

[114] Provencher, N., "The Family as Domestic Church" in *Theology Digest* 30 (1982) pp. 149-152.

Chapter Six

Two most relevant Models for the Future Church: *Basic Ecclesial Communities and Contrast Society*

Introduction

If we look at the Church from the vantage point of the models described in A. Dulles' book *"Models of the Church"*, we could say: there are two models which have come to the fore over the last 30 years. The first is based on the Church as institution; the second is based on the Church as community. There are two modifications to these two basic models. The first, based on the institutional model, is the more traditional view, although it has been revised and adapted to meet new experiences. The latter view, namely the Church based on the community model, is growing in popularity and seems to have a dynamic that could lead to a new understanding of what it means to be Church today. However, it appears that these two images of the Church, currently vigorous, are not easily reconcilable with each other. They could also be construed as the Church in terms of *hierarchical structure* and the Church as *Basic Christian Community*. Some have called the first model *neo-conservative*, in line with the attempt of the official Church to restore the lost image of the Church in the years following the Council. While bearing the characteristics of the Institutional Model, this image has conscientiously tried to incorporate the theology of Vatican II. Hence, it cannot simply be identified with an image of the Church that existed prior to the Council.[1]

The second image, basically built on the model of Church as Community, has come to us through the experience of many movements in the Church today but most articulately through the *Basic Ecclesial Communities* of Latin America and the *Small Christian Communities* in Africa and Asia.

Although the official Church accepted the emergence of these communities, often with great enthusiasm, and regarded this phenomenon as

the working of the Holy Spirit, particularly in Latin America, the BECs
have also experienced stubborn resistance or at least strong resentment
from some official Church leaders. This is most often due to their link
with the Liberation Theology in which the BECs are rooted. J. Marins
pointed out already 20 years ago:

> Some authorities are not happy that the BEC make the people participate,
> that they decentralize decision-making, that they create a new style of priests,
> that they make the faith bear on real life... A part of the Church feels uneasy
> with that trend, which is in conflict with their theological vision which shocks
> their clerical way of life, and so some bishops become spokesmen of that
> mentality and try to disparage the communities.[2]

Reflecting on the Church in Latin America more than 30 years after
the Bishops Conference in Medellin (1968) enthusiastically praised the
emergence of BEC as the hope for the Latin American Continent, Clodovis
Boff sees both Church models operating in Brazil today. In his judgement
it is the Neo-conservative model that gained considerable ground over the
last decades.

> There is a double dynamic at work in the Churches of Latin America today:
> the dynamic of participation, coming from Medellin and Puebla, which finds
> expression especially in the base communities and the dynamic of order and
> authority, of commands of discipline and obedience, with everything com-
> ing from the top down. Unfortunately, this later dynamic seems to be grow-
> ing but at the same time the experience of base communities is something
> which is irreversible in our churches, there is no going back... There has
> been a tendency recently to incorporate them into the parish structure and
> restrict their activity to the renewal of the parishes, as a kind of auxiliary
> service in the parishes, whereas their original thrust and inspiration was to
> transform the parish into a dynamic center of community, to decentralize,
> desacramentalize the parish.[3]

Boff's comment affirms the general observation that the official
Church of Latin America in the pursue of harnessing the Liberation Theology if not stamping it out entirely tries very hard to get these vibrant base
communities under control and to incorporate them into the existing structures once again. How these communities will develop under this restraint
is hard to predict.

The BEC model is built on three important theological principles which
were developed either during the Council or immediately afterwards, when
the bishops tried to adapt to their respective Churches the Council's vision
of the Church and her mission to the world. These can be summarized as

follows: first, the Church must be understood in relation to the world. We must take into consideration not only theological sources but also secular sciences, history and the world in which we live. All attempts to understand the Church that do not take into account her relation to the world are inadequate, one-sided and faulty. Secondly, the Church is not the center of the world; God's salvific will goes beyond the boundaries of the Church. Thirdly, the Church has a concrete role to play in the social-political liberation of human beings in the world. This in no way implies a negation of the human secular autonomy but must be regarded as an assertion of Christian responsibility.[4]

Latin American theologians have written most extensively about these communities.[5] They believe it is from these communities that we can gain a true and genuine understanding of what Church means today, both in its essence as well as in its mission. L. Boff has set forth his most challenging ideas in his book, *Church: Charisma and Power*. He regards the Church as a sacrament of the Holy Spirit and thus charism becomes the organizing principle of the Church. As a sacrament of the Spirit, the Church becomes precisely the sacramental realization of the Kingdom in the world and the instrument of its mediation in history.

Charism is understood as the manifestation of the Spirit's present in each individual member of the community and directing everything for the good of all. Each member of the Church is charismatic, exercising a particular function in the community and enjoying a fundamental equality with other members. As the organizing principle, charism includes the hierarchy. This charism of office is that of exercising leadership within the community. This charism is of prime importance by virtue of the fact that it is responsible for harmony among the many and the diverse charisms within the community. But nevertheless, the hierarchy is to be seen as possessing one ministry among many others charisms which together built up the whole Church.[6]

The Basic Ecclesial Communities are understood as the entities in which the Kingdom makes itself present in its community-creating aspect. These communities consciously seek to practice and live out those features which characterize the Kingdom: equality, participation, fellowship, and communion; or, in the words of the Bible, justice, peace, and joy (Rm 14:17) as the basic elements of the Kingdom historically anticipated.[7] These Basic Ecclesial Communities are the soil from which a new understanding of Church is emerging; then they challenge the way in which it was traditionally perceived.[8]

We need to point out that we are not dealing here with the question which of the two models is right and which is wrong. Both images share the Council's achievement: awareness of the Church as community of 'local Churches', and the relative independence that goes with this awareness, the ministry of the laity, etc. Both views appeal to the authority of the Council and justify their validity by quoting its documents.

Seemingly we are living out two different ecclesiologies found in the documents themselves without being able, at least for the present, to reconcile them with each other. Even during the Council itself observers from the Eastern Churches commented on the impossibility of living out simultaneously on the one hand, the first two chapters of "Lumen Gentium" which have as the basic image of the Church the Pauline concept of 'People of God', and, on the other hand, the third chapter of the same document which portrays the Church in terms of a 'hierarchical entity'. The latter image, which became the dominant concept of the Church after Vatican I, defines the Church primarily in terms of a perfect hierarchical society. The two models could be schematically presented as follows: First model:

– all power flows from the hierarchy
– the laity receives its ministry through delegation from the hierarchy
– the hierarchy is the center around which everything revolves.

Second model:

The organizing principle here is charism in which the charism of leadership expressed by hierarchy is of prime importance. The basic images used are: people of God; creation of the Holy Spirit (charismatic entity); and Body of Christ (living organism).

What we have here are two different models of society and communion: an older one challenged by a newer one, each with its own symbols and juridical structure. The issue, however, is not a matter of structures versus community. We know from the social sciences that society cannot be transformed into communities. Social groupings will search for community but, because of egoism and individualism, laws, order and structures are necessary for any human community. The new model seems to be concerned with the often forgotten fact that community has the primacy and that institution has to be regarded and treated as subordinated in the service of community and communion, and not the other way around.

The new model appeals particularly to new experiences and claims that it can make sense of these in ways the older fails to do. The older one promises continuity, allows for change by internal modification, and claims to be able to integrate these new experiences quite easily without breaking out of its unchanging framework. It tries to accommodate what is felt to be important in these new experiences while at the same time it softens and limits their impact generally. The new model faces the lacuna of not yet having an established framework and, therefore, struggles with forging its language, ritual and juridical structures. A good example of juridical procedure in these images is the following: the old model allows the laity to form a pastoral council with consultative voice and the commissioning of ministers by the parish priest, while the new model operates along the concept of 'discernment of ministry by the whole community'. Similarly with rituals: while accommodation is made in terms of language and common celebration, the performance of the rituals remains strictly priestly and hierarchical in the older model. In sociological language we would say that we are faced with two different views of society: a hierarchical versus a more democratic or 'charismatic' one. Or in theological language: The old model seems to have been organized around the axis of clergy-sacraments, while the new model seems to organize itself around the axis of Gospel-laity.[9]

It is not our intention to go into further detail with this so called Neo-conservative model since our concern is to deal rather with the model of Basic Ecclesial Communities which is most pronounced in the developing countries. But this much can be said: Many Catholics, believing that the best way to face new experiences is to integrate them into this model rather than to change it, continue to subscribe to a hierarchical model of the Church. At the moment we are experiencing a rather powerful resurgence of this model in the Church. Its qualities are:

- it is hierarchical in structure since its power does not come from the people but is held to come directly from Christ
- attentive to people and what they say
- centralized though ready to listen
- interested in the concerns of its members
- found particularly in groups that have a great influence in society and public life

This model has attractive elements that appeal to many Catholics. For instance:

(1) It responds to a concern for the ordinary faithful who are considered unqualified to work out their own personal stand on matters of faith and morals and who need strong directions to enable them to live and deepen their faith. The mission and obligation of the hierarchy are to provide them with this direction.

(2) There is presently a certain growing pessimism about accepting the world either as partner in dialogue or place of divine revelation. Although other cultures are appreciated, the main task of the Church is still seen as that of bringing the faith to the people. The goal of mission work is the building up of a Christian culture. This culture then stands as an expression of a socially attainable faith and also as a directive for personal and public life, which provides symbols, rituals, office, custom and teaching. These offer guidelines and directives as well as a clear and distinct Christian identity.[10]

The European Synod of 1991 on New Evangelization once again brought up the question of faith and inculturation very forcefully. The issue was the "Re-christianization of Europe". The fact that evangelization never occurs outside of a specific culture places great stress on the relationship between culture and evangelization. Each person has been shaped by the historically determined value systems and thought patterns of his or her own culture that surround and limit him/her. In addition he/she is born into a specific social system and participates in a specific life style. Our present technological and industrial culture is determined in its intelligent pursuits by a strong focus on whatever can be clearly mapped out and realized. For this reason, New Evangelization does not only aim at an adaptation of the good news to the respective culture but also at its transformation.

The concrete question at the Synod was how to envision such an evangelization of culture. Shall we support an 'evangelization of culture' only because it is necessary in order to bring the good news to each individual? Or should we say that the evangelization of culture is an integral element of the proclamation of God's Word? We also have to admit that the creation of a more human society and culture is not a tool or a tactical move of the Church in order to secure her own interests. A more human culture is good in itself and not only good because it is a means to an end. This in turn presupposes respect for other views and for the freedom of the individual to express these views unhampered.

This gives rise to the basic difficulty, namely, the presumption that democracy is being built on the philosophical basis of relativism. Doesn't this collide with the claims of the Catholic Church to be the sole possessor of the truth? The Pope himself, without watering down the claim to absolute right of truth, supports dialogue and sincere listening of all in the spirit of discernment and courage. Serious inculturation of the faith demands more than the imposition or even the creation of a Christian Culture which the dialogue partners of other cultures and religious traditions might just perceive as a new way of colonialization.

(3) The Church, visible as a clearly identifiable body with social power, guarantees an effectiveness of working together which can never be obtained through the medium of small communities whose members insert themselves into the fabric of social life. If the Church's mission is the transformation of all social and political realities towards the Kingdom, then it is extremely important that she be heard and exert her influence in public, in places where politics and decisions are made that affect human society as a whole. This has to be regarded as an constitutive element of her mission.

I. Church as BASIC ECCLESIAL COMMUNITIES

This model of Church has been emerging over the last three decades particularly in developing countries. In the words of J. Healey:

> The establishment of Basic Small Christian Communities has had a great influence on the Post Vatican II Church especially in the Third World - as a new model of Church, as a dynamic force for conscientization and as a process for lay people to become active participants in ministry and evangelization. Quite independently on one another, three areas of the Church in the Third World - Latin America, Africa, and Asia - have experienced the extraordinary growth of these communities.[11]

The New Testament background: "House Churches"

A number of authors believe that the emergence of basic Christian communities all over the world has a foundation in the New Testament itself. There are two words *oikos* and *oikia* which are used around 200 times in the New Testament. The reality behind these concepts can best be translated with "household" or "house church." "Household" and its related terms describe the very foundation and context of the Christian movement. According to Hendrickx:

Religiously, the movement originated in and owed its growth either to the conversion of entire households or of certain individuals within households. Generally cultic activities like the Eucharist were celebrated in the house. Economically, the household comprised the context for the sharing of resources among the co-believers as well as the wandering charismatics. Socially, the household provided a practical basis and theoretical model for the Christian organization as well as its preaching.[12]

The house church was the genesis of the Church in any city. It provided space for the preaching of the word and for worship, as well as for social and eucharistic table-sharing. The Greco-Roman household included not only members of the immediate family and their slaves, but also freed persons, laborers and tenants. These household communities contained men and women working as partners in ministries.

Essential for these house churches were these four characteristics without which a gathering could and cannot be called church. These are: (1) *koinonia*/community; meaning that the members are concerned about each other's welfare and have a sense of belonging and being interconnected with all the other house churches. (2) *diakonia*/service or mission; all must serve each other in all needs that may arise since we are all brothers and sisters in Christ. (3) *kerygma*/Gospel-rooted; Kerygma is the name for the Christian Story whose proclamation gathers together a people of faith. For it is the proclaimed Great story that every true church shares with every other true church. (4) *leiturgia*/eucharist; each gathering unit of Christians is a eucharist-celebrating unit.[13]

Since the community met "in households" it was obvious that the *domina* or *mistress* of the house was fully responsible for that community and its gathering in the house church, e.g. Prisca and Priscilla. This would raise once again the question of who presided then actually over the eucharistic celebration in such households gatherings? However, others have this to say:

> In Roman and Hellenistic society the father of the house exercised the authority for all. The structures in ancient times was clearly hierarchical with a patriarchal order. Initially, the Christian community broke with a patriarchal structure since the community consisted of brothers and sisters, united in one faith, one Lord and one baptism. This would have made eminent sense in an enthusiastic movement. Eventually the hierarchical and patriarchal model predominated as the Church developed specific structures even as early as the end of the first century.[14]

The early Christian vision of "discipleship of equals", concretely practiced in the house church, attracted women and slaves especially to Christianity. This led soon to tensions and conflict with the dominant cultural ethos of the patriarchal household. The historical fact is that the *house church* did not survive beyond the first century. The new "household of freedom" which we find in the letters of St Paul had to give way to the old patriarchal pattern found in the normal home of the surrounding culture. The Church adjusted itself fast to the Greco-Roman culture and the "household of freedom" soon belonged to the past. The patriarchal pattern become the pattern not only for structuring the house church but for the universal Church as well. Adaptation to culture does not necessarily always coincide with Christian norms.[15]

The theological background: the council's view of the church as *Local Church*

Although the Council adopted a universalistic perspective most of the time when it talked about the Church, it asserted quite strongly that it is only in and out of the particular churches that the one and single Catholic Church exists (LG 23). This has been called by some theologians "the most important ecclesiological formula of the council."

> It guarantees, or should guarantee, that the relationship between the whole church and the individual churches is seen as one of reciprocal or mutual inclusion, that individual churches are not considered administrative subdivisions of a pre-existent reality, nor is the one church a subsequent federation of individual churches. The many churches are not churches except in the one Church; the one Church does not exist except in and out of the many churches. Since Vatican II, these carefully nuanced and mutually conditioning statements have prompted what some called a Copernican revolution in ecclesiology and a renewed interest in the local churches, whose communion is the whole church.[16]

This view of church is the second most important theological reason for the emergence of the phenomenon call Basic Ecclesial Community.

The concrete situation as the real origin of Basic Ecclesial Communities

In Latin America the emergence of BEC was not programed nor did it follow specific pastoral planning. They just emerged in response to a need: The lack of priests and the advancement of sectarian churches, the social and economical oppression and dependence, and the felt need that, if the people would not take matters into their own hands, the faith may just disappear, all these circumstances have often been the sparks that triggered the emergence of these communities. In hindsight it is obvious that the ultimate inspiration came from the Holy Spirit himself. In Africa, in contrast to Latin America, the BECs were introduced from the top, that means, from the official Church through statements of the bishops. However this responded to the growing awareness of the need by the people to express their own values of community, harmony and solidarity in the context of their Christian faith.[17]

What are basic Ecclesial communities?

Evidence of this new model has been presented to us particularly through the experience of Basic Christian Communities in Latin America, in Asia and in the Small Christian Communities in Africa.[18] Medellin defined the base communities in these words:

> The Christian ought to find the living of the communion to which he or she has been called, in the "base community," that is to say, in a community, local or environmental, which corresponds to the reality of the homogeneous group and whose size allows for personal fraternal contact among its members. Consequently, the Church's pastoral efforts must be oriented towards the transformation of these communities into a "family of God," beginning by making itself present among them as a leaven by means of a nucleus, although it be small, which creates a community of faith, hope and charity. Thus the Christian base community is the first fundamental ecclesiastical nucleus, which on its own level must make itself responsible for the richness and expansion of the faith, as well as of the cult which is its expression. This community becomes then the initial cell of the ecclesiastical structures and the focus of evangelization, and it currently serves as the most important source of human advancement and development. The essential element for the existence of Christian base communities are the leaders or directors. These can be priests, deacons, men or women religious, or laymen.[19]

The base communities are here seen as the "initial cell of the ecclesiastical structures" in terms of the greater institutional Church. For practical reasons I would like to rely here on a definition of BEC's given by the permanent Council of the Conference of Brazilian Bishops in a statement issued in 1982:

> Basic Christian Communities are formed by families, adults and youth, in a tight interpersonal relationship of faith...they celebrate the word of God and are nourished by the Eucharist... they enjoy solidarity and a common commitment... they are cells of a greater community.

Joe Marins defines them in this way:

They are small groups of believers either rural or on the fringes of the larger cities. They are run by lay people with a priest's help and counsel and exist among the poor. Their religious expression tends to be centered on reading and reflecting on the Bible, prayer and mutual help. They are socially committed but not necessarily political.

They are the dynamic reality of an evangelical, liberating and prophetic community opting preferentially for the poor and therefore constituting a new model of Church and the seed of a new model of society.[20]

The East African bishops looking for a term to describe the same kind of phenomenon in Africa coined the phrase *"Small Christian Communities"*.

A SCC community is a caring, sharing, faith-reflecting, praying and serving community in which ongoing Christian formation takes place. It may consists of an existing community, a neighborhood grouping of five to fifteen families, people with common interests or activities, and so on. It is a natural community or grouping based on geographical proximity, blood relationship, occupation, social ties or other affinities. It is the basic place of evangelization and catechesis.[21]

At a plenary session of AMECEA, held in Nairobi in 1976, the bishops held a study day on Small Christian Communities. As a result they set themselves the task of building these communities as a pastoral priority.[22] At a further plenary session in 1979 they reiterated this policy, stating that *"we have been able to clarify, deepen and confirm our conviction that the pastoral option we have taken is indeed one that holds great promise for the Church in Eastern Africa."* This policy represents the most appropriate way of expressing the mystery of the Church as a communion of faith, hope and love, as well as being an excellent means of involving all the members of the People of God in the common task of continuing the reconciling mission of Christ in the world.

In this document the bishops describe Small Christian Communities as *"the most local incarnation of the one, holy, Catholic and apostolic Church"*. The universal Church "must be really present to Christians in their own locality", and the most appropriate way is through the existence of these communities. Through them "the Church is brought down to the daily life and concerns of people to where they actually live. In them the Church takes on flesh and blood in the life situations of people." Christians are able to reflect together on their experiences and can place them under the light of the Gospel. The gifts given by the Holy Spirit are for service and the up-building of the Church. In small communities everyone is able to take part in the life of the Church and so make full use of their gifts. The role of the ordained minister is "to recognize, encourage and coordinate the various gifts of the Spirit"[23]

For the bishops, the resolve to base Christian life and witness on small Christian communities is not just one way among many possible ones; it is not just following a passing fad in the Church today. It is a basic commitment, a serious shift in pastoral emphasis. It is deliberately intended to modify deeply our pastoral system, policy and practice. Up until now, the avowed common system was to base the life of the Church on the parish level, rather on the sub-parish level. In these circumstances of Eastern Africa, what we call missions or parishes cannot be taken as the basic units of the local Church. If so, the Church is doomed to failure. We need to adopt a new system, whereby the basic units of the Church are those smaller communities where the ordinary life of the people takes place.[24] The similarity and closeness to the New Testament term "house church" seems obvious.

A new ecclesiology

The description by the bishops of AMECEA of Small Christian Communities as "the most local incarnation" of the Church points to a shift in ecclesiology within the Roman Catholic Church. Traditionally, a local community of believers belonged to the Church on the basis of its unity with the bishop and through him to Rome. The Church universal is the Church at its fullest. The local Church, which in the language of the Second Vatican Council refers to the diocesan Church united to its bishop (LG 26), receives its authenticity from its union with the universal Church. While preserving this link with the wider Church, the bishops of AMECEA now believe that a small community — a division of the parish which is in turn a division of the diocese — is a manifestation of the Church itself. In practice, this means that, in looking at the those gathered in such a community, we are seeing the Church.

Positive experiences:

The Brazilian bishops mention six elements in particular which are worth incorporating into any renewal of community life in the Church.

(1) The Church in such communities is considered as the "People of God" and "a creation of the Holy Spirit" according to 1 Corinthian 12:7 in which "to each is given some manifestation of the Spirit for the common good."

(2) The Church is considered as sacrament, sign and instrument of a profound union with God and of the unity of the human race (LG1). In this context, the Church is not considered primarily as a society with a visible structure.

(3) The role of the laity, considered in itself and not just as a participation in the ministry of the priest, is deemed constitutive in the life and mission of the Church. Lay people have a ministry of their own and not just through delegation from the hierarchy.

(4) The communities possess a holistic view of history: the story of humanity and the story of salvation are seen as intrinsically interconnected. This view makes the quest for justice and liberation a constitutive element of evangelization.

(5) These communities are the Churches of the poor, not for the poor. Ministry and leadership as well as the social force of these communities come from the poor and are exercised by the poor. This constitutes a new form of being a force for social change.

(6) The prayer and the ministries of these communities derive much from the forms in which the general religious experience of the people in the culture is expressed and nurtured. Even if we accept cultural differences and allow for historical diversities, we can still take these communities as the key to an understanding of how Church life may develop in this present age. Here the local Church is allowed to develop a new relation to itself, to the world, and to the universal Church. These communities still feel the need for an ordained ministry but no longer see a need for a clergy/laity distinction. Charism is seen as the basic organizing principle which gives to each one a function on the basis of being a member of the community. The center and source of these communities is their prayer life.[25]

This prayer is marked by six qualities:

(1) Fundamentally, it is a listening to the Word of God. The Bible plays a decisive role in their prayer meetings.

(2) The power of the Word of God is experienced in their daily life and the people become conscious of it. It is a Word that is alive and addressed to their real problems. When hope is shared with others in a hopeless

situation, the Bible comes alive. The Bible is seen as their book rather than the book preserved for the clergy to be read to the laity.

The Gospel is the calling card of the base ecclesial community. The Gospel is heard, shared, and believed in the community and it in its light that the participants reflect on the problems of their life. This is a typical feature of the community; the Gospel is always confronted with life, with the concrete situation of the community. It is not simply a marvelous and consoling message; above all, it is light and leaven. The Gospel is seen as good news, as a message of hope, promise, and joy for the real situation of the poor.[26]

(3) It is a common prayer in which the freely expressed voice of everyone is welcomed and not hindered by class distinction, whether social or ecclesiastical.

(4) The prayer finds its expression in the experiences and things available to the people: food, drink, songs, meeting place, all those things they themselves have made.

(5) It is a prayer in which the poor are present and active with their popular religiosity, their native religious experience and expression.

These are not just pious prayer groups that sit around and reflect together. As faith moves to actions, a deep process takes place. Most BCCs use the classic *observe, judge and act* model of reflection. Beginning with its local reality, the community evaluates and critiques its experience through discernment and then moves on.

(6) It is joyful and festive, with a joy that springs from the experience of the Kingdom present and the awareness of the power of freedom that the Spirit can give. As it is practiced in these communities, leadership is not guaranteed by office, delegation, or title of power but by charism, discernment and public affirmation within the community.[27]

What kind of community do we have here?

(1) A community in which the poor of the society feel at home and free to express themselves and are able to contribute to the life of others.

The base ecclesial community is also the place where true democracy of the people is practiced, where everything is discussed and decided together, where critical thought is encouraged. For a people who have been oppressed for centuries, whose 'say' has always been denied, the simple fact of having a say is the first stage in taking control and sharing their own destiny. The *'comunidas eclesial de base'* thus transcends its religious meaning and takes on a highly political one.[28]

(2) A community where there is no class distinction.

(3) The mission to the world is seen as the responsibility of the whole community as such and not of the laity as distinct from the clergy.

(4) The holistic view of reality takes this world seriously and results in an awareness of the gratuity of life and of all living things.

Political commitment is born of the reflection of faith that demands change... The base ecclesial community does not become a political entity. It remains what it is: a place for the reflection and celebration of faith. But at the same time, it is the place where human situations are judged ethically in the light of God. The Christian community and the Political community are two open spheres were what is properly Christian circulates.[29]

(5) The mission to the world is undertaken with sensitivity and in an openness to those not of the community. There is an awareness that the Church does not possess all the answers but can suggest some solutions through listening to the Word of God and being open to the Spirit.[30]

On closer analysis, we find three elements which enable the people to hear what the Word of God is saying: the Bible itself, the community, and the real life situation of the people vis-a-vis the surrounding world. In a concrete case it does not matter where one starts. One can begin with the Bible, or with the given community, or with the real life situation of the people and their problems. The important thing is ensure the inclusion of all three factors.[31]

Problems these communities have to face

Since these communities do not as yet have explicit juridical structures, these are the main difficulties they have to face:

(1) The process of discernment is difficult, whether it is a matter of reading the signs of the times, seeing God's presence in a real life situation, or discerning charisms and ministries.

(2) There is the constant risk of substituting democratization for discernment, especially in choosing leaders. The natural leader is not *'ipso facto'* the best and Spirit-willed leader of a BEC. This is an insight many BECs had to reach through painful experiences.

(3) Some communities, especially when they undertake the work of social liberation, can find themselves victims of ideologies of power. This is a concern constantly voiced by the official Church but, at times, exaggeratedly so. The accusation was heard that these communities were at times mere social and political action groups used by ideologies which have no religious bearings at all. Marxism in particular was seen as having dangerously undermined and invaded these communities. The reality of Church at the grass roots level was being seriously questioned.

(4) The independence of local Churches that might arise out of this model of Church could easily lead to fragmentation if bonds between Churches are not fostered.

(5) Given the persistence of mass religion and the genuine piety and need of those who adhere to it, the Christian community has yet to work out its responsibility towards those not interested in accepting its invitation to membership, while at the same time it holds onto the sacraments and other forms of religious expression.

Renewal of the Parish Church through SCC in Africa

The SCCs (Small Christian Communities), the African counterpart to the BECs of Latin America, evolved in the context of pastoral planning.

"The concept of small Christian communities developed as a result of an attempt to put the ecclesiology of Vatican II into practice. The African bishops opted for the SCC pastoral priority as the best way to build up local Churches that are truly self-ministering, self-propagating and self-supporting. The AMECEA Pastoral Priority of SCCs has effectively questioned the whole system by which pastoral ministry is carried out.... the SCCs are the best means for developing African Christianity stating that small communities also seem to be the most effective means of making the Gospel message truly relevant to African traditions."

The Africans were more concerned with inculturating the Gospel message into the fibre of the African community while the BECs in Latin America were more concerned with the liberation of the oppressed from injustices. Although they exercise many ministries, all of them are tied directly into the work of liberation.

On the basis of the Bishops' option for SCC and the pastoral experience made in Africa, the Lumko Institute in South Africa has developed a method of how to build SCC in the local parishes that could lead to a renewal of the African Church. They envision five stages of Church growth which aim at enabling members of a congregation to assess their own stage of growth.[32] In addition, knowing where they have come from, they gain a clearer picture of where they are going. This historical survey is presented in the following five stages (see the diagram on page 120):

The first stage: The Provided-for Church

The dominant person in the parish is the priest who organizes everything himself and offers the laity all the necessary means of salvation. This is the role described for the laity by the Code of Canon Law of 1917. They have the right "to receive from the clerics spiritual goods and strong help for salvation" (Canon 682).

The second stage: A Pastoral Council Church

The laity is recognized as sharing in the mission and work of the Church by working alongside the priest. One way of doing this is through shared leadership in the parish council. At this stage the laity are still often treated as "helpers of the priest" rather than carrying their own responsibility.

The third stage: The Awakening Church

This is a positive title for what is for many people, both cleric and lay, a negative experience. As more lay people become involved in Church life through the exercise of their Spirit-given gifts, the issue of responsibility arises. This in turn raises the issues of power and control. While this can generate a lot of tension in the parish, it can also lead to the non-ordained taking true responsibility and, as true equals, finding a new way of working alongside the ordained.

The fourth stage - The Task Group Church

Having accepted the commitment that arises from their baptism, the laity take responsibility for all that needs to be done, both within the congregation and beyond its boundaries. With the needs of parishioners and their neighbors now being met, many would accept this as a fine model for the parish, a Church at worship and in the service of others. However, the Lumko approach goes further.

The fifth and final stage - The Communion of Communities

At this stage all the believers of a parish are invited to be active members of a Small Christian Community which is situated in their neighborhood. Their regular meetings are based on Gospel sharing and always include reports on their activities since the last meeting and plans for further action on behalf of others. These communities are part of the structure of the parish. One of their number is a member of the Parish Council and all of them are engaged in various liturgical and other activities which keep them linked together and in union with the wider Church.

A SCC community is a caring, sharing, faith-reflecting, praying and serving community in which ongoing Christian formation takes place. It may consists of an existing community, a neighborhood grouping of five to fifteen families, people with common interests or activities, and so on. It is a natural community or grouping based on geographical proximity, blood relationship, occupation, social ties or other affinities. It is the basic place of evangelization and catechesis.

How do ministries arise in these communities?

One of the most important issues of this new ecclesiology is the status of the small communities' leadership. The most local manifestation of the Church in present practice is the parish which is headed by a priest. The priest is ordained and appointed by the bishop who is head of a "particular Church in which the one, holy, Catholic and apostolic Church of Christ is truly present and active" Does this mean that the leaders of the Small Christian Communities must also be appointed "from above"? And what of their non-ordained status? Even if it were acceptable that these leaders could be elected by the members of the small communities themselves, whether that election is ratified by a central authority or not, the question of a community headed by a non-ordained leader introduces a new concept of Church into Roman Catholic theology.

The matter of training for leadership is a further pastoral implication. Holding authority over a local Church, albeit a neighborhood community which has its vital link with the parish through the Sunday celebration of the Eucharist, these leaders represent more than the members of their small community. They would need to be trained in this wider perspective. To leave the content and method of this training to the choice of the local parish priest or animators, and thus open up the possibility of it never taking place, would be to give it insufficient emphasis and open the Church to potential segmentation.

Every ministry arises from the effective participation of the people in the life and mission of the Church and from the needs to which the ecclesial community consciously seeks to respond. The awareness of the needs and the election of the persons to respond to those needs give rise to the ministries and to the corresponding ministers. Normally, the process of formation follows these steps: occasional collaboration, permanent collaboration, becoming conscious of one's role, becoming conscious of one's ministry, confirmation by the community (and the priest or bishop).

Conclusion

The question still lingers: does this model have a future? Will not the general trend in the Church today towards a more conservative reevaluation of the Christian faith hamper the further development of such a model? Those involved with this kind of Church are still optimistic. They hold that these communities

> are writing a narrative theology of liberation and inculturation. A certain searching, experimenting, dying and rising will continue as the grassroots tries to evolve a new model of Church and the seed of a new model of society.

Cl. Boff, addressing the enormous loss of Catholic in Latin America, estimates that every year some 3,500,000 people leave the Latin American Catholic Church for the Pentecostal churches. Some say that 20 years from now most of the population of Latin America will belong to Pentecostal churches and that the largest Catholic continent will lose its religious hegemony. He holds that one of the most effective ways to deal with this challenge and to help people to find in the Catholic faith what they seemingly find in these fundamental sects is the movement of Basic Ecclesial Communities. He writes:

> Basic ecclesial communities are one answer to this fundamental problem: there is a great affinity between the basic communities and the new churches. There is a structural analogy between CEBs and the new churches: 1) the centrality of the Bible, even though in CEBs it is not read in a fundamentalistic

way; 2) the community experience, although CEBs are less charismatic and more democratic communities; 3) participation in the ministries, in church services; 4) missionary spirit, CEBs are spreading, they preach the Gospel and reach out to those who have distanced themselves. Obviously, there are some differences as well. For instance, CEBs encourage social and political awareness, they have a very clear social commitment which is to transform the system, they are open to ecumenical dialogue, not only in terms of traditional ecumenism but also in terms of macro-ecumenism: dialogue with Afro-Brazilian religions, other indigenous religions, etc.

It is clear that the CEBs lack something which instead the new churches have: for example, the emotional aspect which is integrated into the experience of faith. What is missed the most is institutional freedom: CEBs operate within the framework of parishes, dioceses, under the control of the bishop, of the parish priest, and if the bishop, or the parish priest does not want them there is nothing they can do.[33]

But in a talk on *The search for Justice and Solidarity: Meeting the "New Churches"* Clodic Boff added a dimension which base communities certainly contain but which need stronger emphasis today in face of these Pentecostal churches:

> We have to think of a new model of action that no longer presents the heavy, rigid, Marxist features of the past. It has to be a militant model that is more charismatic, more spiritual, more integrated, more flexible. This type of action would not only be more appreciated by the Pentecostals but would also be more biblical, more Christian, more spiritual. It may be that in this way dynamic dialogue and ecumenical growth can be begun.[34]

Karl Rahner, envisioning the Church of the future, voiced the same concern. Facing the crisis of the Church in Europe he insisted that the members of that Church would have to be "mystics". What he meant was that in a world of secularism only those could survive in their faith who had a deep personal experience of God and who in their lives could make this experience accessible to a totally secularized world.

Already 20 years ago Segundo Galilea, a liberation theologian, made a similar observation regarding the Christian of the future in the Latin American context. He writes:

> The 'contemplative' woman or man today is the one who has an experience of God, who is capable of meeting God in history, in politics, in his brothers and sisters, and most fully through prayer. In the future you will no longer be able to be a Christian without being a contemplative and you cannot be a

contemplative without having an experience of Christ and his Kingdom in history. In this sense, Christian contemplation will guarantee the survival of faith in a secularized or politicized world of the future."[35]

Secularism as a widespread ideology today can be described in this way:

Secularism may stem from explicit unbelief, the denial of the existence of God or of any religious dimension to human life. Such unbelief is rarely the product of a formal, atheistic, rational philosophy. More often, it is an allegiance to a popular myth of science as the ultimate theory of everything, a conviction that the only truths are those which are accessible to scientific observation and experiment. Basically, it is a faith in unlimited human progress, apparently confirmed by the spectacular achievements of Western technology..[36]

But as Shorter points out:

... consumer materialism is nowadays the most common cause of secularism. Rather than formal unbelief, it is a religious indifferentism induced by the preoccupation with material things. As Mary Douglas points out, it is the product of a world of impersonal things, a world in which personal relationships are at a minimum and in which symbolism and ritual are discounted as forms of expression in the interpretation of reality.[37]

The question is how to cope with this all pervasive attitude that shapes young and old alike. Basic Ecclesial Communities are different in structures and outlook depending on the situations in which they have emerged. But as a model for an answer to urgent needs, they could be relevant to the Church in the First World as well. Here as well, the need for such small faith communities becomes more and more felt and articulated. They will definitely be different from those in Asia, Latin America or Africa. People feel that the parish structures will not be sufficient for the faith even to survive. What is asked for are communities in which the faith is expressed in a more personal way. Where all participate and share their faith, where all feel equal and are respected not on the level of what they achieve but on the level of being persons. The model of Church as being made up of Basic Ecclesial Communities may well be the one that can address this deeply felt need.

How will the Church look in the near future? This is not a question that is easy to answer. At times we may ask with the Lord who, while looking at Israel, asked his Prophet Hezekiel: "Son of Man, can these dry bones still live?" The prophet had his doubts but it was the Lord himself who gave him the answer: "Yes they will, I will put my Spirit into them and they shall live!" But when the Lord will pour out his Spirit anew over his Church she might look quite different from what we are used to. Her survival will depend on whether she will become truly a world church as K. Rahner anticipated and secondly, whether she will commit herself to take the side of the poor who make up almost 70% of the world's population. As a world church she will have to embrace all cultures and express the Christian message of God's Kingdom in their values and customs. As advocate of the poor her principle of action must remain the one of her master, Jesus himself, *compassion and justice.*

To the first challenge there seems to be no better model available than to see and understand the Church in the model of Basic Christian Communities. This does not exclude other models because there is no one model that expresses the mystery of the Church fully. The use of models depends also on the situation in which the Church finds herself. To the second challenge of globalization and the increase of the poor in today's world, the model of Church as a "contrast society" seems to be best suited to respond to her commitment to the Kingdom which is ultimately defined as a matter of *justice peace and joy in the Holy Spirit* (Rm 14:17).

II. The Church as a "CONTRAST SOCIETY"

The brothers Gehard and Norbert Lohfink proposed a model of the Church which they called "Contrast Society". While the phrase is not found in Scripture, it is a metaphor proposing God's view of how human beings are to live together and what values are to be basic to any given social reality as an alternative to a history that is marred by violence, oppression and injustice. In short, it is seen as a model of how God imagines human society. In spite of all the discussions and the controversies which this term has created among exegetes and theologians, the image highlights aspects needed to understand the Church today, aspects which seem to fulfill all the requirements for a good model because it is *useful, open, fitting, and stimulating* (Luzbetak). The model provides us with a clear idea of how we as Church should see and understand ourselves in a globalized society with its own value system. In this understanding the Church is conceived as a community that is based on a different set of values which she must live and uphold over against a society which does not share these primary values. So perceived, the Church is seen primarily as a community in which justice and compassion are the basic rules of conduct, which must be demanded from society at large as well if the Church wants to fulfill her primary mission to lead all human societies into the Kingdom of God now and to come.

Biblical Basis

By analyzing the biblical origin of the people of Israel we saw that Yahweh's intention was to create this nation as a "counter society." Since the Christian Community stands in direct succession to the Old Testament people, the Church finds her identity in defining itself precisely as contrast society.[38]

Jesus definitely saw Israel as a chosen people that God had made into a contrast society in the midst of all other nations. He understood his mission clearly as gathering the true eschatological Israel into a society, in which the values and the social order of the Kingdom of God would be fully lived. It was not holiness and purity that should determine social reality since this option had only created a fragmentation of the Covenant idea and had ostracized half of the people as renegades and sinners. Jesus' demanded a social reality in which justice and compassion would determine social reality so that God's Kingdom could clearly shine through and all would become the great community of God where there would be no distinction anymore between male or female, neither Jew, nor gentile, neither ruler, nor ruled but all would be one family under the fatherhood of God.[39] The community Jesus envisioned as to be formed by his disciples would be different from the Old Testament community as it had come about. It would be Israel renewed, standing in contrast to all other communities because in it God would reign and the principle for action and behavior would definitely be his own principle of action: justice and compassion.

The Early Church as "Contrast Society"

The question is: Did the early communities understand themselves equally well as a contrast society in relation to the social milieu around them? The experience of the Kingdom as present in their midst definitely set them apart from the way of life found in the society in which they lived. But did they see their communities as contrast societies in opposition to the wider society?

There are a number of texts, particularly in the writings of St. Paul, which support a positive answer to these questions. These attest, first of all, to the experience of being one in Christ and living in a community where all are equal and class distinctions exist no more.

> *So there is no difference between Jews and Gentiles, between slaves and free men, between men and women; you are all one in union with Christ (Gal 3:28).*

> *The group of the believers was one in mind and heart. No one said that any of his belongings was his own, but they all shared with one another everything they had (Ac 4:32).*

It is obvious from these texts that the Church is intended to transcend all other bases of unity such as being of the same race, sharing the same occupation or economic status, adhering to a particular political doctrine, belonging to a certain social class, sharing the same level of educational attainment.

> The political novelty which God brings into the world is a community of those who serve instead of ruling, who suffer instead of inflicting suffering, whose fellowship crosses social lines instead of reinforcing them. This new Christian community, in which the walls are broken down not by human idealism or democratic legalism but by the work of Christ, is not only a vehicle of the Gospel or fruit of the Gospel; it is good news. It is not merely the agent of mission or the constituency of a mission agency. This is the mission.[40]

The early communities experienced themselves as being in contrast with the rest of society. Their whole value system was different. Paul's admonition to the community was: "Do not make yourself like the structures (form) of this age, but be transformed by the renewal of your mind" (Rm 12:2). According to Lohfink this text states that the form and spirit of the churches must not be adapted to the form and spirit of the rest of society.[41]

But the moment the Church became the *Christian society*, the question of a contrast society ceased to be asked. When she became the "official society" under Constantine, there seemed to be no need any longer for the Church to be a *contrast society*. But it did not take too long for her to realize that her new status was a mixed blessing. The idea of the Church as a contrast society was then taken up by groups like religious orders and sectarian movements which either silently or openly protested against a church which had paid dearly for her becoming an agent of the State and had, by necessity and for the sake of convenience, compromised the Gospel's demands.[42]

The Church as Contrast Society today

But in our time the question concerning the conception of Church as a *contrast society* poses a different problem. Critics ask: "Doesn't such a view of Church contradict the very purpose of the Church?" Doesn't being a contrast society automatically close the Church off from the rest of society? Isn't it the Church's mission to be in the world and in its societies in order to transform them? In the word of one such author:

> The question arises: if we define the Church as "Contrast society" are we not declaring the Church to be a separated unity from the world which it wants to serve? Will the Church not become by necessity a sectarian entity which would contradict the whole mission of the Church?[43]

G. Lohfink, who coined the phrase 20 years ago, answers such objections as follows: In the way she conceives of how God wants people to live in society, the Church does not see herself as "counter to" or "against" society as such but a "counter" or a "protest" against a society that does not live up to what it is supposed to be in the eyes of God. The Church poses "an alternative", much as the Old Testament people did in order to fulfill her mission for the world. The idea of Church as *contrast society* aims at the constant attempt by many, inside and outside the Church, to limit the Church and her activity to the purely spiritual, the inner realm of the person, and so deny the Church any right to get involved in the public realm and to claim a say in how society and State have to order their affairs. There is the constant tendency on the part of those authors to make the Kingdom of God "atopic", meaning everywhere and nowhere, as being not located in space and time at all.[44] For them the Kingdom is purely spiritual and an entirely transcendent reality.

Against the second accusation that the definition of Church as *contrast society* would mean to form her into a community of the pure elite, those who help each to become morally better and who then regard themselves superior to the rest, Lohfink counters:

> Church as contrast society does not come into existence because Christians live more determined, more heroic and morally better lives than the rest of humanity... Church as contrast society emerges only then when people let themselves be caught by God's Kingdom present now including their weaknesses and guilt.[45]

We are not living anymore in the cultural setting of the time in which Jesus preached his message. The social reality of Jesus' time was determined by the two catch phrases *holiness and purity*.[46] What shapes modern society and what gains prestige and fame today is *competition and success*. One must be *competitive and successful* to be socially acceptable. The effects of such social reality in our world today are the same as in the time of Jesus: they necessarily lead to exclusion and marginalization of millions of people. But our opportunity as Christians lies just here: to show the world that a different form of society is possible which, however, is not done through words and doctrine but only through concrete practise.

Whatever definition and understanding we may propose for the Church, if she wants to remain faithful to her master, she has no alternative but to conceive herself as a society in which the ultimate norm for social and communal structures must be *justice and compassion*. These are the indispensable principles for action which Jesus demanded from his eschatological community. To create a community in which justice and compassion would reign meant for Jesus the final bringing about of God's plan of salvation for Israel and the whole world. In this he saw the mission he was sent for.

That Jesus wanted a community that includes all and would not develop into an esoteric group concerned only with its own members can be seen in Jesus' own behavior. In bringing about the Kingdom three options were available to Jesus, two of which had already been chosen by others. They are the revolutionary, the sectarian, and the worldly.[47]

Revolutionaries, with their battle cry "Let us grab it," wanted to change the present by overthrowing those who ruled and so bring in God's Reign by force. This option was open to Jesus, but he neither authorized nor accepted it. *Sectarians*, following the motto, "Let us create it", insisted on total withdrawal from society and the creation of a new model of community in which the Covenant would be realized to the full. This was the option of the Qumran community and has been the option of many movements in the Church through the centuries. This option abandons the world because it is seen as being beyond repair. Jesus did not choose this option either. He did not join the Qumran community but stayed where the people were and used their marketplaces for his preaching and his actions. Jesus chose what Dunn called the *"worldly option,"* with its command "Live it!" He showed that the Kingdom is happening now in the midst of human affairs and that human actions may become the carrier of this Kingdom. To accept the Kingdom meant for Jesus to celebrate its presence now in this world, not in withdrawal. Jesus' option can be called "worldly," because it asks us to live wholly immersed in this world yet according to other-worldly values that challenge it to let itself be transformed by what Jesus came to bring.

Consequently, the Church, in the footsteps of Jesus, can not withdraw from the world and close herself up like an esoteric community which cares only for the salvation of its own members. Her mission is the whole world, because the biblical concept "election" always contains the "mandate" to engage actively in God's plan of salvation which aims at saving all.

Every Church community must understand itself from this vantage point and define its mission accordingly: to be a community whose basic principle for action is compassion and justice in contrast to the wider society in which it lives. To be sure, we need to keep in mind other considerations when we define the Church and her mission, but if we forget this essential aspect, the Church has nothing to say to many people today, particularly to the poor and marginalized of our time.

Globalization and Contrast society

There are many reasons today for the Church to opt again for being a *counter society.* One reason in particular is the process called *globalization.* At the moment *globalization* is the "in" word and can be viewed both as blessing and curse. Positively speaking, it recognizes that all countries are interdependent and facilitates communication and collaboration. It is important, however, that we critically examine our assumptions about globalization. Globalization is a double-edged sword which is here to stay. Comments about this social and economic phenomenon fill shelves and lecture halls. Those who extol the virtues of globalization say it is about tearing down borders, eliminating world poverty, uniting divided peoples and securing world peace. But globalization has its seamy underside:

Apparently, globalization does not affect all human populations in identical ways. It has structured the world into haves and have-nots and has created two zones on this globe whose interaction is one of exploitation and dependency. It has also created a new social class: the expendable people, also called *garbage people,* namely those who do not produce and who will not consume.

> Globalization seems to carry the whole world along. But in fact, it leaves more and more behind it in the desert of misery. It uproots people with the promise of plenty, but in fact it saps them mercilessly and allows them to dry out and die. The poor and the weak in our society are increasingly deprived of the security their traditional occupations, however low and menial these may be, provide. They are incapable of competing in a system whose

very nature is to leave behind many as it progresses. The agricultural sector has experienced the heaviest blow of globalization.[48]

At the root of globalization is the *ethic of competitiveness,* which is being promoted as the fundamental and compelling guide for our actions. It really shows its devastating effect mostly in poor countries where it only increases the misery of the majority.

> Economic globalization is based on the exclusion of a growing number of 'useless' persons who do not even have the 'privilege' of being exploited. There are progressively more poor in the global village; never before in human history there are so many poor and so poor like in the actual situation. The presence of more poor in the world continues to challenge Christianity and theology[49]

What seems so frightening for many is the way globalization is presented as a religious belief about how the whole world has to be structured and what values have to be promoted as being absolute.

> Globalization is a mechanistic process (and therefore most easily manipulable by the wielders of power) in the face of which there is no choice, no alternative. The most insidious aspect of this ideology is that it could present itself as the only way. It creates a certain sense of inevitability and absoluteness. In this sense it is akin to the Semitic religious traditions which have the strong tendency for absoluteness and dogmatism.[50]

We do not have to evaluate globalization in negative terms only. If globalization could grow into global *solidarity and co-operation* also with the poor and marginalized, then it would mean greater unity among the peoples of the earth and a greater respect for the person who is created in God's image. It is exactly in this context that the Church today must once again consider herself as a *counter society* which, in contrast to a society of competition and success, will understand itself as being on the side of those who drop out of this process since they can neither produce nor consume. The challenge of the Church today is to be a society of justice and compassion like the one Jesus himself envisioned in the context of his culture and time.

The internal challenge to a Church as Contrast Society

To be a contrast community does not entail living behind closed doors. Rather, it calls for a community with open borders and, at the same time, a burning center. The issue is: given this view of Church, how can we preserve an identity which calls for clear lines and limits and yet is open to those who cannot or will not accept such lines and borders? How can we remain Catholics with our clearly defined doctrines and morals and yet welcome anyone who wants to come in on his/her own terms and understanding? Without a burning center and a closeness to Christ and his vision of the Kingdom such a community will be swallowed up by the values and standards of the society that surrounds it. As a contrast society, the Church is, above all else, a *worshiping community*. Only a constant experience of the Kingdom present in their midst enables the community and the individual to see the presence of God's Kingdom in society at large as well. No mission into the world is possible without a constant union with the Lord who called and sent us.

> Whoever is near me is near the fire,
> and whoever is far from me is far from the Kingdom (Thomas: Saying 82)

The Church as contrast society is not a social action group but a community of those who want to follow the Lord and proclaim his Kingdom.

One need not be a prophet to foresee that, in the near future, the Church will more and more, become a minority group in a society that, for the most part, will not share its values and concerns. In the measure that this happens, the conception of the Church as a "contrast society" or "alternative community" will gain new support and strength and could give her a new identity and new enthusiasm for her mission in the world.

The perception of the Church as a contrast society is, of course, more readily embraced by those Christians who live as minorities among other religious traditions and value systems (e.g., in Asia and Africa), or by those who find themselves in situations of oppression and dependence, or else in surroundings that hardly reflect Christian values anymore (as in parts of Latin America and many First World countries).

The new Christian communities emerging all over the world are precisely the offspring of such a view of Church. They want to offer an alternative community with a set of values different from those held in the surrounding society. However, in order that such Church communities remain truly bound to the universal Church and do not deteriorate into hundreds of diverse sectarian groups, we will have to see and appreciate the need for universal structures and the gift of the Petrine ministry of unity.

The theological value of such a conception of Church

The theological insight gained from such a conception of the Church indicates once again that the Kingdom will remain linked to a community that must see itself in the service of God's ultimate plan of salvation for all. Jesus linked the reign of God, previously belonging to the People of Israel, to the community of his disciples. With this new election of a community, God's purpose for the Old Testament people is now enlarged into the new people composed of Jews and Gentiles. They are now to become a "visible sign of God's intention for the world" and the active carrier of his salvation. They are called out of the nations to take up a mission for the nations. They will fulfill this mission precisely as a "counter society" in the midst of human societies.[51]

From this perspective the Church is vital for the continuation of the Kingdom in the world.

It is the community which has begun to taste (even only in fore-taste) the reality of the Kingdom which alone can provide the hermeneutic of the message... without the hermeneutic of such a living community, the message of the Kingdom can only become an ideology and a program, it will not be a Gospel.[52]

In his book, *Models of the Kingdom*, H. Snyder offers eight models of interpreting the Kingdom of God.[53] One such model he calls the "counter system," which comes closest to the Church as a contrast society. The Kingdom is seen as a counter system, i.e., a way of conceiving and organizing society that is counter to its present dominant form. This model could also be called the "subversive Kingdom" since it consciously seeks to replace society's dominant values and structures. The Kingdom is a reality and a set of values to be lived out now, in the present order in radical obedience to the Gospel and in opposition to the powers of the present age. This model sees the Kingdom as a call to justice in society according to the values of the Kingdom. It shows a particular concern for the poor and oppressed, the victims of society. It reminds the Church of God's special care for the widow, the orphan, and the alien. This view is strongly christo-centric in the sense that Jesus' life and his call to discipleship become the focus of attention. The Church's mission is to be a counter-culture in faithfulness to Jesus Christ. In the words of H. Yoder:

> The alternative community discharges a modeling mission. The Church is called to be now what the world is called to be ultimately... The Church is

therefore not chaplain or priest for the powers running the world: she is called to be a microcosm of the wider society, not only as an idea but also in her function.[54]

Fidelity to Christ is the most important sign of the Kingdom now. To the degree that the values of the Kingdom, justice, peace, and joy (see Rm 14:17) are realized now here on earth, the Kingdom makes itself felt. The final goal of the Kingdom is peace and justice on earth and in all creation. This eschatological reign begins now, but will be fully manifested only when God's Reign comes in glory. Snyder articulates the strength of this model when he writes:

> The genius of this model is its affirmation of God's Kingdom as both present and future and as both individual and social without compromising either the power or the gentleness of the Kingdom. The image is the Lamb and the Lion (Rv 5:5-6).

Conclusion

The two major challenges the Church faces today are inculturation and solidarity with the poor. Both elements assume different urgency and shape in different situations. Both have been regarded by the Church herself as constitutive elements of our Christian faith. Both demand a dialogue with the world of different cultures and religious traditions. Dialogue, not monologue, is called for because the Kingdom is already present among the dialogue partners and can therefore offer to the Church something what she might not yet have. There are many ways to conduct this dialogue in the Church. The two models of Church which have been presented here as the most promising for the future address themselves particularly to the two most urgent challenges today.

First, the Christian faith incarnated itself into different cultures at the grass root so that people can experience and celebrate God's love and concern for them in their own values and customs and so come to know what God has in store for them.

Secondly, all humans are brothers and sisters bound together by a basic human solidarity. In today's world where this truth seems to get black-holed by economic and political values that extol competitiveness and success as ultimate determining social reality, the Church must offer a different view of society in which all those who cannot compete will be regarded first as brothers and sisters in a society in which the ultimate values will be compassion and justice. These are the values which Jesus chose and died for in order to bring God's dream of a society into the world: the great community where everyone counts and everyone is brother or sister to the other. The Church today must become a "contrast society" where the values of the Kingdom count and are not compromised for other values no matter how appealing these values may be presented.

Facing the Indian Church F. Wilfred concludes his article titled: Church's *Commitment to the poor in the Age of Globalization* with these words:

> The lure of globalization and the comforts and the goodies it offers are too powerful to resist. But the real test for the Church is here: Whether it wants to go along with the values, tastes and priorities of the middle and upper classes very much in line with globalization, or whether it wants to be a Church of the poor — making its own the struggles and concerns of the victims. The present-day developments taking place in the country are bound to look very different when seen through the eyes of the poor. Seeing societies through the eyes of the poor and to convert itself to their cause in the age of globalization is the need of the hour, the call of the Gospel which Jesus preached to the poor. The deeply meditated prayer of our great poet Tagore can become the prayer of conversion for every committed Christian and for the whole Church in the country:
>
> > This is my prayer to thee, my Lord — strike, strike at the root of penury in my heart.... Give me the strength never to disown the poor or bend my knees before insolent might.
>
> The poet brings to our mind the two great temptations today: namely to disown the poor and to prostrate before the powers that be. And that is exactly what globalization and economic liberalization do. It is ready to compromise millions of poor for some profit, for some power. Strength is what is required to side with rather than own the victims of our society and to be their voice; strength is what is required before all those powers. When the poet speaks of striking at the root of penury, is he not pointing out the need to radically transform our consciousness and to attune ourselves to the voices of the poor?
>
> In addition to calling for conversion, radical commitment to the cause of the poor also calls for *witnessing*. The glamour of globalization and liberalization can easily make us forget the victims they produce. But the passion of the Lord is an actual reality in the life and struggles of the millions of this country. It is a contemporary experience for a committed Christian and Church. We respond by our witnessing incarnated in deeds. Like Joseph of Aremathea we need to take the poor from the cross on which they are nailed.

Even more, we can no more allow any such inhumanity be done to the weaker ones whom God loves in a special way. And that brings to my mind the challenging words of Ashok Mehta:

"If it is the claim of the Christians that even to this day they feel the agony of Christ on the cross whenever humanity suffers, as it were, it has to be proved in action, not by any statement."[55]

How the world looks today in which we are called to proclaim God's Kingdom as a hope against hope has been expressed in this short passage:

If we should shrink the Earth's population to a village of precisely 100 people, with all existing human ratios remaining the same, it would look like this: There would be 57 Asians, 21 Europeans, 14 from the Americas (North and South) and 8 Africans. 51 would be female, 49 would be male. 70 would be non-white, 30 white. 70 would be non-Christian, 30 Christian. 50% of the entire world's wealth would be in the hands of only 6 people and all 6 would be citizens of the United States. 80 would live in substandard housing. 70 would be unable to read. 50 would suffer from malnutrition. 1 would be near death. 1 would be near birth. 1 would have a college education. No one would own a computer. (Dr. T. Roberts, Tulane University)[56]

But this is the world into which we are called to bring God's Kingdom as God's final design for all. It is this world in which we are called to create communities in which God's presence is experienced and his Kingdom of justice peace and joy shows it first "budding forth" (LG 4). This is the world in which God's Kingdom is already present and within the reach of all those who open themselves to the Spirit that Jesus released like a fire when he sent us the Spirit. Our experience of the Kingdom is not something we can hold for ourselves, our mission is to share this experience so that all my come to see and discover where God is making his plan come true. And where we see its presence we are to celebrate it in order to keep the fire burning and to give expression to our indestructible faith that the power of God's Kingdom is at work to make God's dream for his creation come true no matter how this world may look at the present.

Notes

[1]   Power, David N., "A Theological Assessment of Ministries Today" in *Trends in Mission Towards the 3rd millennium,* ed. W. Jenkinson and H. O'Sullivan (New York: Orbis Books, 1991) pp. 185-201 at p. 197.

2   See J. Healey. "Evolving a New Model of Church", p. 215.

3   Boff, Clodovis, "The Church in Latin America: Between Perplexity and Creativity" *Sedos Bulletin* 27 (1998) pp. 131-141 at pp. 136-137.

4   Height, R., *An Alternative Vision. An Interpretation of Liberation Theology* (New York: Paulist Press, 1985) pp. 163-165.

5   Boff, L., *Ecclesiogenesis. The Base Communities Re-invent the Church* (New York: Orbis, 1986). *Church: Charism and Power. Liberation Theology and the Institutional Church* (London: SCM, 1985) pp. 117-123.

6   *Church; Charisma and Power*, pp. 154-164; Ecclesiogenesis, pp. 23-30.

7   *Church; Charisma and Power*, p. 145f.

8   Wostyn, Lode L., *Exodus Towards the Kingdom. A Survey of Latin American Liberation Theology* (Manila: Claretian Publ., 1986) pp. 91-100.

9   Wostyn, Lode L., *Exodus Towards the Kingdom*, p. 94.

10 Power, D., "A Theological Assessment of Ministries Today", pp. 197-199.

11 Healey, Joseph G., "Evolving a New Model of Church: A comparison of the Basic Christian Communities in Latin America and the Small Christian Communities in Eastern Africa" 26 *Verbum* SVD (1985) pp. 211-225 at p. 211.

12 Hendrickx, H., *The Household of GOD. The Communities Behind the New Testament Writings* (Quezon City: Claretian Publications: 1992) p. 2.

13 Lee, B. & Cowan, M., *Dangerous Memories*, pp. 24-28.

14 O'Grady, John F., *The Roman Church Its Origin & Nature* (New York: Paulist Press, 1997) pp. 69-70.

15 Hendrickx, H., *Household of God*, pp. 129-130.

16 Komonchack, J., "Ecclesiology of Vatican II", p. 765.

17 Healey, J., *Evolving a New Model of Church*, p. 218.

18 M. De C. Azevedo "Basic Ecclesial Communities: A meeting Point of Ecclesiologies" *Theological Studies* 46 (1985) 601-620.

19 Medellin Document: II Conclusion. *The Church in the present Day Transformation of Latin America in the Light of the Council* (Catholic Bishops' Conference: Washington, D.C. 1970) p. 226.

20 Healey, J., "Evolving a New Model of Church", p. 213.

21 Compilation of AMECEA statements in Joseph Healey, *A Fifth Gospel: The Experience of Black Christian Values* (New York: Orbis Books, 1981) p. 37.

22 "1976 AMECEA Plenary on "Building Christian Communities", AFER, 18 (1976) p. 250.

23 AMECEA Pastoral Institute Communities called Church (Eldoret: Gaba Publication 1979) p. 265.

[24] 1976 AMECEA Plenary on "Building Christian Communities", pp. 266-267.

[25] Power, D., "A Theological Assessment of Ministries Today", pp. 193-194.

[26] Boff, L., *Church; Charism and Power*, p. 127.

[27] Neutzling, Inacio, "Celebrationes dans les Communautes de Base," *Spiritus* 24 (1983) pp. 115-155.

[28] Boff, L., *Church; Charisma and Power,* p. 9.

[29] Boff, L., *Church; Charisma and Power*, pp. 8-9.

[30] Healey, J., *Evolving A New Model of Church,* p. 213 he lists here the five similar characteristics as proposed by J. Marins.

[31] Mesters, Carlos, "The Use of the Bible in Christian Communities of the Common People," pp. 119-133.

[32] Prior, Anselm, *Towards a Community Church* (Gemiston: Lumko Publication 1991) pp. 17-27.

[33] Boff, Clodovis, "The Catholic Church and the New Churches in Latin America" *Sedons Bulletin* 31 (1999) pp. 196-201at pp. 200-201.

[34] Sedos Bulletin 31 (1999) *The Search for Justice and Solidarity: Meeting the New Churches*, pp. 202-205 at p. 205.

[35] Galilea, Segundo, *Following Jesus*, Orbis: New York, 1981.

[36] Bertsch, Ludwig, "Inculturation in Europe's Societal Situation: An Introduction", in *Yearbook of Contextual Theologies,* Missio Institute, Aachen, 1993/4, p. 104.

[37] Shorter, Aylward, "Secularism in Africa" *Sedos Bulletin* 30 (1998) pp. 10-14 at p. 11.

[38] Lohfink, Gehard, "The Characteristic Signs of Israel" in *Does God need the Church*, pp. 51-120; Lohfink Norbert F., Option for the Poor The Basic principle of Liberation Theology in the Light of the Bible (Berkeley, California: Bibal Press, 1990) pp. 48-52.

[39] Fuellenbach, John, "Definition of the Kingdom" in *Throw Fire,* pp. 193-218.

[40] Yoder, John Howard, "A People in the World: Theological Interpretation," in James Leo Garrett, *The Concept of the Believer's Church* (Scottdale, Penn.: Herald, 1969) p. 274.

[41] Lohfink, G., *Jesus and Community*, pp.122-132 entitled: "The Church as Contrast-society."

[42] Fr. J. Moloney, *Disciples and Prophets: A Biblical Model of Religious Life.* (London: Darton, Longman and Todd, 1980) pp. 155-170.

[43] Machinek, Marian, "Die Vieldeutigkeit der Rede von Kirche als Kontrastgesellschaft und ihre moraltheologische Implikationen" *Forum Katholischer Theologie* 15 (1999) p. 134-146.

[44] Lohfink, G., *Wem gilt die Bergpredigt?* Heider 1988, "Missverständnisse von Kontrastgesellshaft", 147-160,

[45] Lohfink, G., *Wem gilt die Berpredigt,* 159-60.

[46] Fuellenbach, J., *Throw Fire,* pp. 200-206.

[47] Dunn, *Jesus' Call To Discipleship,* pp. 44-52.

[48] Wilfred, Felix, "No Salvation outside of Globalisation" *Euntes-Digest* 29 (September 1996, pp. 135-144) 137.

[49] Lampe, Armando, "The Globalization of Poverty" *Sedos Bulletin* 32 (2000) pp. 131-135 at p. 132.

[50] Winfred, Felix, "No Salvation", p. 136

[51] Lohfink, Gerhard, *Jesus and Community. Did Jesus Found a Church?* (London: SPCK Press, 1985) pp. 17-29.

[52] Newbegin, L., *Sign of the Kingdom* (Grand Rapids: W.B. Eerdmans, 1980) p. 19.

[53] Snyder, Howard A., *Models of the Kingdom* (Nashville: Abingdom Press 1991) pp. 77-85.

[54] Yoder, Howard J., *The Priestly Kingdom: Social Ethics as Gospel* (Notre Dame: University of Notre Dame Press, 1984) pp. 124-125.

[55] Wilfred, Felix, "Church's Commitment to the Poor in the Age of Globalization", VJTR 62 (1998) pp. 79-95 at p. 95.

[56] Lampe, A., "The Globalization of Poverty", p. 131.

Chapter Seven

Mission of the Church

Introduction

The concern of Jesus was the Kingdom, God's dream for creation. To bring this Kingdom to bear on this world and to transform it into God's final design Jesus chose as his life principle justice and compassion. What counted was a basic human solidarity which would not exclude anyone from God's love and would guarantee that all would be treated as brothers and sisters in the great family of God.[1]

For this vision Jesus gave his life to make it come true. In order to continue his work until the end of time he elected disciples and told them "as the Father has sent me, so I am sending you" (Jn 20:21). The Church as the community of disciples for the Kingdom has been entrusted with the same mission, namely: first, to announce the arrival of the Kingdom; secondly, to create communities in which God's Kingdom as already present in history will be celebrated and effectively experienced in justice, peace and joy; thirdly, to engage in dialogue with all men and women of good will to discover the Kingdom already present in their midst whatever their faith and beliefs may be. This they do in order that God's final dream will reach all and can be experienced already now in the hope that the whole world will become renewed and prepared for the final coming of God and his Kingdom.

The mission of the Church must be seen and understood from this perspective: totally in the service of God's Kingdom designed for the transformation of the whole of creation. Once the Church is no longer seen as the sole holder of the Kingdom, she does not have to define herself any longer as "the Kingdom of God under siege" by the powers of this world. Since Vatican II she sees herself more as *leaven* of the Kingdom or in the *service* of the Kingdom that is broader than herself. In other words, a theology of transcendence gives way to a theology of transformation. With such a view of Church and Kingdom in mind, the mission of the Church has been outlined as follows:

The Threefold Mission

1. To *proclaim in Word and Sacrament* that the Kingdom of God has come in the person of Jesus of Nazareth. Sacrament means that the Church symbolically opens up the everyday world to the ultimate, the Kingdom of God. But, in doing so, the Church is also forced to accept her provisional character. In the words of Schillebeeckx:

The Church is not the Kingdom of God, but bears symbolic witness to the Kingdom through word and sacrament, and her praxis effectively anticipates that Kingdom. She does so by doing for men and women here and now, in new situations (different from those in Jesus' time), what Jesus did in his time: raising them up for the coming Kingdom of God; opening up communication among them; caring for the poor and outcast; establishing communal ties within the household of the faithful and serving all men and women in solidarity.[2]

2. To *create Church communities* (local churches) anywhere and in so doing present the Church community as a place where the Kingdom of God makes itself visible in festive celebration and in the witness to the values of the Kingdom. These communities will offer themselves as *test-cases* of the Kingdom present now in the world through their regard for justice, peace, freedom and respect for human rights. In their concern for a social reality where *compassion and justice* are the dominant values they will become a "contrast society" to society at large. The importance of community building in every culture as the major and fundamental goal of mission has been stressed over and over again: In the words of L. Luzbetak:.

Building Community is a very basic and essential part of the Church's mission. The specific challenge of every Christian Community is non other than to "demystify" the New Testament community model by translating it into the concrete socio-cultural situation and real life here and now. Each society has its way of respecting an individual, its way of bearing another's burden, its way of listening, forgiving, caring, sharing, serving spending oneself for others — in a word, its way of becoming a true New Testament Christian community, here in the Philippines, Thailand, United States or Italy, and now, two thousand years after the first Pentecost. *The building of New Testament Christian communities in our own times is, in fact, one of the most central objectives of mission, if not the very heart of mission. The*

*very key to mission success, and therefore a major and fundamental goal of
mission anthropology as well.*[3]

3. To *engage into dialogue with the world and with the other religious tradition. That means, first, to challenge society as a whole,*
   to transform itself along the basic principles of the Kingdom now
   present: justice, peace, brotherhood/sisterhood and human rights.
   Secondly, to *engage into dialogue with other religious tradition*
   in which God's Kingdom makes itself present as well. These are
   "constitutive elements of proclaiming the Gospel" since the ultimate goal of the Kingdom is the transformation of the whole of
   creation, and the Church must understand her mission in the service of the imminent Kingdom.[4]

This threefold mission finds its expression in the Document
Redemptoris Missio as follows:

> The Church is effectively and concretely at the service of the Kingdom.
> This is seen especially in her preaching, which is a call to conversion. Preach-
> ing constitutes the Church's first and fundamental way of serving the com-
> ing of the Kingdom in individuals and in human society...

> The Church, then, serves the Kingdom by establishing communities and
> founding new particular Churches and by guiding them to mature faith and
> charity in openness towards others, in service to individuals and society,
> and in understanding and esteem for human institutions.

> The Church serves the Kingdom by spreading throughout the world the "Gos-
> pel values" which are an expression of the Kingdom and which help people
> to accept God's plan. It is true that the inchoate reality of the Kingdom can
> also be found beyond the confines of the Church among peoples everywhere
> to the extent that they live "Gospel values" and are open to the working of
> the Spirit, who breathes when and where he wills. (Cf Jn 3:8). (20)

RM regards interreligious dialogue also as a constitutive element of
the Church's evangelizing task. It is "part of the Church's evangelizing
mission" (RM 55); it is one of its expressions and moreover, "a path to-
ward the Kingdom" (RM 57). The document *Dialogue and Proclamation*
adds:

> Interreligious dialogue and proclamation, though not on the same level, are
> both authentic elements of the Church's evangelizing mission. Both are le-
> gitimate and necessary. They are related but not interchangeable (DP 77).

The importance of these two documents concerning the question on interreligious dialogue cannot be overestimated.

> In light of the history of the concept of dialogue over the past century, these documents represent what might be called the complete "domestication" of the previously alien or at least marginal notion of dialogue with the catholic mainstream. From having been a maverick concept less than fifty years ago, interreligious dialogue has now become "an integral elemernt of the church's evangelizing mission.[5]

In these documents RM and DP interreligious dialogue is seen in terms of appreciation of the implicit Christian elements discernible within other religious tradition. On this view, the basis required for dialogue lies in these commonly shared though implicit elements, and the object of dialogue is to bring these elements to light. The Kingdom as God's saving will for all human beings is present anywhere and therefore:

> This respect [for the saving presence of God] in turn impels Christians to engage in dialogue with persons who, while they do not share explicit Christian faith, must supposed to be touched by the Spirit and striving according to their lights to respond to this grace, although they do not know this. It is in this complex sense that dialogue can be said to be integral to the Church's evangelizing mission: mission and dialogue express the single, though differentiated, Christian participation in the single, though diversely advanced, purpose of the triune God.[6]

Since the coming Kingdom of God in the present world always remains a "preliminary" or "proleptic" anticipation of the Kingdom, there will never emerge an "ideal community". Human societies and the Church herself need structures, which will always reveal the preliminary aspect and most often the 'sinfulness' of all human endeavors. Only when the fullness of the Kingdom comes, will all structures of the community be done away with, because the Kingdom in glory is "anarchy", i.e., a community or society that needs no structures anymore, because perfect love has become the guiding rule. As Pannenberg puts it:

> The Kingdom is not yet the way among men; it is not the present reality. Our present world, with its injustices, brutalities, and wars, demonstrates the gap between itself and the Kingdom... But the future of the Kingdom releases a dynamic factor into the present that kindles again and again the vision of man and gives meaning to his fervent quest for the political forms of justice and love... The function of the Church is a preliminary function. By this we mean that the existence of the Church is justified only in view of the fact that the present political forms of society do not provide the ulti-

mate human satisfaction for individual or corporate life. If the present social structures were adequate, there would be no need for the Church. For
then the Kingdom of God would be present in its completeness.[7]

Or in the words of Jürgen Möltmann:

The Church in the power of the Spirit is not yet the Kingdom of God, but it
is its anticipation in history. Christianity is not yet the new creation, but it is
the working of the Spirit of the new creation. Christianity is not yet the new
humankind but it is its vanguard, in resistance to deadly introversion and in
self-giving and representation for man's future.[8]

The two ways of mission

The Church's ultimate goal is to serve the Kingdom and to lead humankind to its final destiny. Wherever the Kingdom shows itself in the
world the Church must help to promote and to bring it to its fulness. The
mission of the Church in the service of the Kingdom is, therefore, basically twofold:

First, we are called to make God's Kingdom present by proclaiming
its presence in word and sacrament. This happens through the creation of
Christian communities in which God's Kingdom shines forth like a symbol, a sign or a parable, where its presence can clearly be discerned and its
final goal appears like a foretaste of what is to come in fullness in God's
own time. The disciples in such communities are to celebrate the presence
of God's Kingdom in their midst and let themselves be set on fire again
and again. Especially when they remember the Lord in the table fellowship of the Eucharist, the disciples should make present once again that
compassion of God which Jesus showed in such feasts to be the heart of his
own God-experience. The Kingdom can therefore never be separated from
the Church, which, after all, is God's chosen instrument for his Kingdom
here on earth. The following quotation might sound strong but it is certainly correct:

The Kingdom is, of course, far broader than the Church alone. God's Kingdom is all-embracing in respect of both points of view and purpose; it signifies the consummation of the whole of history; it has cosmic proportions
and fulfills time and eternity. Meanwhile, the Church, the believing and
active community of Christ, is raised up by God among all nations to share
in the salvation and suffering service of the Kingdom. The Church consists
of those whom God has called to stand at His side to act out with Him the

drama of the revelation of the Kingdom come and coming. The Church constitutes the firstling, the early harvest of the Kingdom. Thus, though not limited to the Church, the Kingdom is unthinkable without the Church. Conversely, growth and expansion of the Church should not be viewed as ends but rather as means to be used in the service of the Kingdom. The Church, in other words, is not a goal in and of itself; but neither is it, as some at present would seem to imply, a contemptible entity that should feel ashamed of its calling and seek its redemption in self-destruction. The keys of the Kingdom have been given to the Church. It does not fulfill its mandate by relinquishing those keys but rather by using them to open up the avenues of approach to the Kingdom for all peoples and all population groups at every level of human society. It makes no biblical sense whatever to deny, as many do, that the up building of the Church everywhere in the world is a proper concern of the proclamation of the good news of the Gospel; and it is high time for a forthright repudiation of such nonsense.[9]

Secondly, we can see that neither Jesus nor his Spirit have abandoned the world; they continue to be present and active among people. In us, the community of believers and followers of Jesus, his action which is present everywhere acquires a visibility and symbolic reality. Because of this, we are called and sent into the world to serve and to promote the ongoing action of Jesus and the Spirit. From this the second dimension of our mission follows: to be at the service of, and to promote collaboratively God's own continuing action in the world and among people outside the Church community. It is our task to discover God's Kingdom here, to rejoice over its presence, learn from it and bring it to completion.

If the Church community "feasts" on the presence of God's Kingdom in its midst most intensely in the Eucharistic meal celebration, then there must also be a "feast" aspect in the Church's second missionary task. We are, therefore, called to promote "feasts" where people of all races, cultures religious tradition and world views are coming together to enjoy each other's company in life-giving relationships and genuine compassion. It is precisely in these values that God's Kingdom makes itself felt outside the periphery of the Church community and can be experienced as present in the midst of human affairs.

The two "feast" aspects are two interrelated ways of pursuing the one goal of mission which is the realization of the 'New Heaven and the New Earth' that is God's promise to all peoples. In these common feasts we want to celebrate the Kingdom which is already present there among these people and to help them to see and to experience in their own way the presence of God who wants all people to be reached by his love. Here we may say that it is in getting actively involved in promoting God's transformative action in the world that the Church-community will build itself up as an authentic symbol of and witness to that action.[10]

Here we face a question: which is the more urgent at the moment? The building up of Church communities in all parts of the world? or our witness to God's Kingdom every where in the world? Michael Amallados thinks the second is the more important missionary task at the present. The fact is that most of our missionaries, particularly in situations where the Church is a minority, are primarily involved in building up Church communities and feel lost when they are expected to engage in dialogue with the world and other religious traditions. They are just not trained and, therefore, are often unable to even see mission work in the second way as the one most necessary today. If the Kingdom of God is operative ever where in the world and not just in the Church, then our mission is to witness to this presence and to 'sniff it out', raise people's awareness of it and celebrate it wherever it becomes tangible. If our mission is that of Jesus, namely to proclaim and to bring God's Kingdom into the world, then that very Kingdom calls on us to pursue these two ways.

The Church, the "Universal Sacrament of Salvation" as mediator of the Kingdom

With regard to the salvation of non-Christians the following question still arises: if the Kingdom as God's universal will to save all people is active outside of the Church, is this activity still mediated through the Church? or is it independent of her in some way? The answer varies according to whether or not we identify the Kingdom now with the Pilgrim Church.

Those who maintain a distinction between Kingdom and Church argue as follows: Pope John Paul in *Redemptoris Missio* (RM10) asserts that "for those people (non-Christians), salvation in Christ is accessible by virtue of a grace which, while having a mysterious relationship to the Church, does not make them formally part of the Church, but enlightens them in a way which is accommodated to their spiritual and material situation. This grace comes from Christ."

This text is seen as a clear rejection of *ecclesio-centrism*. The necessity of the Church for salvation is not to be understood in a way that means access to the Kingdom is only possible through the Church. One can partake in the Kingdom of God without being a member of the Church and without passing through her mediation of it.[11] Theologians who take this stand in no way deny that the salvation of any human being is based on Christ's death and resurrection. For them all grace is christo-centric. They hold that God's saving grace in Jesus Christ reaches the non-Christian not directly through the Church but by circumventing the Church "in ways only known to God." Schnackenburg seems to indicate this indirectly by saying:

> The Kingdom of Christ is... a more comprehensive term than "Church." In the Christian's present existence on earth his share in Christ's Kingdom and his claim to the eschatological Kingdom... find their fulfillment in the Church, the domain in which the grace of the heavenly Christ are operative... But Christ's rule extends beyond the Church... and one day the Church will have completed her earthly task and will be absorbed in the eschatological Kingdom of Christ or of God.[12]

Theologians who hold to the identification of the Kingdom on earth now with the Pilgrim Church cannot accept this position. For them all saving grace passes through the Church, otherwise the Church could not be called "the universal sacrament of salvation". Basing their view on a careful reading of the main Documents of Vatican II, they maintain that we cannot deduce from these documents that Vatican II distinguished between the Kingdom present now in history and the Pilgrim Church here on earth. Their arguments are the following:

The Council describes the Church as being by its very essence the *universal sign of salvation.* This description, which holds a prominent place in the *Dogmatic Constitution on the Church* (LG 48), is quoted both in the *Decree on the Church's Missionary Activity* (AG 1) and in the *Pastoral Constitution on the Church in the Modern World* (GS 45). When calling the Church a sacrament, the Council understands a symbolic reality established by Christ, a sign that contains and confers the grace it signifies. The Church, therefore, is not merely a cognitive sign, which makes known something that already exists, but an efficacious sign that brings about the redemption to which it points. Since the Church is seen as a universal sacrament, i.e., as *"an instrument for the redemption of all"* (LG 9), we must assume that the salvation of all human beings depends, in some way on the Church. The Church is involved in the salvation of all who are saved (LG 16). Whatever faith or belief people may confess, we must assume that the grace which saves them is in a *mysterious way* linked to the Church. They are, in the words of the Council, through this grace ordered to the Church. That means the saving grace they receive outside the Church gives the recipients a positive inclination towards the Church, so that all who live by God's grace are in a certain sense affiliated with the Church.[13]

The question that now arises is: does the Church simply save by being the reality towards which people are oriented? or does she act deliberately to bring about the salvation of such persons? The perception of the Church as "a universal instrument" of salvation (LG1) suggests that the Church is actively at work in the salvific process; however, it does not explain by what activities the Church accomplishes this result.

Francis Sullivan puts the question this way: "In what way can the Church be said to exercise an instrumental role in the salvation of all those people who apparently have no contact with the Church?" Referring to the encyclical *Mystici corporis* of Pius XII, the teaching of the Council (*Constitution on the Liturgy* SC, 83) and the eucharistic prayers, Sullivan sees the Church mediating salvation to non-Christians through prayer and intercession. Consequently, we can say that the Church, at least by means of intercessions, especially during the Eucharist, prays and offers Christ's sacrifice for the salvation of all people. Thus her intercessory mediation extends to all who are being saved. In Sullivan's own words:

> On the basis of the teaching of the council, and the eucharistic prayers which reflect this teaching, we have sound reason for affirming that because of the church's role as priestly people, offering to the Father with Christ the High Priest the sacrifice from which grace of salvation flows to the whole world, the church is rightly termed the universal sacrament of salvation in the sense that it plays an instrumental role in the salvation of every person who is saved.[14]

The orientation of the Church towards the Kingdom is most beautifully revealed in the central act of worship, the celebration of the Eucharist. Mark's account of the Last Supper closes with Jesus' words: *"Truly, I say to you I shall not drink again of the fruit of the vine until that day when I drink it new in the Kingdom of God"* (Mk 14:25). Thus the Eucharist is situated within the context of the eschatological Kingdom. In his handing on of the story of the origins of the Lord's supper, Paul also clearly sees its celebration within an eschatological context: *"For as often as you eat this bread and drink the cup, you proclaim the Lord's death until he comes"* (1 Cor 11:26).

But the link between Church and Kingdom in the Eucharist is still more profound. It is with his blood that Jesus establishes the new covenant (Lk 22:20; 1 Cor 11:25), the divine order of eschatological grace for all humanity. Only by virtue of the universal efficacy of the blood of this covenant (Mk 14:24) is it possible for human beings to be saved. In the celebration of the Lord's Supper, the Church is clearly presented as belonging to his Kingdom; she celebrates this covenant, established by the blood which, according to the Lucan account, is poured out "for us" (22:20). The eschatological benefits of salvation are intended "for us", which must be understood as including those believers in Christ who are actually celebrating the Eucharist. But these benefits do not extend to Christians alone; they reach out to all human beings whose salvation is ultimately guaranteed through the death and resurrection of Christ[15].

Kingdom consciousness and the mission of the Church

As the community of those chosen to carry on the vision of Jesus, the Church must define itself in relation to the Kingdom, which is meant for humankind and the whole of creation. Her mission is to reveal through the ages the hidden plan of God (Eph 3:3-11; Col 1:26) and to lead humankind towards its final destiny. She must be seen to be entirely at the service of this divine salvific plan for all human beings and all of creation which is operative and present wherever people live, no matter what religion or faith they may confess.

> The Church is not placed at her own service: she is entirely oriented towards the Kingdom of God that is coming. For only the Kingdom, as the fullness of God's manifestation, is absolute... The abiding vocation of the Church does not consist in the qualitative increase of her members. In dialogue and collaboration with all the people of good will (who may belong to other religions and spiritual families), she is called to manifest and foster the Reign of God which... keeps happening through the religious history of humankind, well beyond the visible boundaries of the "People of God."[16]

The identity of the Church depends ultimately on her Kingdom consciousness based on Scripture. This she would reveal in her sensitivity to the priority of the Kingdom. According to Snyder such Kingdom consciousness includes the following five elements.[17]

1. Kingdom consciousness means living and working in the firm hope of the final triumph of God's reign. In the face of contrary evi-

dence Kingdom Christians hold on to the conviction that God will eventually swallow up all evil, hate, and injustice. They firmly believe that the leaven of the Kingdom is already at work in the dough of creation, to use Jesus' own parable. This gives Christians an unworldly audacious confidence that enables them to go right on doing what others say is impossible or futile.

Looking at the world of today there is reason to doubt that the human species has the requisite capacity to change. Many view the present world situation with despair. Christian faith has been one important way in which people have lived with hope in the midst of apparently hopeless conditions. But those who open themselves to the Kingdom will discover there is a power at work in us that can transform even our distorted wills. This transformation is not subject to our control but comes as a gift. We call it grace, and we can place no limits on the extent to which grace can make us into new men and new women.[18]

2. Understanding God's Kingdom means that the lines between "sacred" and "secular" do not exist in concrete reality. God's Kingdom means that all things are in the sphere of God's sovereignty and, therefore, of God's concern. All spheres of life are Kingdom topics.

3. Kingdom awareness means that ministry is much broader than Church work. Christians who understand the meaning of God's reign know they are busy about the Kingdom, not about the Church. They see all activity as ultimately having Kingdom significance.

4. In the Kingdom perspective, concern for justice and concrete commitment to the Word of God are necessarily tied together. An awareness of God's Kingdom, biblically understood, resolves the tension between two vital concerns. First, those committed to the Kingdom want to win people to personal faith in Jesus Christ, since the Kingdom is the ultimate longing of every human heart. Secondly, they are also committed to peace, justice, and righteousness at every level of society because the Kingdom includes "all things in heaven and on earth" (Eph 1:10) as well as the welfare of every person and everything God has made.

5. The reality of the Kingdom of God can be experienced now through the Spirit who gives the believer the first fruits of the fullness of the Kingdom in the here and now. Particularly in their liturgy,

Kingdom people anticipate its joy. The different charisms given by the Holy Spirit witness concretely to the Kingdom as present. They are appreciated by all as clear manifestations of the powerful presence of the Kingdom in the midst of their daily life.

Conclusion

The Church is inseparable from the person of Jesus and has a mission of salvation for the world. As the 'sacrament of the Kingdom', she is God's choice, not ours and is called to accomplish with the Holy Spirit his plan for creation: the salvation of the whole world. She exists in the world and for the world as Jesus' chosen agent to carry on his mission to *gather all people into the one family of God*. Not only does she have to celebrate the Kingdom already in her midst and everywhere to create communities in which the Kingdom is explicitly experienced but she must also seek out the Kingdom present beyond her boundary. Here she seeks to rejoice in its presence and to help people discover the God of the Kingdom in their own midst who wants the salvation of all his children. It is this last task of the Church which can really fully be seen and, with conviction and joy, be taken up in the measure we come to realize that God's Kingdom here and now is more comprehensive than the Church. The Church is in the service of the Kingdom that embraces all of reality and not only the graced reality called Church.

Notes

1 Nolan, Albert, "the Poor and the Oppressed" pp. 21-29; "The Kingdom and Solidarity", pp. 59-67 in *Jesus before Christianity* (New York: Orbis Books, 1978).

2 Schillebeeckx, E., *Church: The Human Face of God*, p. 157.

3 Luzbetak, Louis J., *The Church and Cultures: New Perspectives in Missiological Anthropology* (Maryknoll, New York: Orbis Books, 1988), pp. 391.

4 McBrien, R., *Catholicism*, p. 717.

5 DiNoia, Joseph A., "The Church and Dialogue with Other Religions. A Plea for the Recognition of Differences": in *A Church For all People*, pp. 75-89 at p. 79.

6 DiNoia, Joseph A., p. 80.

7 Pannenberg, W., "The Kingdom and the Church", pp. 80-82.

8 Möltmann, J., *The Church in the Power of the Spirit* (New York: Harper & Row, 1977) p. 196.

9 Verkuyl, Johannes, "The Biblical Notion of Kingdom: Test of Validity for Theology of Religion", in *The Good News of the Kingdom: Mission Theology for the Third Millennium*, Chr. Van Engen, Dean S. Gilliland, Paul Pierson, Editors (New York: Orbis Books, 1993, pp. 71-81, at p. 73.

10 Amallados, M., "New Faces of Mission," 21-33.

11 Dupuis, J., *Jesus Christ and the Encounter of World Religions*, p. 6.

12 Schnackenburg, R., *God's Rule and Kingdom*, p. 301.

13 Dulles, A., "Vatican II and the Church's purpose", *Theology Digest* 32 (1985) pp. 344-345.

14 Sullivan, Francis, *The Church to Believe in* (New York: Paulist Press 1988) p. 128).

11 Henn, W., "The Church and the Kingdom of God" in *Studia missionalia* 46 (1997) p. 130.

16 Geffre, C., as quoted by J. Dupuis, "Dialogue and Proclamation", p. 158.

17 Snyder, H. A., *Models of the Kingdom* (Nashville: Abingon Press,1991) pp. 154-155.

18 Cobb, J., *Sustainability*, pp. 7-19.

Epilogue

Simon Peter the fisherman's net, the Church, is not for catching a small select group, some kind of spiritual elite. It is the net for a universal Church, capable of offering a home to all peoples and every kind of human being.

Throughout her history the Church has needed reminders of this again and again. The great demands and challenges of the Gospel led to repeated attempts at establishing churches for small groups, elites of specially selected men and women. This church was meant to clearly distinguish itself from the masses through exceptional holiness, special insights into God's mysteries and a way of life that demanded very high standards. These attempts also witness to the deep longing of those who have the sincere wish to live up to the high expectations of Christ's Church.

Yet the image of the net teaches us that the Church was not meant to be an elite community. Without taking anything away from the demands of the Gospel, her ultimate purpose is to be open and welcoming to ordinary people, the poor, the sick, those who do not count, but who are able to enkindle a tiny flame of faith and open themselves to the small light of love.

We are talking about a Church whose shepherds bear the responsibility of having a "big heart". They should be endowed with understanding, compassion, mercy and a broad vision. They need to point to ways that even the weakest and least talented can walk. Only when they do this, are they seriously on the way towards a Church that resembles the image of Peter's net, filled with the biggest catch ever made.[1]

---

[1] Adapted from: Carlo Maria Martini, *Mein spirituelles Wörterbuch*. Pattloch Verlag: 1998

SELECTED BIBLIOGRAPHY

Arens, H.   "Das Prohetische am Ordensleben" *Ordenskorrespondenz* 33 (1992) 8-22.

Ashley, B. M.   *Justice in the Church: Gender and Participation.* Washington. D.C.: Catholic University Press, 1996.

Auer, J.
& Ratzinger, J.   *Dogmatic Theology 8; The Church: The Universal Sacrament of Salvation.* Washington, D.C.: The Catholic University Press, 1993.

Azevedo, M.   "Basic Ecclesial Communities: A meeting Point of Ecclesiologies" *Theological Studies* 46 (1985) 601-620.

Bas van Iersel,   "Who according to the New Testament has the say in the Church" *Concilium* 148 (1981) 11-17.

Baum, G.   "The Meaning of Church" in *The Credibility of the Church Today.* New York: Herder & Herder, 1968.

Bellagamba, A.   *Mission & Ministry in a Global Church.* New York: Orbis Books, 1992.

Bertsch, L.   "Inculturation in Europe's Societal Situation: An Introduction", *Yearbook of Contextual Theologies*, Aachen: Missio Institut, 1993/4.

Boff, C.   "The Church in Latin America: Between Perplexity and Creativity" *Sedos Bulletin* 27 (1998) 131-141.

_____,   "The Catholic Church and the New Churches in Latin America" *Sedons Bulletin* 31 (1999) 196-201.

_____,   "The Search for Justice and Solidarity: Meeting the New Churches" *Sedos Bulletin* 31 (1999) 202-205

Boff, L.   *Church Charisma and Power. Liberation Theology and the Institutional Church,* London: SCM Press, 1985.

_____   *Ecclesiogenesis. The Base Communities Re-invent the Church,* New York: Orbis Books, 1989.

Bonhoeffer, D.   *Gesammelte Schriften.* vol. 3, München: Kaiser Verlag, 1958.

Borg, M. J.   *Jesus, A Vision, Spirit, Culture, and Life of Discipleship.* San Francisco: Harper & Row, 1987.

_____.   *The God we never knew.* San Francisco: Harper, 1998.

Brown, R.   *Biblical Exegesis & Church Doctrine.* New York/ Mahwah: Paulist Press.1985.

_____.   *Priest and Bishop, Biblical Reflections.* New York: Paulist Press, 1970.

_____,   "Not Jewish Christianity and Gentile Christianity but Types of Jewish/ Gentile Christianity" *The Catholic Biblical Quarterly* 45 (1983) 74-79.

Brueggemann, W.   *Prophetic Imagination.* London: SCM Press, 1992.

Casaldáliga. P.
& Vigil, J. Maria,   *Political Holiness.* New York: Orbis Books, 1994.

Chenu, M. D.   "The New Awareness of the Trinitarian Basis of the Church", *Concilium* 146, (1981) 14-22.

Cobb, J. B.   *Sustainability, Economics Ecology & Justice.* New York: Orbis Books, 1992.

Congar, Y.   *Lay People in the Church.* London: Bloomsbury Publishing Co. Ltd., 1957.

Covell, R.   "Jesus Christ and World Religions" in *The Good News of the Kingdom: Mission Theology for the Third Millennium.* eds. Charles Van Engen, Dean S. Gilliland, Paul Pierson, New York: Orbis Books, 1993, 162-171.

Cullmann, O.   *Christ and Time.* Philadelphia: Westminster 1950.

DiNoia, J.D.   *The Church and Dialogue with Other Religions. A Plea for the Recognition of Differences: in A Church For all People,* 75-89.

Dulles, A.   "The Church and the Kingdom" in *A Church for all People*. ed. Eugene LaVerdiere, Collegeville, Minnesota: The Liturgical Press, 1993, 13-27.

_____.   *A Church to Believe In. Discipleship and the Dynamics of Freedom*. New York: Crossroad, 1982.

_____.   *Models of the Church*. Expanded Edition, New York: Image Book Doubleday, 1987.

_____,   "The Succession of Prophets in the Church", *Concilium* 4 (April 1968) Vol. 4, 28-32.

_____.   "Successio Apostolorum", *Concilium* 148 (1981) 61-67.

_____.   "Vatican II and the Church's purpose", *Theology Digest* 32 (1985) 344-345.

Dunn, J. D.   *Jesus and the Spirit*. London: SCM Press, 1975.

Dupuis, J.   "A Theological Commentary: Dialogue and Proclamation," in Burrows, William R., *Redemption and Dialogue, Reading Redemptoris Missio and Dialogue and Proclamation*. New York: Orbis Book, 1994, 119-158

_____.   "Evangelization and Kingdom Values: The Church and the 'Others'" *Indian Missiological Review* 14 (1992), 4-21.

_____.   "Religious plurality and the Christological debate" *Sedos Bulletin* 28 (1996) 229-333.

Duquoc, C.   "Jesus Christus, Mittelpunkt des Europa von morgen", in P,. Huenermann (Hg.) *Das Neue Europa, Herausforderung für Kirche und Theology* (QD 144), Freiburg i. Br., 1993, 100-110.

_____.   *Provisional Churches An Essay in Ecumenical Ecclesiology*. London: SCM Press LTD, 1986.

Ferguson, E.   *The Church of Christ: A Biblical Ecclesiology for Today*. Grand Rapids: Eerdman's Publication Company, 1996.

Fuellenbach, J.   *Throw Fire.* Manila: Logos Publication, 1998.

_____.   *The Kingdom of God.* New York: Orbis Books, 1995.

Galilea, S.   *Following Jesus.* New York: Orbis Books, 1981.

Grassmann, G.   "The Church as Sacrament, Sign and Instrument," in *Church Kingdom World.* by G. Limouris, Ed. Geneva: World Council, 1986, 1-16.

Granfield, P.   "The Concept of the Church as Communion", *Origin* 28 (1999) 753-758.

Healey, J. G.   "Evolving a New Model of Church: A comparison of the Basic Christian Communities in Latin America and the Small Christian Communities in Eastern Africa" 26 *Verbum* SVD (1985) 211-225.

Height, R.   *An Alternative Vision. An Interpretation of Liberation Theology.* New York: Paulist Press, 1985.

Hendrickx, H.   *The Household of GOD. The Communities Behind the New Testament Writings.* Quezon City: Claretian Publications, 1992.

_____.   *A Key to the Gospel of Matthew.* Manila: Claretian Publications, 1992.

Henn, W.,   "The Church and the Kingdom of God" in *Studia missionalia* 46 (1997) 119-147.

John Paul II,   *Redemptoris Missio.* Vatican City: Liberia Editrice Vaticana, 1991.

Kasper, W.   *Theology and Church.* New York: Crossroad, 1989.

_____,   "The Church As Communio" *New Blackfriars* 74 (1993) 232-244

Kasper, W.
& Sauter, G.   *Kirche Ort des Geistes.* Freiburg: Herder, 1976.

Kehl, M.   *Die Kirche: Eine katholische Ekklesiologie.* Würzburg: Echter Verlag, 1992.

Kirchschläger, W   *Die Anfänge der Kirche: Eine Biblische Rückbesinnung.* Graz: Styria Verlag 1990.

Komonchak, J.   "Ecclesiology of Vatican II," *Origin* 28 (1999) 763-768.

Küng, H.   *The Church.* New York: Sheed and Ward, 1967.

_____,   "Paradigm Change in Theology: A Proposal for Discussion," in: *Paradigm Change in Theology: A Symposium for the Future.* Edit by Hans Küng and David Tracy, Edinburgh: T&T Clark LTD, 1989, 3-31.

Kuzmic, P.   "The Church and the Kingdom of God: A Theological Reflection" in *The Church. God's Agent for Change.* Edited by Bruce J. Nicholls, Flemington Markets, Australia: Paternoster Press, 1986.

Ladd, G. E.   *The Present of the Future. A revised and Updated Version of Jesus and the Kingdom.* Grand Rapids, Michigan: Eerdmans Pub. Company, 1974.

Lambino, A. B.   "A New Theological Model: Theology of Liberation". *Towards Doing Theology in the Philippine Context*, Manila: Loyola Papers 9, 1977, 2-25.

Lampe, A.,   "The Globalization of Poverty" *Sedos Bulletin* 32 (2000) 131-135.

Lee, B. J. & M. A. Cowan,   *Dangerous Memories. House Churches and our American Story.* Kansa City: Sheed & Ward, 1986.

Lochman, J. Milic,   "Church and World in the Light of the Kingdom of God", *Church - Kingdom - World. The Church as Mystery and Prophetic Sign, Faith and Order* Paper no. 130, Gennadios Limouris Ed. Geneva: World Council of Churches, 1986, 58-72.

Lode L. Wostyn,   *Exodus Towards the Kingdom. A Survey of Latin American Liberation Theology.* Manila: Claretian Publ., 1986.

Lohfink, G.   *Does God Need the Church.* Collegeville Minnesota: Glazier Book, 1999.

_____. *Wem gilt die Bergpredigt?* Freiburg: Herder, 1988.

_____. *Jesus and Community. Did Jesus Found a Church?* London: SPCK Press, 1985.

_____, "Did Jesus found a Church?", *Theology Digest* 30 (1982) 231-235..

Lohfink, N. "Where are today's prophets?" *Theology Digest* 37 (1990) 103-107.

_____, "Religious Orders: God's Therapy for the Church," *Theology Digest* 33 (1986) 232-244 .

_____. *Option for the poor.* Berkeley, California: Bibal Press, 1987.

Lonergan, B. "Theology in its new Context" W.E. Conn, Ed., *Conversion.* New York: Alba House, 1978, 3-21.

Luzbetak, L. J. *The Church and Cultures: New Perspectives in Missiological Anthropology.* New York: Orbis Books, 1988.

Machinek, M. "Die Vieldeutigkeit der Rede von Kirche als Kontrastgesellschaft und ihre moraltheologische Implikationen" *Forum Katholischer Theologie* 15 (1999) 134-146.

McBrien, R. P. *Catholicism.* London: Geoffrey Champman, 1981.

Merton T. *Prophets in the Belly of Paradox.* ed. G. Twomey, New York 1978.

Metz, J. B. "For a Renewed Church before a New Council: A Concept in Four Theses," in *Towards Vatican III: The Work that Needs to Be Done.* ed. David Tracy, New York: Seabury, 1978.

_____. *Followers of Christ. The Religious Life and the Church.* London: Paulist Press, 1978

Michiels, R. "Church of Jesus Christ, An Exegetical-Ecclesiological Consideration", *Louvain Studies* 18 (1993) 297-317.

Minar, P. S.   *Images of the Church in the New Testament.* Philadelphia: Westminster Press, 1977.

Moloney, F.   *Disciples and Prophets: A Biblical Model of Religious Life.* London: Darton, Longman and Todd, 1980.

Möltmann J.   *The Church in the Power of the Spirit.* New York: Harper & Row, 1977.

Nardoni, E.,   "Charism in the Early Church Since Rudolph Sohm: An Ecumenical Challenge" *Theological Studies* 53 (1992) 646-662.

Neutzling, I.   "Celebrationes dans les Communautes de Base," *Spiritus* 24 (1983) 115 -155.

Newbegin, L.   *Sign of the Kingdom.* Grand Rapids: W.B. Eerdmans, 1980.

Nolan, Albert,   "The Poor and the Oppressed" pp.21-29; "The Kingdom and Solidarity" pp.59-67 in *Jesus before Christianity.* New York: Orbis Books, 1978.

O'Grady, J. F.   *The Roman Church Its Origin & Nature.* New York: Paulist Press, 1997.

Pannenberg, W.   *Theology and the Kingdom of God.* Philadelphia: Westminster Press, 1977.

Power, D. N.   "A Theological Assessment of Ministries Today" in *Trends in Mission Towards the 3rd millennium.* ed. W. Jenkinson and H. O'Sullivan, New York: Orbis Books, 1991, 185-201.

Provencher, N.,   "The Family as Domestic Church" in *Theology Digest* 30 (1982) 149-152.

Rahner, K.   *The Church and the Sacraments.* London: Burns & Oates, 1963.

_____.   *Spirit in the Church.* London: Burns & Oates,1979.

_____,   "Towards a fundamental theological interpretation of Vatican II" *Theological Studies* 40 (1979) 716-27

_____, "Concern for the Church," *Theological Investigation* XX. New York: Crossroad Publ.,1981, 77-102.

Rahner,K.
& Ratzinger, J.   *The Episcopacy and the Primacy.* New York: Herder & Herder 1963.

Rossi de Gasperi, F   "Continuity and Newness in the Faith of the Mother Church of Jerusalem", *Bible and Inculturation, Inculturation Working papers on living Faith,* Rome (1983) 17-69.

Schillebeeckx, E.,   *Church: The Human Face of God.* New York: Crossroad, 1990.

Schmaus, M.   *Dogmatic 4: The Church its origin and Structure.* London: Sheet and Ward, 1977.

_____.   *The Church as Sacrament.* London: Sheed & Ward, 1975.

Schnackenburg, R.   *God's Rule and Kingdom.* New York: Herder and Herder, 1968.

_____,   "Signoria e regno di Dio nell'annuncio di Gesu e della Chiesa delle Origini", *Communio* 86 (1986) 41-42.

Schoelles, Patricia,   "Liberation Theology and Discipleship: The Critical and Reforming Tendencies of Basic Christian Identity", *Louvain Studies* 19 (1994) 46-64.

Shorter, A.   "Secularism in Africa" *Sedos Bulletin* 30 (1998) 10-14.

Schreiter, R.J.   *Constructing Local Theologies.* New York: Orbis Books, 1985

Schüssler Fiorenza, E. *Foundational Theology: Jesus and the Church.* New: 1984.

Schweizer, E.   *The Holy Spirit.* Philadelphia: Fortress Press, 1980.

_____.   *The Church as the Body of Christ.* Atlanta: John Knox Press, 1976.

_____. *Church Order in the New Testament*. London: SCM Press, 1961.

Snyder, H. A. *Models of the Kingdom*. Nashville: Abingdom Press 1991.

Sobrino, J. *Christology at the Crossroads: A Latin American Approach*. New York: Orbis Books, 1978.

Song, C. S. *Jesus & the Reign of God*. Minneapolis: Fortress Press, 1993.

Stafford, J. F. "The inscrutable Riches of Christ: The Catholic Church's Mission of Salvation" in *A Church for All People. Missionary Issues in a World Church*. Ed. E. La Verdiere Collegeville: Liturgical Press, 1993, 31-50.

Sullivan, F. A. *Charisms and Charismatic Renewal: A Biblical Theological Study*. Dublin: Gill & Macmillan, 1982.

_____. *The Church We Believe In*. New York: Paulist Press, 1988.

Theisen P. J. *The Ultimate Church and the Promise of Salvation*. Collegeville, Minnesota: St John's University Press, 1976.

Torres, S. & Eagleson, J. Eds. *Challenge of Basic Christian Communities, Papers from the International-Ecumenical Congress of Theology*, February 20-March 2, 1980, Sao Paulo, Brasil, New York: Orbis 1981, Chapter 19: Final Document, No 33, 236-237.

Venetz, H. J. *So fing es mit der Kirche an. Ein Blick in das Neue Testament*. Zürich 1981.

Verkuyl, J. "The Biblical Notion of Kingdom: Test of Validity for Theology of Religion", in *The Good News of the Kingdom: Mission Theology for the Third Millennium*. Chr. Van Engen, Dean S. Gilliland, Paul Pierson, New York: Orbis Books, 1993, 71-81.

Viviano, B. T.   *The Kingdom of God in History*. Wilmington, Delaware: Michael Glazier, 1988.

Werbick, J.   *Kirche, Ein Ekklesiologischer Entwurf für Studium und Praxis* (Freiburg: Herder 1994) pp. 76-80.

Wilfred, F.   "Once again. Church and Kingdom," *Vidyajyoti* 57 (1993) 6-24.

———,   "No Salvation outside of Globalization", *Euntes-Digest* 29 (September 1996) 135-144.

———,   "Church's Commitment to the Poor in the Age of Globalization", *Vidyajyoti* 62 (1998) 79-95.

Yoder, J. H.   "A People in the World: Theological Interpretation," in James Leo Garrett, *The Concept of the Believer's Church*. Scottdale, Penn.: Herald, 1969.

———.   *The Priestly Kingdom: Social Ethics as Gospel*. Notre Dame: University of Notre Dame Press, 1984.

OCCASIONAL PAPERS

The Nature and Purpose of the Church, Faith and Order Paper No 181, Bialystock, Polan: Ortdruck Orthodox Printing House, 1998.

Shvani-Kendra Reseach Seminar 2000, "A Vision of Mission for the New Millennium", *Sedos Bulletin* 32 (2000).

International Theological Commission: Text and Document 1969-85, edited by M. Sharky, San Francisco: Ignatius Press, 1989.

Union of Superiors General, *Consecrated Life Today. Charisms in the Church for the World,* Montreal: St Paul, 1994.

Extraordinary Synod of Bishops, "The Final Report," II,C, 1 Origins 16 (1985).

Congregation of the Doctrine of the Faith, "Some Aspect of the Church Understood as Communion," *Origins* 21 (1992).

Medellin Document: II Conclusion. *The Church in the present Day Transformation of Latin America in the Light of the Council*, Catholic Bishops' Conference: Washington, D.C. 1970.